W9-BVJ-837

Growing into God

OTHER BOOKS BY JOHN R. MABRY

Faithful Generations:
Effective Ministry Across Generational Lines

Salvation of the True Rock:
The Sufi Poetry of Najat Ozkaya

Sermons That Connect:
A Beginner's Guide to Crafting and Delivering
Powerful, Excellent Sermons

The Kingdom: A Berkeley Blackfriars Novel

People of Faith:
An Interfaith Companion to the Revised Common Lectionary

The Way of Thomas:
Nine Insights for Enlightened Living from the Secret Sayings of Jesus

The Monster God: Coming to Terms with the Dark Side of Divinity

Noticing the Divine:
An Introduction to Interfaith Spiritual Guidance

Faith Styles: Ways People Believe

God Has One Eye: The Mystics of the World's Religions

God is a Great Underground River:
Articles, Essays, and Homilies on Interfaith Spirituality

I Believe in a God Who is Growing:
Process Perspectives on the Creed, the Sacraments, and the Christian Life

Who Are the Independent Catholics? (with John P. Plummer)

Crisis and Communion:
The Re-Mythologization of the Eucharist

Heretics, Mystics & Misfits

God As Nature Sees God: A Christian Reading of the Tao Te Ching

Growing into God

A Beginner's Guide to Christian Mysticism

John R. Mabry

QUEST

BOOKS

Theosophical Publishing House
Wheaton, Illinois * Chennai, India

BOCA RATON PUBLIC LIBRARY
BOCA RATON, FLORIDA

Copyright © 2012 by John R. Mabry

First Quest Edition 2012

All rights reserved. No part of this book may be reproduced in any manner without written permission from the publisher except for quotations embodied in critical articles or reviews. For additional information write to

Quest Books
Theosophical Publishing House
PO Box 270
Wheaton, IL 60187-0270

www.questbooks.net

Some of the mystics' biographies are adapted from *Heretics, Mystics & Misfits* by John R. Mabry (Berkeley: Apocryphile Press, 2004). All rights held by the author and used by permission.

All scripture quotations from the New Revised Standard Version, unless otherwise identified.

Cover design by Kirsten Hansen Pott
Typesetting by Wordstop Technologies, Chennai, India

Library of Congress Cataloging-in-Publication Data

Mabry, John R.
Growing into God: a beginner's guide to Christian mysticism / John R. Mabry.—1st Quest ed.
    p.   cm.
Includes bibliographical references and index.

ISBN 978-0-8356-0901-2

1. Mysticism.   2. Spirituality.   I. Title.
BV5082.3.M24 2012
248.2'2—dc23   2012009022

5 4 3 2 1 * 12 13 14 15

Printed in the United States of America

Dedication

For my dear wife,
Lisa Fullam,
who "gets it"

Contents

Notes and Acknowledgments

This book began—as so many of my books do—in a fit of frustration over the lack of appropriate materials for a class I was teaching, specifically a Christian mysticism class at John F. Kennedy University in Pleasant Hill, California. It arose from my sympathy for my students, who had to wade through nearly 400 pages of Evelyn Underhill's *Mysticism: A Study of the Nature and Development of Man's Spiritual Consciousness*. Now don't get me wrong, *Mysticism* is a classic, a masterwork, an unparalleled document in the field of world mysticism. It's also difficult to read—sublimely evocative and maddeningly opaque, written in a stilted early-twentieth-century style with one foot firmly planted in Victorian academia, which is a friend to nobody.

Thus, it was my intention with this book to adapt Underhill, to create a reader-friendly version of *Mysticism*. I claim little wisdom of my own; Evelyn Underhill is my master, and I feel privileged to have been able to sit at her literary feet. If you like this book, I recommend you turn next to its inspiration and source. You won't be sorry. I have used some of Underhill's more outstanding quotations, placing her among the mystics. This is, I think, entirely appropriate, as she was a practicing Anglican and a very mystical soul indeed. Her feast day is celebrated in the Anglican Communion on June 15. She's not officially St. Evelyn, but for many of us, she's close.

I'm also indebted to several other authors, translators, and compilers whose work sorting and presenting excerpts from the writings of the mystics made my job of selecting quotations so much easier—especially Bear & Co.'s *Meditations With . . .* series, John Anthony McGuckin's *The Book of Mystical Chapters*, and Bernard McGinn's *The Essential Writings of Christian Mysticism*. I also want to acknowledge Chris O'Neill's *Meditations with Thomas Merton*, an unpublished master's thesis for Holy Names College (1988). Even when I chose not to quote from these authors directly, they pointed me in the right directions.

The foundation of the text that follows was laid during a series of sermons delivered to my parish, Grace North Church, in Berkeley, as well as several lectures for my JFK students. I'm grateful to my parishioners for their interest in the subject, their encouragement, and their suggestions. Likewise, to my JFK students, who asked great questions and delighted in putting me on the spot.

My thanks to Vernice Solimar for asking me to teach the Christian mysticism class, and to Lola McCrary for her enthusiastic encouragement. I am also indebted to my interfaith spiritual guidance students at the Chaplaincy Institute for Arts and Interfaith Ministry and the Institute of Transpersonal Psychology, as well as my spiritual direction clients, in whom I watched so much of this book's contents "made flesh and dwelling among us."

The questions for the "Question and Answer" chapter were not generated by me, but were real questions submitted by friends who read this book. Thank you, John C. Robinson, Gina M. Steele, Kevin Filocamo, Deni Harding, Faith Freed, Grace Gilliam, Nancy Schluntz, Sharon Lehman, Sharon Moody, Tony Lorenzen, Pamela Falkowski, and Keith Johnston. They also pointed out typos. Thank you! Thanks also to my research assistants who worked so hard to help me meet the deadline for this manuscript, especially Jackie Gamble, Rachel Bauman, and Keith Johnston. Also many thanks to Bishop Michael Milner for keeping me honest and for his assistance during the final stages of this manuscript. If I forgot anyone, I owe you dinner.

A final note regarding inclusive language in this text, or the lack of same. I consider myself a feminist—one of those occasionally tiresome folk who are of the opinion that women are the equal of men in every way. In theory, I agree with the importance of inclusive language in liturgy and God-talk. In practice, however, this is an exceedingly clumsy proposition. Any attempt to remove masculine pronouns—such as using gender-neutral language—distances God and obliterates or diminishes the relational character of one's language. Changing the pronouns from masculine to feminine is equally problematic—it is so jarring that it leaves the reader thinking only about the oddness of the language, distracting from the point of the text.

For all of its evils, I have decided to retain the masculine references to God in this text, as changing them all would have done violence to the intended language of every mystic I quote. They all wrote using masculine imagery and pronouns for God, and I would rather err on the side of being thought backward and sexist than resort to untoward revisionism, distortion, and distraction. I hope that you will be a forgiving reader and allow grace where greater errors might easily have followed had I chosen a different strategy.

Whoever believes, fears.
Whoever fears is humble.
Whoever is humble becomes gentle.
Whoever is gentle
pacifies the unruly forces of desire and aggression
and begins to keep the commandments.
Whoever keeps the commandments is purified.
Whoever is purified is illuminated.
Whoever is illuminated
is made a spouse of the divine Logos-Bridegroom
and shares with him
the bridal chamber of mysteries.

—Maximos the Confessor

A pear seed grows up into a pear tree,
a nut seed grows up into a nut tree—
but a seed of God grows into God, to God.

—Meister Eckhart

Introduction

In the second century Acts of Thomas, there is a wonderful story about a young prince who is second in line to the throne. His royal parents send him to Egypt to retrieve a valuable pearl from a wicked serpent. So he takes off his beautiful robe and sets forth. Eventually he finds the serpent, but before he can procure the pearl, the locals distract him with fine food and rich wine. The young prince falls into a deep sleep, and when he awakens, he is in a stupor and does not remember who he is or where he came from. He lives like the Egyptians, seeking only pleasure, oblivious to his royal heritage.

His parents are deeply grieved when they hear what has happened, and they send him a letter, signed by all of the nobles of his home country, reminding him of his royal identity, inviting him to wake up, to fulfill his mission, and return home to his family and subjects.

Upon reading this letter, the spell of Egypt is broken, and the prince's memories come rushing back. He rises up, lulls the serpent to sleep, retrieves the pearl, and returns home. His royal robe is restored to him, and with pearl in hand, he ascends the steps of the temple to present it in offering to his father, the king.

If the outlines of this story seem familiar, there's good reason. It's an expansion of the Prodigal Son story. The hymn is a metaphor for the spiritual journey, and it's one of the earliest explications of Christian mysticism. The prince symbolizes all of us—we are all of royal heritage, we are sons and daughters of God. We come from God, and to God we seek to return. We come seeking spiritual maturity, and this must be won by effort. Yet this earth distracts us—we forget that our true nature is in God, and we are like those who sleep.

But the good news is that through scripture, tradition, and the writings of those fellow pilgrims of the soul—the mystics—a wake-up call is offered to us: there is more to life than the world we see; our destiny is greater than we ever could have dreamed. Do you want to know what it is?

That is the call of Christian mysticism. We come from God, and to God we long to return. But how? The Christian tradition is filled with saints and sinners just like us, pilgrims and mystics who have travelled this road in search of spiritual maturity. They have sent us letters outlining exactly how to wake up, how to remember our true nature, and how to return to the Divine presence.

The problem is that many of the writers who have documented the journey are hard to read; they use a bewildering variety of symbols and metaphors and often leave modern readers scratching their heads. This book, then, is written in the language of Egypt—for those just starting out on the mystical path, it lays out the route in simple terms, in a friendly manner.

People often have the idea that mysticism is the domain of those in the past or very holy women and men, that it is something unattainable by average people. But this is not true! It takes work, but so does anything worth doing well: playing the guitar, learning to dance, or mastering another language—things people do all the time. In the same way, average folks like you and me can turn from business-as-usual and set out on a new path toward God.

THE MYSTICISM OF JESUS

In the New Testament gospels, Jesus encountered many "spiritual" people who asserted that God's favor was only for some people—that only those who were holy, or who kept the religious Law, or were of a certain heritage were worthy of God's friendship and grace. But Jesus refuted these people at every turn, and he went in search of those who had been disenfranchised by the religious establishment. He found outcasts, looked down upon as sinners, sneered at as foreigners, and he revealed to them a truth that changed their lives forever: that God loved them just as they were, and that God wanted a relationship with them, to be family, to be united in love with them, regardless of what anyone else said. He touched the unclean in order to heal them, making himself ritually impure in the eyes of many. He ate meals with sinners, which no self-respecting rabbi at the time would do; to eat with someone implied that you approved of them. And for a rabbi to eat with someone implied that God approved of them as well! And that's exactly what Jesus was trying to get across: God accepts and loves you and invites you into his family. And in doing these things, Jesus gave people their dignity back, he restored their humanity, and he healed their souls.

And his message is just as clear today: friendship with God is not for "holy" people only, or just for religious professionals. It is for everyone, everyone, everyone—even you. God wants to be united with you forever. This relationship is something that God desires more than anything, and there is a part of us that also fervently wants this—otherwise you would not be reading this book.

The Meaning of Mysticism

Too often when people hear the word *mysticism* they think of dark, occult secrets or untouchable saints who never spill tomato soup on their white robes. But that's not what mysticism is about at all. *Mysticism is the pursuit of—or enjoyment of—union with God.* As Julian of Norwich put it, "And thus I saw God, and sought God. I had God, and at the same time I wanted God. And this is, and should be, what we are all working towards."[1]

Every religious tradition has its varieties of mysticism. In some systems, such as Advaita Vedanta, Buddhism, or Taoism, divinity is depicted as impersonal; the effort involved in the mysticism is mostly related to *awareness* of an already existent unity.

In theistic traditions, however, such as Judaism, Christianity, Islam, or devotional Hinduism, where divinity is understood as a *person*, union may or may not be a given, but the mystical process is seen as involving the growth of *relationship* between a person and the Divine. In these systems, the Divine is first and foremost interested in one thing: intimacy with the human soul. And the metaphors commonly found in such traditions are likewise intimate.

The Christian mystical tradition belongs to anyone for whom the life and teachings of Jesus have meaning. You don't have to be a Christian to do this practice—Jesus wasn't a Christian and no one who ever knew him or followed him during his life was a Christian. Jesus was concerned with only one thing, intimacy with God, and was adamant that this intimacy was the birthright of every human being, regardless of your religion or beliefs or your alleged "moral" state. Jesus said that God is like the father in the story of the prodigal son—God is here for you now, with his arms open to embrace you, if only you will return the embrace.

What Is the Goal of Mysticism?

If mysticism is the pursuit or enjoyment of union with God, what form does this union take? For what end is God wooing us? Is the goal of mysticism a union of wills—to unite God's will with our will? Or is it a union of essence—a gradual or given identification, or identical-ness, the "us-ness" of God and the "godness" of us, and indeed, of the whole creation?

The early Christians insisted on a differentiation between our essence and God's. They saw the purpose of mysticism as the unification or identification of our will with God's—so that our wills would be knit together, so that what God desires we would desire, so that God's plans would manifest for the universe. As Methodist mystic Henry Martyn put it so poetically, "I wish to have my whole soul swallowed up in the will of God."[2]

This is congruent with Evangelical Christian teaching today: although the Holy Spirit indwells the human bodies of believers, the

Holy Spirit does not indwell unbelievers. There is an absolute distinction between creator and creation.

For Orthodox Christians, though, humans are not identical with God now, but we are partially identified and will eventually be completely and wholly divine through the redeeming work of God—as will all of nature. Our nature is being transformed *into* God's, through the process of deification.

Among the medieval mystics of the West, however, we see another sort of mysticism: we and God are already one thing, of the same essence or substance, but because of human sin, we are ignorant of our true nature. Meister Eckhart specifically refuted the "union of wills" position in favor of the "union of essence" when he wrote, "There are some who say that blessedness consists not in knowing but in willing. They are wrong; for if it consisted only in the will it would not be one."[3]

Regardless of their era or the kind of union they espouse, mystics generally fall into one of two varieties: *apophatic* and *kataphatic*. These are Greek-derived words that refer to whether or not images are used in contemplating the Divine.

Apophatic mystics (literally, "without saying") favor the negative way in mysticism, believing, as Meister Eckhart put it, that "God is found through a process of subtraction."[4] Their mysticism, therefore, is about shedding images of God until one is left with only silence, with no ideas or images at all. When Eckhart wrote, "I pray God that he may quit me of god,"[5] this is what he means: he wants to get rid of his images of God so that he can encounter the reality of God unmediated by mental abstractions and images.

Kataphatic mystics (literally, "with saying"), on the other hand, believe that humans *need* metaphor, words, and images in order to approach the great Mystery, because the unmediated Divine is incomprehensible. Their experience of Divine communion is therefore one of *relationship*. They relate to God as *an Other*, even though they may believe that, ultimately, this is a false distinction. But due to the limits of human understanding, this is how it *seems*, and so this is how they must approach God. These mystics speak of their relationship with God as a love affair, a marriage of their soul with God's Spirit.

In the chapters that follow, we will see three metaphors emerge again and again to describe union with God: (1) *birth* (or rebirth)—our own or the birth of the Word in us; (2) *deification*, the transmutation of our will or essence into that of God's (favored by apophatic mystics and Orthodox Christians); and (3) *sacred marriage*, the erotic enfoldment of our will or nature into the Divine (favored by kataphatic mystics and many Roman Catholic Christians).

Feeling overwhelmed? Not to worry—there is no need to keep all of this straight right now. We'll revisit these themes with much more context as we go along.

Spiritual Direction

In the world, it is possible for a person to do either good or bad. As a result of the latter, a body is placed in many afflictions. To lessen them, a person should therefore act according to the judgment of a spiritual director, lest one find only the bitterness and not the sweetness of life.[6]
—Hildegard of Bingen

The problem with intimacy with God is that human beings—even the best of us—are really complicated, messed-up creatures. We have *issues* with intimacy. Our biggest obstacle to intimacy with God is our own sense of shame. We too often hold God at arm's length because we don't feel worthy of a relationship with him; we don't feel like we deserve that kind of love. We have internalized all of those negative religious messages that said, "You're a sinner!" and so we push God away.

Have you ever broken up with a girlfriend or boyfriend because you didn't feel worthy of someone who was that good to you? Have you ever deflected a compliment because you didn't feel worthy of it? These are knee-jerk reactions that go deep and can completely derail us from the most significant and transformative relationship in our lives—our relationship with God. The mystics know this feeling well. Julian of Norwich wrote, "Many times our trust is not complete: for we are not sure that God hears us, because we think ourselves unworthy, and we feel like nothings. . . . It is because we feel such foolishness that we are weak. I have felt this in myself."[7]

We push God away because of fear. Perhaps we have been wounded by abusive religious teachings or communities. We often confuse God with the destructive and even downright evil things that people do in his name. I love the bumper sticker that says, "God, save me from your followers." That's actually a pretty good prayer.

We all have our own reasons that we push God away, and the sad truth is most of us do it. Often we're just not aware of it. The Christian tradition developed a ministry designed to specifically help us overcome resistance to intimacy with God, a ministry called Spiritual Direction.

In formal spiritual direction as it is practiced today, two people meet face to face, in the presence of God. One person is understood to be a little more experienced than the other, often referred to as the "director." The other person, often referred to as the "directee," comes to the director seeking help or insight into his or her spiritual journey. The two of them meet, acknowledging the presence of God in their midst, and talk. And in their conversation, the director looks for the movement of God in the life of the directee.

Very often, we're too close to our own journeys to see them clearly. Because we see every moment pass, we are often not aware of the large scope of movement or change—like parents who are not as aware of how much their children have grown as the grandparents who only see them every few months.

It's the same in spiritual direction. A director and directee meet about once a month usually, and in that time, as they talk, motion toward or away from God can be detected. It is the spiritual director's job to notice when people are moving away from God or when someone is resisting God in some way. Part of what the director does is to point out when he or she sees this kind of resistance.

Seeing a spiritual director is the most efficient way of ensuring, gauging, and encouraging someone's growth toward God. Your spiritual director can help you as you work through this book. The spiritual journey is often confusing, discouraging, and scary. A spiritual director is there to hold your hand, to walk beside you on frightful roads, to give you a reality check, and to make sure you are on the right path.

It doesn't matter what religion your spiritual director is. As long as a director has been through a reputable training program, he or she will be able to help you just fine. If you have trouble finding one, go to the Spiritual Directors International website (www.sdiworld. org) and click on "Find a Spiritual Director." Interview a couple of them and work with whoever seems like the best fit. You will not be sorry.

A Mystic's Story: Origen

How do we get from where we are to where we want to be? How do we cultivate this relationship with God? Where did the mystics' road-map come from and what does it look like?

The map really begins with the work of a very early, very odd, very brilliant fellow named Origen. Born in the second century, he was raised during a period of extreme persecution of the Christian Church. To be a martyr was the highest honor a Christian might hope for, as it brought with it the promise of immediate and assured entry into heaven. Origen's father had been martyred and Origen dreamed of following in his footsteps.

In fact, he so longed for martyrdom that he was prepared to rush out into the street when the imperial forces raided his city, searching for Christians. The only reason he failed to do so was that his mother hid his clothes and Origen was simply too modest to be martyred without his loincloth.

The soldiers did such a good job of purging the region of able-bodied Christian men that the local school of Christian philosophy was without faculty. And it is because of this that Origen, at the ripe old age of eighteen, was elevated to headmaster of that school.

Fanatical but also brilliant, he was fully equal to the new task. A compulsive studier with a photographic memory, he read a book once and retained the entire contents for easy and instant retrieval. However, his significant challenge came from within, for he felt his own body betrayed him. He was, after all, a teenager who was suddenly put in a position of authority over others very near his own age. In addition, his school was co-ed, which meant that many of his students were women.

And this was very nearly (in his own imagination, at least) his undoing. He simply did not trust himself. He was afraid he would not be able to avoid temptation. So in order to avoid any possible disaster or even any "appearance of evil" (as St. Paul puts it), Origen took to heart Jesus's admonition, "If thine hand offend thee, cut it off." Only, in his case, it was not his hand that offended, but a much *tenderer* member.

Whether he paid a surgeon to castrate him or whether he wielded the knife himself, history does not tell us. But after a suitable recovery period, Origen was on his feet again, teaching women without offense and (according to St. Jerome) writing more books than any human being could ever hope to read.

And it is his writing that is his real claim to fame, for Origen was the first to suggest that the Bible needed to be read on two levels: the superficial, historical level (which was the normal way of understanding it), and the esoteric, spiritual level (which was his own innovation). Origen never denied the authority of scripture; he just decided he could pick and choose which level was authoritative!

One familiar example of Origen's interpretation pertains to the biblical book, The Song of Solomon or The Song of Songs. For most of its history, the Church has interpreted this erotic love poetry as being about the relationship between Christ and the Church. What most people are not aware of is that this is entirely Origen's idea and is typical of his approach to scripture.

Origen was particularly fond of those writings attributed to Solomon and considered Solomon's three books to be the cornerstone of biblical teaching, providing the paradigm for spiritual growth.

Origen taught that spiritual growth had three stages: The first stage is Virtue, which is addressed by the book of Proverbs. The second stage is Detachment, which is elucidated by the book of Ecclesiastes. The third stage is Contemplation, which can be read into the Song of Songs.[8]

Origen's formulation was reinterpreted by later writers as the three-step process of Purgation, Illumination, and Union, which is the map that we'll be following (see chart below). In the first stage, Purgation, we rid our lives and our thoughts of all things that are illusory. In the second stage, Illumination, we glimpse—for ourselves, experientially—the universe as it actually is, bathed in and inseparable from divinity. Finally, in the third stage, Union, we learn to live in this awareness, with profound inner and outer results.

CHRISTIAN MYSTICAL GROWTH

stage	sub-stage	practices
3. UNION	Deification or Sacred Marriage	*Action*
	Dark Night of the Spirit	
2. ILLUMINATION	b. World-in-God	*Quiet: Acquisition*
	a. Illuminated World	Quiet: Depravation
	Dark Night of the Senses	
1. PURGATION	b. Mortification	
	a. Detachment	Recollection
0. AWAKENING		*Inbreaking*

Key to Practices:
Regular type = active, we do it.
Italics = passive, God does it.

These three stages are a gross oversimplification of the process, and we'll go into much more detail about this in the chapters that follow. Evelyn Underhill, in her classic book, *Mysticism*, adds a preliminary stage—Awakening—which offers us a glimpse of the God-drenched world and reorients us toward the Real, motivating us to begin the journey of discovering Reality.

In the past, writers have called this Jacob's Ladder, or the Ladder of Divine Ascent, images of which imply that one goes step by step to higher and higher levels of spiritual attainment. This is indeed how previous generations have often seen the spiritual journey, although many people today see these stages as overlapping (happening simultaneously with emphases on the successive stages) or even cyclic (going deeper every time through the process).[9]

But even if we do view the journey in a linear, developmental way, we know that roads are never exactly straight. As Lao Tzu (a Chinese Taoist mystic) once wrote, "The road ahead seems to go backwards." That's why I call it a roadmap; although it is a good guide to where we will eventually be going, most of us will take a meandering or "two steps forward, one step back" approach to getting there.

This journey is not about spiritual athleticism, although certainly there have been people in the history of Christianity who have approached it that way. It is not about attainment. Instead, true mysticism is about relationship, and genuine relationship always takes time. It is always messy. It also involves mistakes, missteps, pain, causing pain to others, forgiveness, reconciliation, compassion, and rest. This is not a contest. It is about making a home with God.

So how do we effect this homecoming? How do we grow into God? It usually doesn't begin with us, but with something that God does *in* us, or *for* us. It's a profound experience that Evelyn Underhill calls *Awakening* . . .

• For Questions and Answers that clarify points in this Introduction, turn to page 121.

The next day Jesus decided to go to Galilee. He found Philip and said to him, "Follow me." . . . Philip found Nathanael and said to him, "We have found him about whom Moses in the Law and also the prophets wrote, Jesus son of Joseph from Nazareth." Nathanael said to him, "Can anything good come out of Nazareth?" Philip said to him, "Come and see." When Jesus saw Nathanael coming towards him, he said of him, "Here is truly an Israelite in whom there is no deceit!" Nathanael asked him, "Where did you come to know me?" Jesus answered, "I saw you under the fig tree before Philip called you." Nathanael replied, "Rabbi, you are the Son of God! You are the King of Israel!" Jesus answered, "Do you believe because I told you that I saw you under the fig tree? You will see greater things than these." And he said to him, "Very truly, I tell you, you will see heaven opened and the angels of God ascending and descending upon the Son of Man."

—John 1:43–57

Chapter One

Awakening

In the passage on the facing page from the Gospel of John, Jesus issues a call to his future disciples Philip and Nathanael. He calls them to follow him and he gets Nathanael's attention with a very minor miracle: he knew what Nathanael was doing when Nathanael was alone. But he promises that if he comes with him, Nathanael will see much greater things.

Nathanael is not unique—this is something that happens to a lot of people; perhaps it has even happened to you. It seems to be the way God works: he shows us just a little bit, enough to turn us from our intended course, and promises that if we will come with him, he will show us much, much more.

This is the essence of Awakening. It is a minor miracle—sometimes dramatic, sometimes subtle, but usually it is just enough to make us go, "Whoa! What was that?" and start us searching in a direction we might not have gone otherwise.

It is, in a sense, an experience of conversion, but not in the way we normally think about that word. For it is not a conversion to a set of doctrines or beliefs, but a conversion—a transformation, if you will—of one's very perception of Reality.

"You Must Be Born Again"

When we are born the first time, it is into a world that revolves around ourselves. When we have an Awakening experience, we are born again, but this time into a world in which the locus of importance is elsewhere—in fact, *everywhere*. Awakening is a momentary flash of insight when we are granted a glimpse of the universe as God sees it.

In college, I struggled mightily with the fundamentalist teachings I had grown up with; I was terrified that God would reject me. I was reading a lot of Anglican poets, theologians, and mystics, so when a friend said, "Let's go see what those Anglicans mean by 'church,'" I was primed for the experience.

Primed maybe, but not ready. The church of my childhood harbored a deep distrust of art or beauty, especially in worship spaces, so my jaw dropped when I encountered the gothic sanctuary covered with tapestries, icons, and statuary, as well as the enormous, gory crucifix staring down at me in all its agony—mesmerizing and deeply moving.

But what really shook me was when the priest gave the call for communion. I cannot say why, but I raced for the communion rail and knelt, certain that I had found what I had been searching for all of my life.

And that's when it happened. I heard the voice of the Holy Spirit speaking to me. As the priest placed that wafer on my tongue, I felt a presence wash over me like an ocean wave and I heard an audible voice: "This is my mercy for you. You can feel it. You can taste it. It is real." Not only had I not been rejected by God, I had been *chosen*. I had been *called*. And I glimpsed something of God that completely reoriented my life. I was *awakened*.

Awakening takes different forms for everyone. For some it may be a half hour in which everything seems to glow with transcendent import. Or perhaps it is a moment in which you seem to see right into people's souls and feel such profound compassion for them your heart feels likely to burst. Perhaps it is an inrushing of energy that leaves you dazed and tingling. Perhaps, like me, you are actually *in* church and the voice of the Spirit whispers to you audibly in a way you cannot ignore or deny. Or perhaps a walk in the woods turns into a more sacred experience than any church service you've ever been to, as in this account from Quaker mystic Rufus Jones:

I was walking alone in a forest, trying to map out my plan of life and confronted with issues which seemed too complex and difficult for my mind to solve. Suddenly I felt the walls between the visible and the invisible grow thin and the Eternal seemed to break through into the world where I was. I saw no flood of light, I heard no voice, but I felt as though I were face to face with a higher order of reality than that of the trees or mountains. I went down on my knees there in the woods with that same feeling of awe which compelled men in earlier times to take off their shoes from their feet. A sense of mission broke in on me and I felt that I was being called to a well-defined task of like to which I then and there dedicated myself.[1]

Such an experience can utterly undo a person. It can be disorienting, frightening, inspiring, and dangerous. In spiritual direction, we call it a Spiritual Emergence, or even a Spiritual Emergency—and indeed people often flee to the emergency room, fearing that they are going crazy or are physically ill.

Some people are glad when the experience passes. "Thank God *that's* over," they say as they go back to life as usual. And for some people it's not so dramatic. But whether the experience is subtle or intense, there are many who do not go back to business-as-usual; for these people it is the beginning of the end—in a good way. Because in that glimpse they realize that the way they have been living has little meaning in the grand scheme of things, that they are not who they thought they were; they've had a little taste of God, and they want more. They are *hooked*.

AN INVITATION

If you want to grow spiritually, if you want to walk the mystic's path, be careful and beware what you ask for. You may be singing with REM, "It's the end of the world as we know it, and I feel fine," and, indeed, you may be so drunk on divine ecstasy that you're lighting the flame-thrower yourself, but your world *will* end. And worlds do not end without tears.

When Philip and Nathanael followed Jesus, they left everything and everyone they knew behind. They left their jobs, their homes, their families, their *lives*. What God may be calling you to may not be so extreme—but then again, it might be. That's a risk you take on this journey. Just how far down does the rabbit hole go?

But here is the comfort—the only things coming to an end are unreal things—nothing real is ending, only illusions of security, or competence, or grandeur. Everything that you thought you were, but that you are *not*, in fact, is called into question by this experience, and it can be both liberating and scary as hell.

The Awakening experience is actually very common. Some people run from it as far and as fast as they can. But those who are truly mystics, who embrace the experience, set their feet upon a path that has no end. There will be more hardships, sure, more worlds to end, you can be sure of that, but also joy and the greatest gift God can bestow upon a human being: the knowledge of our true selves, our true nature, our true purpose.

The experience of Awakening is, in a way, an *Invitation*—not to a safe and warm and fuzzy spirituality, but to Judgment Day. For in this fleeting glimpse of capital *R* Reality, the true nature of our lives is revealed. In the few precious moments that the veil is drawn back, we see the ultimate worth of our lives and the relative meaninglessness with which we fill them.

A MYSTIC'S STORY: JULIAN OF NORWICH

Awakening often begins with a vision of the Real, and Julian of Norwich desperately wanted to have such a vision. As a young woman in the fourteenth century, she prayed for a threefold favor from God: First she wanted to behold the crucifixion, to be as one who stood at the foot of the cross so that she might better comprehend Jesus's suffering and share his compassion for the world. The second favor she asked was to be made deathly ill before she was thirty years old so that she might be purged of herself and be able to live more fully in the life of Christ. The third petition was that God grant her three wounds: the wound of compassion, the wound of contrition, and the wound of willful longing toward God.

We are conscious of the fact that prophecies are often self-fulfilling, so it is not too surprising that her request was granted. At the end of her twenty-ninth year she fell ill with an unspecified disease that brought her to the very brink of death. A priest was summoned; he suspended a crucifix above her head and gave her the last rites.

And as she lay there, staring at the face of the crucifix, shuddering with fever, the crucifix came to life and Julian was granted sixteen "shewings," or visions. We know about these visions because soon after she recovered, Julian wrote them down. Then, twenty years later, she wrote them down again, only this time with the benefit of many years' reflection. Thus we have a short manuscript and a longer manuscript from Julian. Both are valuable, but it is generally the longer version that is read popularly.

Pick up a copy. It is widely available and should be read by everyone on a spiritual path. Because she lived in the fourteenth century, Julian writes in Middle English, and along with Geoffrey Chaucer, she is one of early English's literary pioneers. In fact, hers is the first book written in English by a woman, and though she calls herself "unlettered," she is, in fact, a literary, political, and religious genius. Feminists (and I include myself here) have much to rejoice at—not only Julian's literary achievements but also her theological chutzpah.

Who was this amazing woman? Her real name is lost to us. We call her Julian only because of her association with the Church of St. Julian in Norwich, England. Visions are a dime a dozen in the history of religions and the Church has always been suspicious of them. Yet Julian's visions were immediately recognized as being genuine, although it is true that not everyone appreciated what she had to say—some of which was shocking in her day as well as in ours.

It is difficult to pin down one main teaching, but several threads are discernible in Julian's work. One of the most amazing concerns God's wrath. She writes, "Seeing these things I thought it was necessary to see and know that we are sinners . . . deserving pain and wrath. And yet, in spite of this, I saw that, in fact, our Lord was never angry and never will be. For he is God: Good, Life, Truth, Love, Peace . . . God is the Goodness that cannot be angry."[2]

What is she doing here? Julian is an obedient daughter of the Church. Her self-image is that she is wholly and completely orthodox, reluctant to err in any way or to contradict Church teaching. But she is in a quandary: her project is to relate what she saw of God in her visions, and the difficulty for her is that very often the things she saw did not agree with the teachings of the Church. As we saw above, Awakening experiences often have the effect of jolting us out of our comfortable religious paradigms, revealing to us things that the orthodox would consider . . . well, *unorthodox*. Julian tries to be true to her vision and yet does not want to rock the boat, and she has to pedal pretty hard to have it both ways.

She writes, "I thought it was necessary to see and know that we are sinners . . . deserving pain and wrath," but then she has to admit the truth that she did not behold any wrath in God when she had her vision. The God Julian beheld on her sickbed was a God filled only with goodness. That which separates us from God is not God's wrath or his offended honor or God's need for justice, but simply our own shame, which God pleads with us to let go of so that we can enjoy communion with him.

This is in marked contrast to the theologians of Julian's day (who placed the block to communion between God and humanity in God— God refuses communion with humans because of human sin). Julian says that God embraces us always; it is *we* who turn away from him. We do this not because God holds our sin against us, but because we live in shame of our sin and cannot let go of it. It is not that God will not forgive us; it is that we cannot forgive ourselves.

Julian says that there is a part of every person that does not consent to sin and never will, and that is our true soul, which is at one with God and ever shall be. Julian writes, "As long as we are in this life . . . our Lord God touches us tenderly and calls to us blissfully, saying to our soul: 'Let be all your love, my dear and worthy child: turn to me—for I am enough for you—enjoy your Savior and your salvation.'"[3]

Likewise, Julian tap dances deftly around the subject of hell. She says that, in her vision, "I wanted—as much as I dared—to see Hell and Purgatory. I did not intend to doubt anything belonging to the Faith, for I truly believe that Hell and Purgatory serve the purpose that Holy Church teaches they do. But I wanted to learn everything I could about my Faith so that I might live more faithfully to God and do well. But despite my desire, I could see nothing of them."[4]

She doesn't come right out and say, "There is no Hell." Instead, she says, "The Church teaches that Hell and Purgatory are real, and so of course, it must be so; but *I could see nothing of them.*" Thus, she cleverly protects her orthodoxy and challenges it in the very same statement.

But for all of her boldness, Julian's writings are most rewarding because of her deep mysticism. She invents many words in her book, no doubt because she needed them and they did not yet exist. One word she uses repeatedly is "oneing."[5] God "ones" us to himself, God is "oneing" the universe. Today we may say "uniting" or "atonement" (at-one-ment) but these have different shades of meaning. For Julian, all the universe resides in God. "See!" she writes, "I am God. See! I am in all things. See! I do all things. See! I lift never my hands off my works, nor ever shall. See! I lead all things to the end I ordained it to from the beginning, by the same Might, Wisdom and Love through which I made it. How should any thing be amiss?"[6]

And this is the great comforting kernel of Julian's work: as distressing as sin, suffering, and evil are, as difficult as it is to reconcile these things with God's love, in the end Julian is convinced that "all things work together for the good,"[7] and in her visions she is told to be at peace. God is in control, God embraces the world in love always, and nothing and no one will ever be lost. "All shall be well," she is told. "All shall be well, and all shall be well, and all manner of thing shall be well."[8]

Julian gives us an image of God as mother, cradling the world, cooing at it like her child, comforting it, and promising to keep it safe. She calls Jesus "our mother in nature and in grace."[9] The cross was his travail of childbirth and we his children. The milk by which we are suckled is the sacraments, and the bosom to which we cling is his wounded side.[10] We can run to him when we are hurting, and as Julian says, "The dear gracious hands of our Mother are ever about us, and eager to help."[11]

Julian is thus not only one of the first women ever to write in English, but she is most assuredly the first feminist theologian.

If we must have a single image with which to typify her visions, it would be her description of the hazelnut. She writes that God "showed me more, a little thing, the size of a hazelnut, on the palm of my hand, round like a ball. I looked at it thoughtfully and wondered, 'What is this?' And the answer came, 'It is all that is made.' I marveled that it continued to exist and did not suddenly disintegrate; it was so small. And again my mind supplied the answer, 'It exists, both now and for ever, because God loves it.' In short, everything owes its existence to the love of God."[12]

Julian's fever dream was a true Awakening experience because in it she saw a God very different from the one she was given: instead of a God of wrath, she saw only a God of love; instead of hell, she saw only mercy; instead of sin, she saw only illusion. Julian's God is big enough to hold the whole universe in the palm of his hand, and yet he nurses and supports it out of pure and eternal love. Yes, sin is troubling, she says, but all will be well. Yes, the Church teaches God is wrathful and people go to hell, but I could not see it. Yes, God is our father, but Jesus is our mother; he gave birth to us and he cradles us in love now and forever.

Because of this experience, Julian turned to a life of constant contemplation as an anchoress. "What is an anchoress?" you might be asking, and the answer may shock you. An anchorite (or anchoress if she was a woman) was a person who allowed him- or herself to be shut into a single room for the rest of his or her life. The Church has since condemned this kind of "morbid seclusion" but in medieval times, it was quite common.

Julian did not actually have that lonely a life, however. One side of her room had a window into the Church so she could participate in the Mass. Another window allowed her to commune with nature, receive her meals, and offer spiritual direction to the many pilgrims who came for advice. She also had the company of her beloved cat; Julian is sometimes shown with her cat in icons.

Soon after her vision, she asked to be shut up in the Church of St. Julian to better devote her life to prayer and meditation upon her visions, a request that was granted when she was installed on May 16, 1373. Her Awakening experience led her in a radical new direction. It started her on the road to a deep mysticism that changed her forever and contributed to the literature of mysticism in an invaluable way that continues to benefit us today.

- *For Questions and Answers that clarify points in this chapter, turn to page 131.*
- *To read what the mystics say about Awakening, turn to page 183.*
- *To try some exercises around Awakening, turn to page 237.*

Then the people of Jerusalem and all Judea were going out to [John], and all the region along the Jordan, and they were baptized by him in the river Jordan, confessing their sins. . . . He said to them, ". . . I baptize you with water for repentance, but one who is more powerful than I is coming after me; I am not worthy to carry his sandals. He will baptize you with the Holy Spirit and fire. His winnowing-fork is in his hand, and he will clear his threshing-floor and will gather his wheat into the granary; but the chaff he will burn with unquenchable fire."

—Matthew 3:5–10

Chapter Two

Purgation

About ten years ago, my wife, Kate, and I owned a sweet but rather dim-witted black cocker spaniel named Abigail. Abbey was one of those dogs who would eat anything small enough to get her teeth around, so keeping our house dog-proof was a constant challenge. In preparation for an extended visit from my friend Colby—who lives in Europe and is not a dog person—we hired a professional housecleaner to "de-dog" the place with a good polish.

So imagine my surprise when, Colby in tow, I opened the door of our house to an unimaginably noxious odor. I stepped in and nearly killed myself on our slippery hardwood floor—which was covered with a greasy, filmy substance.

My first clue as to what was up was Abbey—lying on her side, tongue out, moaning like a goat in labor. Colby uttered a blasphemous expletive and exited the house, while I investigated further.

It turned out that the evening before, Kate had been deep-frying spring rolls and had left the cast-iron pot of used oil on the stove burner. When the housekeeper came in, she moved the pot to the floor in order to clean the stove, unwittingly giving Abbey access to a gallon and a half of yummy used oil. She drank every last drop and over the next several hours was thoughtful enough to oil our floors as it leaked out the other end.

For the next several days, she was one sick puppy. She was also as cleaned out as is possible for a dog to be and live to tell the tale. For seventy-two hours she barely moved, and every now and then I went over to check that she was still breathing. She was, and I hoped that the experience gave her a smidgen of insight, but knowing Abbey, I tend to doubt it.

To be sure, this was an experience of Purgation, and as Abbey found out the hard way, this is not always pleasant. It is necessary, however, if we are serious about walking the mystic's path.

Like Abbey, we tend to be hungry for things that are not good for us—greedy for them, even. We consume without thinking, swayed by peer pressure and the media—which is just peer pressure writ large—and by our own insecurities and our inexplicable inner longings. We consume because there is a place in us that feels empty, but very rarely do the fillers actually satisfy us. Like Abigail, we eat and eat and eat—or we buy, buy, buy, or we work, work, work. But eventually such consumption will only make us ill.

Abigail had no choice but to excrete all she had consumed—and in such a considerate and convenient manner—and there was very little thought behind it. But with us, it is different.

In our last chapter we talked about Awakening, an experience that ushers us—however briefly—into the Divine presence. It is often a profound and unsettling experience. But it is also an invitation. To borrow imagery from one of Jesus's parables, in our Awakening experience, we have received our invitation to a wedding feast. We have a choice: are we going to go to this feast or not? If we decide to go, what next? Why, we take a bath of course.

Purgation is the first step on the intentional path of Christian mysticism. Awakening is something that happens *to* us, but Purgation is something we set out to do. The invitation has been received, but we have to actually get up off our butts and get moving if we're going to get anywhere.

It's not a pretty sounding word—Purgation. It smacks of plumbing or unseemly bodily functions. Perhaps a more effective word these days might be *cleansing*.

This is exactly what John the Baptist was calling people to do in the reading above. He proclaimed the imminent arrival of the Messiah and bid his people to get ready, by cleansing themselves of all their impurities.

If we want to be mystics, if we want to experience unity with God, then we, too, must consent to be cleaned out. We would not go to a wedding feast in dirty clothes. It is impossible to progress spiritually unless we allow ourselves to be cleansed.

A Call to Discernment

In the temple [Jesus] found people selling cattle, sheep, and doves, and the money-changers seated at their tables. Making a whip of cords, he drove all of them out of the temple, both the sheep and the cattle. He also poured out the coins of the money-changers and overturned their tables. He told those who were selling the doves, "Take these things out of here! Stop making my Father's house a market-place!"

—John 2:14–16

The scene of Jesus cleansing the temple is one of the most arresting and troubling images in all of the Gospels. We hardly recognize the mild-mannered savior we've all come to know and love. Isn't Jesus supposed to be forgiving, meek, gentle, and all of that?

This scene delights me precisely because it shows us a side of Jesus we don't often see: a very human side that gets angry, goes a little out of control, and does things that, upon sober reflection, perhaps he ought not have done. It's a Jesus that I can relate to. But it's also a symbolic snapshot of what God is longing to do. The biggest difference is that I'm sure the moneychangers didn't consent to having their businesses tossed; God, however, wants our permission to bust our place up.

But he wants to do it just the same. Even when we think symbolically, it's a strange image. Why would God want that? It's a violent scene and it's scary to think that God has such violent feelings toward us.

Chapter Two

The good news is that God's violent feelings aren't really about us; the bad news is he still wants to trash the place, and the place in question is our lives. He wants to shake it up—not just a little bit, a lot. What God is really up to is a huge spring cleaning.

Once we have our Awakening experience and we get serious about wanting to follow the mystics' path, we instantly come to the hard part—moral preparation. Before God can live in us, we have to clean the guest room.

But clean it of what? Sin? In my opinion, too much is made of sin, and at the same time, not enough. Christianity has done a terrible job in its teaching about sin, elevating sexual sins to a place of ultimate importance and almost completely ignoring social sins such as our casual acceptance of hunger, war, disenfranchisement, or turning the mentally ill out onto the street.

For those of us who have been really wounded by over-moralistic versions of Christianity, the language of sin is not all that helpful. So instead imagine it in terms of Reality and unreality. God can only really deal with what is Real. So if we want to work with God, the unreal has to go. We must do the difficult work of separating the wheat from the chaff in our lives—gathering the wheat and burning the chaff—and discovering in the process what is really us and what is not, what is Real and what is illusory. We must be willing to discard or cleanse from our lives everything that is not authentic.

In Hindu iconography, the goddess Kali appears as a horrific, violent deity with a flaming sword and a necklace of human skulls, dancing on a corpse. And at the same time, she is the sweet and loving mother of the world. A contradiction? No, because her ferocity is directed only against illusion. Her violent action is always for our highest good. If you have ever seen a picture of Kali, I'm sure you'll agree that she's someone you want on *your* side.

Sin and illusion are not the only ways of viewing the stuff that needs to go. What we need to be cleansed of is *anything that separates us from God*. And that's going to be different for different people.

What separates me from God might not be a problem for you. For Antoinette Bourignan, a Flemish mystic in the seventeenth century, a single penny was enough to create a barrier between herself and God,[1] but for others, wealth is not an obstacle because it is simply not that important to them.

This is a call to *discernment*—for we are discerning what is real from what is not, what separates us from God from what supports our intimacy with him. To help us make these discernments, the mystics recommend a little practice called Recollection.

SPIRITUAL PRACTICE: RECOLLECTION

Recollection is the medieval Christian name for a spiritual practice that will probably be very familiar to you. We call it "meditation." It is, essentially, sitting quietly before God. We are gathering together—re-collecting—our scattered attention, and focusing our whole awareness into a single point. It doesn't really matter what that point is—it can be the visual contemplation of a leaf, the repetition of a sacred word or phrase (similar to a mantra), or the concentration on one's breath going in and out.

Like all meditation, it is hard work, but what does it do for us? How does this contribute to our Purgation?

When we sit in silence, it is revealed to us how very little we actually need, how little there is to actually be concerned about, and how our lives are dependent upon the love of God. In Recollection it is revealed to us how little of our obsessive consumption is necessary or helpful and how much we need the love, companionship, and care of God. As the Greek ascetic Evagrius of Pontus wrote, "Someone who is tied up cannot run. Just so, the spiritual intellect that is still a slave to its obsessive desires can never see the domain of spiritual prayer, because it is dragged all over the place by compulsive ideations and cannot achieve the necessary intellectual stillness."[2] Recollection reveals to us what we can let go of, what our lives need to be purged of—in other words, how to be simple—for it is only when we are standing in our simplicity that we can progress to the next stage of mystical awareness.

But let's not get ahead of ourselves. Purgation starts with getting quiet. Hopefully this will not be as fraught with gastric distress as Abbey's "quiet period" after her unfortunate purgation, but you never know. Few children *like* being told they have to take a bath or clean their rooms. Part of growing into spiritual maturity is being willing to do something even when it isn't fun or pleasant or easy.

Armed with Recollection as a practical tool for discernment, the prospective mystic can embark on a two-step process of deep and productive Purgation. The two steps are Detachment and Mortification (don't worry, it sounds more medieval than it is). But before we embark on a detailed exploration of these sub-stages, let's hear from the Orthodox mystical tradition about the importance of Recollection to the beginning mystic.

A Mystics' Story: The Way of a Pilgrim

One of the greatest classics of Russian Orthodox spiritual literature is a curious little book called *The Way of a Pilgrim*. First published in 1884, it tells the story of an anonymous Russian Christian, wandering the countryside, searching for spiritual guidance. No one knows whether the book is fiction or nonfiction, whether it tells the story of a real person, a fictional person, or a composite of many seekers encountered by its anonymous author.

Like all great myth, however, regardless of whether the book depicts historical fact, it certainly tells a *true* story, in that the unnamed Pilgrim is, in the end, *us*, and his questions and struggles are *truly* ours.

The book follows no overarching plot line, but instead is a series of episodes, each of which serves to instruct the Pilgrim—and us, of course. For our purposes, a few scenes from the first chapter will illustrate the kind of adventures the Pilgrim meets with, as well as the practice of Recollection.

The Pilgrim seeks out a devout nobleman and asks his advice. "St. Paul says we must 'pray constantly,' but how is that even possible?" he asks. The nobleman gives this some thought and tells him that he must ask God to teach him how to do this, but to be patient, because it takes time. The nobleman then generously gives the Pilgrim some food and a place to sleep for the night.

The next day while the Pilgrim is walking he comes across a monk who is heading in the same direction. The monk invites the Pilgrim to stay at his monastery that night and the Pilgrim gratefully accepts. As they walk, the Pilgrim shares his struggle with prayer with the monk, who cheerfully tells him to be at peace. Once at the monastery, the monk teaches the Pilgrim how to do the Jesus prayer:

> The ceaseless Jesus Prayer is a continuous, uninterrupted call on the holy name of Jesus Christ with the lips, mind, and heart; and in the awareness of His abiding presence it is a plea for His blessing in all undertakings, in all places, at all times, even in sleep. The words of the Prayer are: "Lord Jesus Christ, have mercy on me!" Anyone who becomes accustomed to this Prayer will experience great comfort as well as the need to say it continuously.[3]

The monk then tells him about a book called the *Philokalia*, a collection of writings from early Christian mystics about the spiritual life. Showing him a copy, he opens it and reads,

> Sit alone and in silence; bow your head and close your eyes; relax your breathing and with your imagination look into your heart; direct your thoughts from your head into your heart. And while inhaling say, "Lord Jesus Christ, have mercy on me," either softly with your lips or in your mind. Endeavor to fight distractions but be patient and peaceful and repeat this process frequently.[4]

Chapter Two

The Pilgrim is ecstatic. Finally, he has found an answer to his question! He finds a hut to practice in, and begins. Immediately, though, he runs into trouble. He feels bored, sleepy, and lazy. Dark thoughts trouble him. So he goes back to the monk for advice.

The monk greets him cheerfully and seems to think that his experience is entirely normal. "A war is being waged for your soul, brother!" he declares. "You must persevere, and not let the world of darkness defeat you!" He then gives the Pilgrim a rosary to help him count and tells him to say the Jesus Prayer 6,000 times per day.

With excitement, the Pilgrim returns to his hut and starts. The first two days are tough, but then something begins to shift. He notices that not only is praying getting easier, but whenever he is *not* praying, he feels an internal pressure to get back to it.

It becomes easier and easier until the prayer becomes second nature and begins to pray itself. When he reports this to the monk, his friend is affirming. "This is great! Now, don't waste this opportunity. Step it up, and pray it 12,000 times per day."

It is hard, but if the Pilgrim begins early in the morning, he is able to finish all 12,000 repetitions just before it is time to blow out the lamp and get some sleep. The Pilgrim seems to enter an altered state in which the Prayer wakes him, speaks itself throughout the day, and causes him such great joy that he can barely contain it. When he returns to the monk for spiritual direction, he is told, "You have done it! You are praying without ceasing. You can now pray it as many times as you like, and live every moment in the presence of God, who will now direct your every move."

Not long after, the monk dies, and with tears in his eyes the Pilgrim hits the road again. No longer having access to the wisdom of the *Philokalia*—for he had been reading the monk's copy—he spends all that he has on a beat-up used copy.

Although he has more questions and adventures, this practice of Recollection—called Hesychastic Prayer by Orthodox Christians—provides the Pilgrim with a sure foundation for his continued growth into God. As he sums it up, "So now I walk and say the Jesus Prayer without ceasing and it is more precious and sweet to me than anything else in the world. . . . I walk in a semiconscious state without worries, interests, and temptations. My only desire and attraction is for solitude and the ceaseless recitation of the Jesus Prayer."[5]

Of course, few of us will be able to pray the Jesus Prayer 12,000 times in a single day, but praying it for even one round of the rosary will help and instruct us, for it will quiet the mind, will re-collect our thoughts, and will allow us to focus our attention—an essential skill for any aspiring mystic.

STEP ONE: DETACHMENT

None of you can become my disciple if
you do not give up all your possessions.

—Luke 14:33

Be passersby.

—Gospel of Thomas, 42

In the classic book of Jewish mysticism, the *Zohar*, there is the story of how Abraham came to know the true God. One morning he arose and saw the sun rising in the east. It instantly occurred to him that this great orb of light must be God. "This is the King that created me!" he cried, and he worshipped the sun all day.

That same night, the sun went down and the moon rose in its place. Abraham's faith was shattered and he said to himself, "This silver orb must rule over the golden one I worshipped all day, since the golden one was darkened before it and does not shine anymore." So he prostrated himself to the moon and worshipped it all night.

Then, in the morning, he saw the darkness flee and the light growing in the east again, and he wept for joy, saying, "Of course! There is a King who rules over all of these orbs!" and in that moment he gained knowledge of the true God and began to worship him aright.

What I like about this story is that no one is blaming Abraham for worshipping the wrong thing as God—it's a process of trial and error, and he eventually finds his way around to the truth. Christian mysticism is a kindly process. I'm not saying it isn't hard work or that it isn't painful, just that it isn't inhuman. We make mistakes, we learn from them, we go on to make other mistakes, we learn from them, and eventually we find ourselves closer to God than we were before. No shame, no blame, just herky-jerky progress.

The important thing about Abraham's story is not that he made mistakes—but that he *learns* from them. He doesn't cling to his mistakes, he doesn't get hung up on the fact that he's made them or get down on himself for them. He does not, out of some misdirected sense of pride, insist that he was right all along. Though he's excited about that sun, he's quick to discard it once the moon comes along, but he's not attached to that moon, either. When a greater truth is revealed, he just as eagerly grabs onto that and gets on with the task at hand.

It's a story paralleled in the story of Jesus's baptism. People are eager to latch onto John the Baptist to proclaim him the Messiah, but he dissuades them. "Don't get attached to me!" he is saying, "another one is coming, and I'm not worthy to tie his shoes!"[6] And sure enough, when Jesus gets there, he proves his messiah-ness by casting out those gnarly demons right out there in public. Once people get over their shock, they say, "See ya later, John"—or at least some of them do. Some of them continue to follow John, but more of them, like Abraham in the story from the *Zohar*, are able to recognize their error and chart a new course toward a greater light.

This is what the Purgative Way in Christian mysticism is asking us to do: to recognize that what we thought was God, what we thought was "religion," what we thought was *us*, has all been an illusion. In our Awakening experience, we're given a momentary glimpse of the Real, of the universe *as it really is*. Then we have a choice: are we going to ignore this new revelation and pretend that everything is just as it has always been or are we going to drop the pretenses we have been living with and chart a new course?

Through Recollection—meditation—we focus our mind so that we can glimpse more of this Real World. Awakening is like the sun that Abraham saw; Recollection is like the moon, leading him further and further toward Truth. The next step in our Purgative journey is Detachment—the ability to let previous revelations go completely—so that a deeper, truer view of God, the universe, and ourselves can emerge.

When I hear the word *Detachment*, I think of the Buddhist attitude of letting go; this is similar to what the Christian mystics are trying to get at. In the Gospel of Thomas, Jesus commands us to "Be passersby," to not get too attached to things here in this life.

The Catholic tradition has long insisted on three arenas in which we must practice detachment: *poverty, chastity, and obedience:*

Poverty refers to the complete surrender of your goods, the conscious process of stripping away all those finite things that you unduly value—such as money or social position. (In case you thought this was going to be easy!) *Chastity* refers to a complete surrender of your body, of all that you are, to God—a commitment to be God's lover and to be faithful only to him. *Obedience* is the complete surrender of your will to the Divine will, being willing to simply "go with the flow" regardless of what floats your way. These are actually three aspects of one act of surrender—of all that you have, all that you are, and all that you want—to God.

Why is this necessary? Because when Christ arrives, he cannot lodge in an inn if there are no vacancies. As Meister Eckhart wrote, "No container can hold two kinds of liquid. If it is to hold wine, we must necessarily pour out the water; it must become empty and void. If, therefore, you are to receive divine joy and God, you must necessarily pour out the creatures."7 God cannot pour himself into a jar that is already full—it must first be emptied of all attachments, all selfhood, all desire, and all illusion—before it can be filled with what is Real.

Why is this? Is it because God is a tyrant who does not want us to have any sense of self or pleasure? Far from it. God wants us to break through the illusion that there is anything that is *not* God. Poverty is easy; letting go of your ideas about who God is or what God wants—that's hard. Face it, friends, none of us is Abraham—I'd probably have been worshipping that sun for a month or more before I got that whole moon thing.

This is not just a poverty of possessions we are being called to, but a poverty of the spirit as well. We must let go of the idea that we know anything or that we have achieved any spiritual merit—for these, too, are illusions. As Nicholas of Cusa wrote, "It is therefore clear that all we know of truth is that the Absolute Truth, as it is, is beyond our grasp. The more mindfully we learn this lesson of ignorance, the closer we draw to truth itself."[8] For many of us, self-worth comes from what we know or what we have accomplished rather than from the things we have accumulated, so letting go of our privilege is just as much intellectual as it is physical. These non-corporeal belongings must be surrendered, too.

By surrendering ourselves to detachment, we open ourselves to being stripped of everything that is not Real. Our possessions are not ours; if we cling to them, they must go. Our spouses are not our possessions; we have them for a time and they are gone. Only God is with us forever. The human will is a fickle thing. Only the will of God is constant and we must give up the idea that we know what we are doing. Finally, even our ideas of what Reality is, who God is, and who we are has to go. Everything illusory must be stripped away until the only thing left is what is Real—and I do mean Real with a capital *R*.

DON'T PANIC—YOU HAVE TO BE READY

"This is *way* too hard," you may say. "I can't give up *everything*. How will I live?" Don't panic. The truth is that it *is* that hard and it *isn't*. The irony is that you don't have to give up any of it so long as you're not attached to any of it. If you don't care at all for your family or your car or your job, you can keep them. Only those things that you value *more than God*, that will get in the way of total surrender to God, must go. Chew on that for a while.

This is what Jesus meant when he said, "anyone who does not hate his father and his mother is not worthy of me" (Luke 14:26). This is hyperbole—he doesn't really want you to hate anybody, including yourself. What he's asking you to do is to evaluate your priorities—remember, this stage is about discernment—so anything that you value more than God will become an obstacle on this path and has to go.

But this is a *willing* letting go. If you're not ready to let it go, don't let it go. Be where you are. God will meet you there. It will be fine. But when you are ready, when you are able, when you are tired of living in Plato's cave with only shadow-puppets for your companions, when you are hungry for the real and harsh light of day, step on out. God will be waiting.

There is a wonderful story in the Desert Fathers. Some bandits come to raid the cave of one of the hermits. They hold the old man at knifepoint and tell him, "We've come to take everything you own." "Take whatever you see," says the hermit. So they pile everything they can find on their donkey and go on their way. But they unknowingly leave behind a little bag that has fallen behind a rock. Seeing the bag, the hermit picks it up and runs after them, shouting, "Hey, you forgot this!"

God is the Great Thief, ready to take all that is not Real. So when you are ready to hand back, with a smile, everything you have ever known, then we can get serious about this Detachment thing. Are you there yet?

Don't worry. If you are serious about the spiritual path, if you are sincere and have brought your desire to God earnestly, then it is already underway. Quietly, slowly, in doses we can tolerate, God is revealing to us the unreality of our lives. We have only to decide whether we will cooperate, whether we are willing to let go of what's not Real. Usually we don't notice it, but God is working on us all the time. That's a comforting fact that you can trust.

And don't be discouraged if you don't do it perfectly—as the great Orthodox mystic John Climacus wrote, "Do not be surprised if you fall back into the old ways every day. Do not be disheartened but resolve to do something positive, and without question, that angel who stands guard over you will honor your perseverance."[9] This kind of growth happens only in fits and starts.

Also, keep in mind that few of us can let go of things as heroically as the Desert Fathers or Saint Francis or even Martin Luther (more on them later). But truthfully, heroes are overrated. Jesus didn't come to call on heroes; just normal folks like you and me—people who put their pants on one leg at a time, people who blaspheme when we slam our hands in the car door, people who love God as much as we can with the woundedness that we carry. Thanks be to God.

Okay, that's a lot. But you do realize we're only getting started, right?

STEP TWO: MORTIFICATION

The angel said to her, "The Holy Spirit will come upon you, and the power of the Most High will overshadow you; therefore the child to be born will be holy; he will be called Son of God. And now, your relative Elizabeth in her old age has also conceived a son; and this is the sixth month for her who was said to be barren. For nothing will be impossible with God." Then Mary said, "Here am I, the servant of the Lord; let it be with me according to your word."

—Luke 1:35-38

The Desert Fathers and Mothers emerged in the fourth century due to a completely unforeseen tragedy that rocked the fledgling Christian Church. And just what was that tragedy? According to some, it was the worst thing that could have possibly happened to the Church, an event that effectively destroyed Christianity as they had known it. Have you guessed it yet? The tragedy was *acceptance.*

In one fell stroke, the Emperor Constantine took the embattled little Church and made it legal, legit, and worst of all, *popular.* Suddenly gone were the intimate services held in people's homes by candlelight. Gone was the sense of danger and the specialness that comes when you think that you alone are God's faithful people.

Suddenly the bishops were moving from their hovels into palaces, trading their homespun for Roman finery. The services moved from house-churches to enormous government buildings, the basilicas. And not only that, they incorporated lots of elements from the local native traditions—the Greek and Roman mystery religions.

"Nonsense!" the old-time Christians shouted. "All this stuff is nonsense! Where did our religion go?" They felt that, in making their faith legal, Constantine had stolen it away from them.

It forced them to do some heavy-duty discernment, to reevaluate their lives. What was congruent with the Truth they had received, and what was not?

When their discernment was completed, they left the cities—and Constantine's "new and improved" Christianity. They sold their houses, gave the money to the poor, and took up residence in caves in the Egyptian desert. This took a lot of guts. They said "yes" to God—with their lives.

A little girl named Mary did the same. When the angel appeared and told her what God had planned for her, it was not some kind of romantic, beautiful revelation, seen through the gauzy haze of piety and religious romanticism from the safety of being 2,000 years removed from the event.

Imagine that *you* are Mary, a thirteen-year-old girl, being told that you will bear a child out of wedlock, that you will shame your family forever, that your child will be a bastard, that every shred of safety and decency and respect is from this moment yanked away from you. How do *you* respond?

If Gabriel had come to me (which would make for a miraculous birth indeed), I would have said, "Are you nuts? Find another incubator, smart guy, because I have plans." Which is, no doubt, why God chose Mary and not me to bear his son.

What amazes me, though, is the magnitude of what was being asked of her—the son of God was to be born in her, and to say yes to that would completely turn her life upside down. And she said, "Yes." Amazing.

Yet this is what God asks of all of us. We have seen the things we cling to that are not Real—so what? We must let go of them. Not just in our heads, but in our lives. The next step is changing how we actually *live*.

The mystics call this second stage of Purgation by an odd name: Mortification. Now, like you, when I hear this word I think of medieval processions filled with stringy-haired pilgrims whipping their own backs into bloody strips, and that is indeed one meaning of the word. But the mystics mean something more subtle—and infinitely more useful—than turning our backs into hamburger.

Mortification means disciplining our lives so that they are congruent with the revelation of Reality we have discerned. Once we have seen what is true and what is false in our lives, the next step is to do something about it, to live differently, in a way that honors and conforms to Reality as we now understand it.

This might mean something as dramatic as selling your house, leaving everything behind, and moving to the desert. If you are a little girl named Mary, it might mean abandoning your dreams of having a normal, respectable life. But more likely it is going to be something more individual, more idiosyncratic.

What might it mean for you? When the seed of God is planted in you, when you are given a glimpse of the Real, when you have seen what is essential and what is dross, how will *your* life change?

For now, perhaps it is enough to simply acknowledge that God wants to be born in you. Will you consent, like Mary, knowing that it might require changes you cannot even dream of right now? Will you say "yes," or will you say, "Are you nuts?" Both are legitimate responses and both are eminently justifiable. God, after all, is like the camel and the tent. Once the camel gets its nose in the tent, it is soon wearing the tent.

Just so, it's very hard to say "yes" to God just a little bit. It's hard to say, "Yes, but just this far . . ." because that probably sounds a lot like "no" to God, who is not famous for his subtlety.

This mysticism thing is not safe; it is not something you can do in a controlled fashion. It's kind of an all-or-nothing thing. So maybe you're not ready yet. That's okay. But maybe you are. Remember that this road to God is not laid out in a straight line. We are invited to grow again and again, and each time, God asks us to see as much as we can in the place we are at and to change as much as we are able. You may be ready for a lot of change, you may be ready for a little, but the question is, are you ready?

If you have seen that your life is out of sync with the mystical vision you have been given, what are you willing to do about it? (Relax—you don't have to answer right now. Just think about it.)

As a child, I used to imagine that God was a friend I could snuggle up to and I used to scoot far to the edge of my single bed to make room for him. I have a much bigger bed, now, but I would like to think that I still make room for God—that I am willing to change how I live, how I act, even how I sleep, in order to be faithful to the Truth I have received. Not perfectly, of course, not every time, every day, not like Mary would have done, certainly, but sincerely, with all that is in me. That's all that God asks of any of us.

A MYSTIC'S STORY: ST. FRANCIS OF ASSISI

Francis never set out to be a saint—in fact, it was a most unlikely vocation for him. The son of a wealthy merchant, he spent his idle youth carousing with his friends, enjoying wine and music, and showing off his fine clothes. Even though he never showed much aptitude for business, it was understood that he would one day take over his father's textile operation, and he seemed not just content, but delighted with his lot in life.

As it is for many young men, the glory of war was seductive for Francis, and when his townsmen set themselves against a rival city, he and his friends donned their polished armor and rode off to battle. Unfortunately, the carefree Francis who went off to war never returned.

He was captured by the enemy and spent more than a year in prison, during which time he suffered a chronic illness. Eventually he was released and, perhaps to assuage a bruised ego at having been unsuccessful in his first military outing, he signed up again to fight abroad. But apparently his illness had weakened him substantially and on the sea voyage to war he fell ill again. He was told in a dream to return to Assisi and this he did.

However, once home, Francis was a changed man. He no longer sought the rowdy company of his friends and he seemed perpetually distracted. He stopped wearing fine clothes and began to eschew excess in all forms.

One day, as Francis was praying in a ruined church called San Damiano, the crucifix came to life and spoke to him. "Go, Francis, and repair my house, which, as you see, is falling into ruin." Francis instantly set about fixing up the ruined church. He went to his father's shop, gathered a load of cloth on a donkey, and went to the marketplace and sold it at a discounted rate.

He took the money to the priest at San Damiano, but the clergyman refused it. In anger, Francis threw the money on the ground and returned home, where his father, who was even more angry, beat the young man within an inch of his life for stealing the cloth.

Francis ran away from home and holed up in a cave where his father would not find him. Finally, covered with dirt and thin as a rail, he returned home, whereupon his father beat him again and locked him in the cellar.

When his father was away, his mother rescued Francis and he returned to San Damiano, where the priest gave him a place to stay. His father was not yet satisfied and dragged Francis before the magistrate and later the bishop in order to strip him of his inheritance rights.

These Francis was all too willing to relinquish. For there before the bishop and all who were watching, Francis stripped off every stitch of clothing he wore and handed them to his father, saying, "Up to now I have called you my father on earth. From now on, however, I only want to address 'Our Father, who art in heaven.'" Naked, he walked out of the town to a nearby monastery, where he was given shelter (and, presumably, some clothes).

Francis soon returned to Assisi though, and taking the cross's instruction to "repair my house" literally, he began begging for stones for the repair of San Damiano. One by one he carried them and set them in place. On one wintry morning in 1208, while resting during the daily Mass, he heard the gospel reading for the day: "Carry no purse, no bag, no sandals. . . . Whenever you enter a town and its people welcome you, eat what is set before you; cure the sick who are there, and say to them, 'The kingdom of God has come near to you.'"[10] As if struck by a brick, Francis realized that his true calling was to poverty and, after Mass was over, he threw away those few things he still possessed: his shoes, his coat, his walking stick, and even his empty wallet.

Feeling elated and strangely, wonderfully free, he covered himself in beggars' robes and began to walk the streets of Assisi singing love songs to his Lady Poverty. Nobody was laughing at him now. In fact, people began to feel inspired by his example and, one by one, other young men walked away from their budding careers and took up beggar's robes to be with him.

Chapter Two

Seeking God's guidance for himself and his followers, Francis entered a church and opened the book of Gospels at random. He did this three times and each time the passage instructed them to leave all behind and follow Jesus. "This is our Rule of Life," Francis told them.

Francis and his followers were far from severe. Ascetics they were, but they were merry ones, to be sure. They roamed the streets begging and singing songs of praise. They preached and encouraged people wherever they went. They worked alongside laborers in the field to earn a bit of bread and rebuilt several churches. They also cared for outcasts and lepers, washing and bandaging their sores and offering them friendship and pastoral care.

More and more young men joined them, until it was impressed upon Francis by his local bishop that they were of such a size that they needed to be recognized. Francis and several of his friars journeyed to Rome to solicit the pope's support for their order. The pope originally rejected his request for an audience, but after having a dream of Francis sustaining a crumbling papal palace, he recalled the young man and heard him out. The Holy Father was significantly moved by the meeting and he gave the friar his blessing.

Upon their return, Francis sent his friars out two by two, just as the Gospel commanded. They saw themselves as the Lord's minstrels, singing hymns of joy and praise, preaching the freedom of poverty, and proclaiming the good news of God's love to every creature.

Soon, a young woman named Clare begged to be admitted to his order. Francis agreed and, under cover of night, Clare and her sister ran away from home to be with the friars. They held their liturgy in the street where Clare and her sister took their vows, had their hair shorn, and entered a convent prepared for them.

(Men felt safe to roam around, which is the way of friars. It was not thought safe for women to do so, so women Franciscans—called Poor Clares—led a more cloistered life as nuns in convents.)

Purgation

Francis lived out the rest of his days preaching holy poverty and trying to the best of his ability to live the Gospel as he understood it. His calling was first and foremost one of Purgation. He practiced Detachment by letting go of all that he did not need, all that served to separate him from the life of freedom promised in the Gospels. And he practiced Mortification by radically changing his style of life in order to be congruent with the vision he had received.

At the same time he lived richly. Though he owned nothing, all things in heaven and earth were his. He had the sky for his blanket and the earth for his carpet. He owned no creature, yet saw every creature as his family and, indeed, as his friend. Eschewing all things, he rejected nothing, embracing even difficult things such as hunger, poverty, and death as precious, cherished siblings. Sister Poverty and Sister Death were loved ones to be embraced in their turn, each bringing good gifts to those who cling to nothing.

- *For Questions and Answers that clarify points in this chapter, turn to page 143.*
- *To read what the mystics say about Purgation, turn to page 186.*
- *To try some exercises around Purgation, turn to page 238.*

And the Spirit immediately drove him out into the wilderness. He was in the wilderness for forty days, tempted by Satan; and he was with the wild beasts; and the angels waited on him.

—Mark 1:12–13

Chapter Three

Transition:
Dark Night of the Senses

When I was in my late teens, I experienced a traumatic abuse of power at the hands of my pastors, an experience that has shaped my religious life to the present day. They demanded absolute obedience of me and my parents, and when my parents refused, my family was excommunicated from the Church.

My bedrock was shattered and what ensued was a crisis of faith that took years to resolve. I was uncertain about my very identity and purpose. My reason for being, for living, had been revealed to be untrustworthy and I had no place to stand. Hurled into a deep depression, I finally found myself poised over the bathroom sink, sharp implement in hand, ready to end my life.

Thank God some part of me heard wisdom that convinced me to simply slink off to bed. But I still quiver when I think how close I came to the brink that night. Fortunately, I was able to tell my parents about it and they got me immediate professional help. That truly saved my life and I am grateful for the miracle of modern psychopharmacology. It might have permanently crippled my liver but it got me through this very early crisis, this dark night of the soul, and it gave me a future. I have had other difficult patches in my life, but as I look back, this was probably the worst.

At the time I was clueless, but the experience was lined with grace. It has given me a great deal of compassion toward others when they were in the midst of their own dark nights. When you really have been there, it makes a difference. It's not something you can put on your pastor's résumé, but it ought to be, because being present with people who are going through crises is an important part of what we clergy do.

And there's a good deal of call for it. When we are in the midst of a crisis, we tend to think that we are somehow unique, that no one has it as bad as we do. But the truth is everyone who reads this book has been through their own dark nights because pain, darkness, and disillusionment are part of everyone's life. What's important is how we cope.

Even Jesus wasn't immune. In his baptism, he underwent a horrific crisis of identity. Jesus comes to the Jordan River to be baptized, and what happens? A theophany happens. Imagine what it must have been like: the heavens break open; the voice of God booms loud enough to cause avalanches in the Judean hills; strange, luminous birds alight upon your head and everyone stares at you like you're from Mars. It's surreal. It's upsetting. And what's more, if you didn't already think you were some kind of supernatural freak, it could really mess with your sense of self.

Jesus is so shaken by the experience that he high-tails it for solitude in the desert, and who can blame him? The desert is another metaphor for the rough patches in our lives and just as evocative as the dark night.

The dark night of the soul is a phrase that has passed into common usage. It comes from St. John of the Cross, a Roman Catholic Carmelite monk in Spain during the sixteenth century. Thrown in prison for trying to reform the Carmelite order, he experienced his own significant dark night. And he wrote about it. His poem and commentary, *Dark Night of the Soul,* is one of the great works of Christian mysticism (more about him, later).

St. John actually meant something very specific by "the dark night of the soul." He spoke of two distinct and very singular experiences known as the "Dark Night of the Senses" and the "Dark Night of the

Spirit." But before we explore these very specific terms, I think it is important to acknowledge what the catch-all *dark night of the soul* has come to mean.

We tend to save this term for the worst of the worst, to describe those times that don't just upset us, but shake us to our core, that make us confront hard questions about our purpose and our identity. And even if they are not mystical experiences *per se*, such dark nights can act as a catalyst to move us closer to or further away from God.

And that is the thing to pay attention to. When we are experiencing our dark nights, where does it leave us on the other side of these events? Leaning on God like never before or with a sense of isolation and estrangement? A lot of it has to do with the degree of hopelessness we feel. For where we feel no hope, it is hard to muster any degree of faith.

When I am going through rough patches, it's easier to have hope if I can just remember that the feelings I am having are not permanent, that emotions rise and fall, and that there is an end to them. Which is not to say that I shouldn't be feeling them, or that you shouldn't, or that anyone shouldn't.

We have this idea in our culture that difficult feelings are bad and that we shouldn't feel them, but I don't think that is true. Negative feelings are useful and important. It was a good and helpful thing for Jesus to go off into the desert. In fact, he didn't do it just once; he was always taking off for some alone time in the hills. When bad things happen, it is only human, it is only right, it is only *good* to feel bad.

When we find ourselves in places of crisis or loss, the most important thing to do is to be in them as fully and completely as we can. When something or someone we loved or trusted has died, the best thing we can possibly do is to grieve. When your own identity and sense of purpose or self has died, a little desert time, a passage through the dark night, is the most appropriate thing. But it's important to remember that we are only visiting; we are not there to stay. The dark night gives way to morning, the desert eventually finds the sea.

Grief is prolonged only if we seek to avoid it or to push it out of consciousness. If we do that, it can dog us for the rest of our lives and the dark night may never end. But if we can grieve consciously, deeply, and well, the desert can do its work, the dark night can purify us in a way that is mysterious and profound.

Although we all have dark night of the soul experiences, unless we are serious about the mystical path, very few of us will experience the specific states for which St. John of the Cross invented the term. The first of these that we encounter as part of the mystical process is the Dark Night of the Senses.

THE DARK NIGHT OF THE SENSES

He called the crowd with his disciples, and said to them, "If any want to become my followers, let them deny themselves and take up their cross and follow me. For those who want to save their life will lose it, and those who lose their life for my sake, and for the sake of the gospel, will save it. For what will it profit them to gain the whole world and forfeit their life?"

—Mark 8:34–36

Long before the Jewish mystical system of Kabbalah was conceived, Jewish mystics practiced something called Merkobah mysticism. *Merkobah* is the Hebrew word for "chariot," and Jews of a mystical bent in the early centuries of the Common Era loved to speculate on the great chariot of God, symbolized by the sun. They believed that by hard work at specific mystical disciplines, they could gain access to the chariot, which would carry them into the heavens, reveal to them the secrets of the universe, and even usher them through the gates of paradise.

The most famous of the Merkobah mystics was Rabbi Akiva, and there is a tale about him and three other rabbis who attempted to storm the gates of heaven. All four of them were successful, but unfortunately, only Rabbi Akiva returned to tell the tale.

What happened to the other three? One's mind snapped and he went stark raving mad, spending the rest of his life in restraints in a cell. Another, having accessed the throne room of God, beheld not one God, but two! Upon his return he was exiled as a heretic.

But the final rabbi is the one we are most concerned with. This rabbi gained entrance to paradise and when he came back, he simply lost all interest in anything else. Food lost its flavor, study seemed empty, worship seemed rote. Even sex caused him to shrug his shoulders and go "eh . . . ," which could not have pleased his wife. Nothing on this earthly plane could in any way compare to the glorious vision he'd beheld, so he simply stopped eating, wasted away, and died.

What this unnamed rabbi experienced was very similar to what St. John of the Cross in the Christian mystical tradition refers to as the Dark Night of the Senses.

The dark nights are kind of the wild cards of the mystical path. You never know when they're going to hit or when they will lift. They are trickster stages because they offer one thing on the surface, but actually impart something completely different. They are painful and hard but the gifts they bring are pure grace. They're kind of like lima beans—you don't really like them, but you have to eat them because they're good for you.

The Dark Night of the Senses first hits around the time of a mystic's transition from Purgation to Illumination. Purgation, as we've discovered, can be really tough. But here's where the gift of the Dark Night of the Senses comes in. We are knuckled under, working really hard to battle all of our temptations and stay on the straight and narrow. And then all of the sudden, *boom!* The Dark Night of the Senses descends upon us, and it is both a burden and a grace. It's a burden because, like Rabbi Akiva's companion, we lose all interest in the things of this world. M&M's, who needs 'em? Steak? No, thanks. *Buffy the Vampire Slayer*? Nah . . . another time. Sex? Not in the mood, really. In fact, in the Dark Night of the Senses, *nothing* holds any appeal except maybe prayer or going to church.

It's kind of an extreme version of what Jesus was referring to when he said, "Those who want to save their life will lose it, and those who lose their life for my sake and for the sake of the Gospel will save it." The person who has seriously set out on the mystical path is ready and willing to make that exchange, even if it hasn't happened yet. The Dark Night of the Senses is the moment of surrender, when the old life we know is let go of, is lost, and the mystic is ushered into a new life where the only thing that truly matters is God.

And that is why it is a grace. Because up to that point, it has been a struggle to let go of those sensuous things that we so much enjoy. But when the dark night hits, it eradicates every shred of temptation. It takes with it all of our craving. It is a grace because the struggle is suddenly gone. We are simply left face to face with God, wanting nothing, nothing, nothing but that.

Even though it may come as a relief to someone who is seriously walking the mystics' path, the Dark Night of the Senses is never a pleasant experience. Anhedonia—the inability to take pleasure in anything—is a diagnosable mental disorder and we should be wary and concerned when it hits, lest, like Rabbi Akiva's companion, we shrivel up and blow away.

I wish I could tell you that you only have to go through it once, but dark nights are unpredictable. There may be periods, even after the mystic has entered Illumination, that Purgation reasserts itself and a new Dark Night of the Senses descends. Up to this point, we may lose interest in everything but prayer, but in later stages, the Dark Night of the Senses may take on a different flavor, in which even spiritual pursuits fail to provide any consolation. It isn't just movies, food, and sex that seem empty and dry, but prayer, meditation, and church as well.

This is a particularly difficult time for the mystic. St. John of the Cross says that mystics in the grip of this advanced stage can expect to be afflicted by three spirits: dizziness (because you just don't know which way is up, anymore), blasphemy (because at this point you are cussing God for doing this to you), and fornication (because, hey, why not?—anything to feel a little better at this point).[1]

The mystic's only way forward is to let go of trying and surrender in complete trust. None of the things that used to provide comfort are working—prayer, rituals, etc.—so the mystic is forced to look elsewhere for consolation. Food or sex or distraction? A step backwards. But God alone? If the mystic can stay the course, the purpose of the dark night will be fulfilled and a deeper and more advanced stage of Illumination is possible (see "Acquisition and Quiet" in the next chapter).

The dark nights are the most unpleasant parts of the mystical journey. They are the proverbial "valley of the shadow of death." But it is important to remember that God does not impose them in order to be mean or spiteful, nor are they the actions of a capricious and arbitrary deity. They are, instead, the very school of hard knocks necessary to allow us to progress.

A Mystic's Story: St. Ignatius of Loyola

One day in the sixteenth century, a young Spanish soldier named Ignatius was fighting alongside his fellows at the siege of Pamplona. Ignatius was brave, he was handsome, and he was wealthy. In fact, things could hardly have been going better. Then he caught a cannonball in both legs.

Obviously, that's just not something you get up and walk away from. Awash in grime and gore, Ignatius was carried from the battlefield and began a very long and tedious convalescence, where his true battle began—the battle for his soul.

Up until that time, he had not been particularly devout. At least no more than most young men with means and ambition. The Church was just part of the furniture. God was in Heaven the same way the King was on his throne. One paid taxes and one went to Church and no one questioned or grumbled about either one of them, at least not in public.

Chapter Three

But sitting on your butt for months, waiting for a shattered leg to mend gives a guy lots of time to think, to read, and, yes, even to pray. Ignatius's Purgation was not a willing process. Everything he had valued was taken away by that cannonball. And in the emptiness that followed, he began to see what was Real and what wasn't. Unwelcome grace? It was certainly uninvited, but it was grace just the same.

Ignatius started praying—really praying—and when that happened, he was quiet enough to notice some very interesting phenomena: the fantasies that used to occupy his thoughts left him feeling bored and dry. But when he read books about the lives of the saints, he felt comforted and energized. When he prayed for healing so that he could return to his former life—a life of carousing, of male camaraderie, and female pursuit—he felt empty. His fantasies left him feeling hollow. "It aroused within me a spirit of desolation," he said.

When, however, he prayed for God's will to be done, when he read of the surrender that the saints enjoyed and fantasized about a life focused on God, he felt very different. This kind of prayer left him with what he called "a spirit of consolation."

He noticed that as he prayed for what he wanted, a strange and subtle process of discernment was taking place. He discovered that his prayer wasn't speeding his healing, it wasn't getting him what he wanted, it wasn't affecting *anything* "out there." Instead, it was changing *him*, from the inside out.

He discovered that what he *thought* he wanted wasn't what he wanted at all and that his soul's true desire was being made known to him. And when he figured this out and clued in to what God was doing in him, he was overwhelmed by the grace that was being shown to him. And he was able to cooperate with the process so that it accelerated and turned him into a very different creature from that guy who had become cannon fodder.

By paying attention to his emotions—to what bored or energized him, what depressed or comforted him—Ignatius discovered his soul.

All his former desires fell away and the only thing left was his desire for God.

When he felt well enough, he made a pilgrimage to the Black Virgin of Montserrat, where he hung his sword up forever before her altar. (And where you can still see it, by the way.)

Ignatius's Dark Night of the Senses was not at an end, however. He went to dwell in a cave to be more intentional about his Purgation, and another dark night left him so depressed that he seriously contemplated suicide. Soon, however, this experience ushered him into a state of Illumination in which, newly energized, he made another pilgrimage—to Jerusalem to see the places where Jesus had been. His Illumination continued in a more conventional way as he pursued a formal theological education. This was a real struggle for someone who had previously aspired to nothing more than a courtier's life.

Eventually he triumphed and founded the Society of Jesus—also known as the Jesuits—an order known for their "availability to God," willing to pick up and go anywhere in the world at a moment's notice. Jesuits are known as exceptional educators and tireless missionaries.

- *For Questions and Answers that clarify points in this chapter, turn to page 158.*
- *To read what the mystics say about the Dark Night of the Senses, turn to page 196.*

Jesus took with him Peter and James and his brother John and led them up a high mountain, by themselves. And he was transfigured before them, and his face shone like the sun, and his clothes became dazzling white. Suddenly there appeared to them Moses and Elijah, talking with him. . . . Suddenly a bright cloud overshadowed them, and from the cloud a voice said, "This is my Son, the Beloved, with him I am well pleased. Listen to him!" When the disciples heard this, they fell to the ground and were overcome by fear. But Jesus came and touched them, saying, "Get up and do not be afraid."

—Matthew 17:1–8

Chapter Four

Illumination

In the short story "The Shoddy Lands," C. S. Lewis plays himself—an English professor. A former student stops by his office to say hello, with his fiancée in tow. While they are talking, Lewis drifts off momentarily and finds himself in a very strange place—a very *shoddy* place, actually. The sky is gray, the trees are indistinct, and the streets are nondescript.

It looks very much like an impressionist painting rendered entirely void of color. And yet, much to his surprise, he is drawn to a patch of color. As he gets closer, he discovers it is a jewelry store where everything is bright, in crisp focus—a startling contrast to everything else in this shoddy world.

Then he sees *her*, his student's fiancée. He recognizes her as *her*, but she's different. She's idealized, as if you had crossed the real her with a fashion model. And she is, of course, full of color and detail. She's also enormous.

With a start, Lewis is jolted back to his own world and realizes that, for just a second, he had fallen into his student's fiancée's head, her consciousness, and he saw the world as she sees it. And he is—as indeed, we are supposed to be—appalled by the vanity and the superficiality, indeed, the *shoddiness* of her little world.

Some people have accused Lewis of being misogynistic in this tale—and even though it is true that Lewis has his misogynistic moments, I'm not sure that is a fair assessment of this story, because Lewis isn't making a statement about women with this story, but about people in general—indeed, about himself. We all have our shoddy lands. We all have interior worlds where those things that bore us are simply a blur. If you could drop into any one of our heads in a shopping mall, I wonder how many shops would be intelligible.

But Lewis isn't just making a statement about human blinders. He is concerned with issues of ultimate value. He is using a fictional analogy to point out how human limitation and human sin blind us to the brightness, the beauty, and the reality of the world as it appears to God.

This is the task of Christian mysticism—to point out to us how our view of the world, including ourselves, is limited and then to assist us in overcoming this limitation so we might see the world as God sees it.

In the story of the Transfiguration, the disciples experience the veils being pulled from their eyes, allowing them to behold the glory-filled universe as it is. They see Jesus in his true glory, they see the mountain shining with the reflected glory of God, they see Moses and Elijah testifying about Jesus's ministry.

These are Jesus's closest disciples, who have already left everything behind to follow their Lord. They have worked hard to strip away their illusions and false conceptions. They have come to the top of Mt. Tabor to pray, and in the silence, they experience the third step in our spiritual journey, Illumination.

In this step, we are graced with increasingly longer glimpses of the world-as-it-is, the world as God beholds it. The world that the disciples beheld is the same one we are living in now. It is a transfigured world, shining with glory, brimming with divinity, touching, fulfilling, sustaining, and loving all things. The only problem is we don't see it. And the reason we don't see it is that we are living in our own Shoddy Lands.

We do not have to stay here. Indeed, the call of God is that we all go to Mt. Tabor, that we commit to the arduous process of Purgation, that we cleanse the doors of our perception (as Aldus Huxley phrased it).

What would we find if we did? Unfortunately words cannot begin to describe the spiritual reality that is shining through the most mundane objects at every moment. Fortunately that didn't stop the mystics from trying. It is in the Illuminative state that the mystics spend most of their time, and it is on this state that they waste most of their ink, trying to describe it.

We'll go into more detail about how Illumination manifests itself later, but for now, let us simply say that the dualism that seems to drive our world—the distinctions between us and them, you and me, matter and spirit—are, in the Illuminated state, revealed to be the illusions that they are. All things are revealed to be pulsing with the life that fires the stars. All people are revealed to be the lovers, the spouses, the sweethearts of God. We are revealed to be worthy of more love than we ever dared hope for.

A MYSTIC'S STORY: BROTHER LAWRENCE

Brother Lawrence was born in France in 1610, and as a young man, he fought in the Thirty Years' War, where he was almost mortally wounded. His recovery was slow and, unfortunately, partial. His wounds left him crippled and in debilitating pain for the rest of his life.

Fortunately, that is not the whole of the story. As with Francis and Ignatius before him, the trauma of battle had a lasting effect on Lawrence and reoriented his life toward the things of the Spirit. As soon as he was able, he took to the wilderness, where he was determined, despite being crippled, to live like one of the Desert Fathers.

As you might imagine, that did not go well. He was no more successful as a morbidly ascetic hermit than he'd been as a soldier. With two strikes against him and coming up fast on middle age, Lawrence took one more try at "finding his purpose in life" and joined a monastery. And wouldn't you know it, there his hopes were instantly, horribly dashed.

For the wise and esteemed fathers who ran the monastery did not see the brilliant mind or the adventurous spirit in their midst. They saw a broken, crippled middle-aged man who would mostly be a burden on the community. Instead of giving him a position of honor or responsibility as he had hoped, they consigned Lawrence to the kitchen and told him to wash dishes.

Out of luck and out of chances, Lawrence tried to make the best of it. The trouble was he *hated* doing dishes. But he kept at it, he threw himself into his work, but most importantly, he told God how he felt about it. Out loud. All the time.

The upshot of this was that as Lawrence became accustomed to talking to God as he worked, and the more he talked, the more aware he was that God was there. And the mere awareness of God's presence began to transform him: Every moment was charged with significance. Everything he touched seemed to glow with divine life. And God seemed more fully and really present in a more and more profound way as he continued in this awareness.

Before long, his conversations with God consisted less and less of complaining and whining and more and more of worship and praise. Lawrence began to see that every duty, no matter how lowly or despised, could usher one into the divine presence, if one were only attentive to it.

STEP ONE: BEHOLDING THE ILLUMINATED WORLD

Like most mystics, Brother Lawrence went through the stages we have been discussing. In the wake of his injury in the military, he had his spiritual Awakening. In his time in the wilderness, he had a traumatic experience of Purgation. And finally, as a lowly dishwasher in a monastery, he experienced the third stage of mystical attainment—Illumination.

Of course, Illumination, like most of the stages, is broken down into substages as well, and Brother Lawrence came to rest in the first of two substages of Illumination, the awareness of God in all things, also known as the Illuminated World.

Remember that the disciples did not seek out Jesus. Instead, Jesus went out to find *them*. And Jesus didn't meet the disciples in holy, rarified places like the desert. He met them at work, in the midst of their daily lives. He met them while they were casting their nets, sorting their fish, resting under fig trees. He met them not in the temple but in the most ordinary surroundings.

The Good News of Jesus is that God is not aloof. God is not found only on the mountaintop or in the cathedral. In Jesus we meet Emmanuel, the God-who-is-with-us, in the warp and woof of our ordinary, everyday lives. It is only to those who have never experienced it that mysticism seems a rare and exotic kind of spirituality, full of occult mystery, dependent upon secret initiations in consecrated sanctuaries.

True mystics know that just the opposite is the case—that, as Mohammad revealed in the Koran, God is closer to us than the vein of our own neck; that it is not only in the temples and the sanctuaries that God becomes present to us, but in the rearing of children, in the commute to work, in the washing of dishes, in the cuddling of spouses. For if God is not real to us in our actual lives, where we actually live, then what good is God to us?

The choice before us is not one of vocation, of choosing to be a monk or a nun or some other kind of religious professional who lives in the temple or the sanctuary in order to be close to God; the choice is whether we will make the effort, in the midst of our busy, conflicted, confusing lives, to notice that God is there, too.

And it *requires* effort. All real spiritual endeavors do. But the returns are enormous, giving back far more than we put in. This is where Brother Lawrence's example is so helpful. For he isn't advocating some strenuous method of meditation or some subtle and incomprehensible system of spiritual correspondences, as occult traditions so often do. He is recommending something much simpler, much more reliable, something that you don't need to be a full-timer or need a PhD in philosophy to grasp.

He says this: Pretend like God is there and God will show up. Whatever you're doing, stop and notice that you are not alone. Talk to God about how you are feeling, even if you're feeling lousy, and not in churchy, prayer-ific language—nobody talks like that. Just talk, as if you were griping to your sister about something. Lawrence says that something amazing will happen if you do.

God will show up. And the more you are able to do this, the *more* God will show up, until you are aware of God's presence in every moment, in every activity—shining forth from the person you just said "hi" to, radiating from the table you are sitting at, filling that donut you're noshing like divinity jelly. As St. Simeon the New Theologian wrote, "I move my hand, and my hand is wholly Christ, for God's divinity is united inseparable to me. I move my foot, and lo! It glows like God himself."[1]

You will not just become aware of God sometimes, in some things, but you will become aware that God is present at *all* times, shining forth from *all* things, filling every moment, every person, every place you happen to be in. You will see the world as it actually is, "charged with the grandeur of God," as Gerard Manly Hopkins put it, or as Martin Luther wrote, "Heaven and earth are [God's] sack; as wheat fills the sack, so he fills all things."[2]

The more we can become aware of God's presence in and with and through all things, the more our lives will be transformed, because the illusion that we are separate beings, that God is away out there somewhere, that life is a meaningless succession of disconnected events will be increasingly shattered as we experience firsthand that our life is God's life, that our work is God's work, that the people we love reflect back to us the very love of God, not just sometimes, but all the time, not just in some places but in all places, not just some people but *all* people.

In our culture we are constantly being seduced by the media—drawn to glamorous surroundings, model-beautiful people, and high-powered jobs—but this is the very illusion that needs shattering if we are ever to progress on the mystical path. Like Brother Lawrence, we might poo-poo such unglamorous jobs as doing the dishes. But the truth is that if we do even the most humble activities right, if we do them with prayer, if we do them with intention, we will not be able to contain the power and the glory that will fill us.

SPIRITUAL PRACTICE: QUIET AND DEPRIVATION

For God alone my soul waits in silence; from him comes my salvation.

—Psalm 62:1

As I was researching this section, I dimly remembered a story from *The Phantom Tollbooth*, the marvelous children's book by Norton Juster. As I remembered it, the boy Milo and the watchdog Tock were sitting in Milo's toy car all ready to go, but the car wasn't moving. The boy and the dog discuss the car's lifelessness, but neither of them can think of a way to make it go. Having exhausted all of the possibilities they fall silent, and only then does the car begin to move. "Of course," Tock exclaims, "it goes without saying."

Our spiritual lives are very much the same. The state of Illumination is certainly reachable by anyone who sets his or her mind to it and is sincere. But it's not as simple as just *wanting* to. Purgation, if you recall, was a lot of work, and reaching Illumination is no piece of cake, either, but it requires a very different kind of effort.

The discipline involved in Purgation was a moral discipline—eliminating those behaviors and possessions from our lives that were not congruent with the Real. In Illumination, we achieve the first stage by eliminating something else—all of those *thoughts* that are not congruent with the Real. And because all thoughts, and language-making in general, are products of the illusion of our separateness, this means that what has to go is *thought itself.*

The discipline by which we approach the Illuminated World is called by the mystics "Quiet," and we'll spend the next few pages exploring its implications and substages. The important thing for us to remember right now is that no awareness of God in All Things is likely to occur to us unless we can become quiet enough to notice it.

This is a profoundly countercultural act. Quiet is hard for us, and most of us fight tooth and nail to avoid it. We have the radio on in the car, the stereo on in the house, or the television or Internet. We find the silences between people almost unbearable, and we feel impelled to make inane small talk rather than endure them. We are assaulted by the media with flashy images and noise in an incessant barrage that distracts us, throwing us into information overload. And if the media isn't chattering at us, if our neighbor isn't chatting at us, then our own brains are chattering at us with an incessant stream of judgment and commentary.

Which is fine, except that it *is* incessant. I mean I love a good action movie as much as the next red-blooded American guy and I don't see anything wrong with loud music or MTV or, for heaven's sake, critical thinking. *But,* there is that little thing called *moderation.* Brother Lawrence's conversation with God compensated for a life too much filled with loneliness and quiet. Our problem is usually *too much* stimulation.

As a matter of fact, when I went back to *The Phantom Tollbooth* to look up the story that I remembered, I was horrified to find that it wasn't there. Instead, the car refused to move because Milo *wasn't thinking.* And as soon as he started thinking, the car started on down the road. Which is a fine metaphor all by itself, but I thought it particularly poignant in contrast to the way I had remembered it, and I realized that my false memory held more wisdom for me than the actual story. *Thinking* I do well enough, and more than enough of. What I *need* is to take a break from it now and then.

Because as long as I am *thinking*, as long as my brain is chattering away at me, or someone else is chattering away at me, or the media is chattering away at me, I am *not present* to what is actually happening around me. Most important, I am not aware that *God* is *present*.

God's presence is a subtle thing—it is real and profound, but it requires silence in order to discern. The reason most of us are not aware of God in our everyday lives is that we have made no room for him. If there is always a loud voice chattering away at us, we cannot hear the still, small voice that whispers to us, "I am here. You are loved. All is well." And I'm sure you don't need me to tell you how wonderful it would be to hear those words now and again.

The Psalmist David knew this truth. "For God alone my soul waits in silence."[3] That's the way you do it. That is how all of the great mystics became aware of God's unfailing presence. For when David achieved this quiet, when he became aware of the Holy One, he perceived God as his rock, his salvation, his fortress, which made him unshakable.

That is the language of certainty and it does not come through speculation or blind faith. It comes from a real and direct experience of the Holy, achieved only through the willingness and the ability to shut up long enough to notice that that Rock is even there.

This is a tough point to grasp, even for those studying to be spiritual directors. When I am teaching spiritual direction classes, I am constantly reminding my students that they must not go into a session with a plan, with any idea of what they are going to do, or they are likely to upset what God actually *is* trying to do.

"But," they complain, "what if the client doesn't say anything?"

"Then you sit in silence," I tell them. At which point they look at me like I have completely lost my mind.

"But if we're just sitting in silence, we're not doing anything!" they say.

"Exactly," I reply. "God is doing the work, here. You're just holding space." I then explain that silence may be exactly the thing their client most needs. As I said, our culture doesn't encourage silence. To sit with another soul, giving him or her permission to simply sit in silence isn't irresponsible, as my students fear. It is, in fact, *ministry*.

People often come to spiritual direction because they are having trouble connecting with God. Usually people have trouble connecting with God because they do not make space in their lives for Quiet, the quiet needed to even *notice* God. So, when they come for spiritual direction, sometimes we just sit in silence. And there, in the presence of another person, they feel they have permission to just do nothing, to discern, to observe their own soul, to hear the subtle whisper of the Holy Spirit.

I experienced this myself recently. About a week before this writing, it seemed that everything that could go wrong *did* go wrong. My Internet connection went down, we were having a flea infestation at my house, and my laptop battery kept dying, none of which is insurmountable. But add to this a full week of pastoral visits and spiritual direction, a reading load from the new semester starting up, preparing for two classes, clients standing me up, and a backup of writing and editing projects, and you can see how I might start to buckle.

I was lying in the bathtub whimpering about it all, when it occurred to me that I felt utterly alone. I felt like someone had cut a hole in the sky and sucked God and everything sacred right out of the world. Once I was able to articulate that, I realized that God had not, in fact, been vacuumed out of the universe—thank goodness. I was just too busy to notice that he was there.

At this realization, my whole body relaxed. I didn't have too much to do—I always have a lot of projects. The problem was I was *too busy*, which is a different thing altogether. Once I just stopped and noticed, made some room for Quiet, for God, everything shifted. As I relaxed, as I sank into Quiet, God showed up again. "For God alone my soul waits in silence," and the Lord was there. And then everything else seemed to fall into place, too. My overwhelm subsided and my calm returned.

The mystics call this stage of Quiet "Deprivation" and they describe it as a kind of death. And it is. It is death to the constant, obsessive busy-ness our culture insists upon. It is death to the illusion of the solitary soul. For when we wait in silence upon God, no matter how bad things seem, no matter how far away God seems to be, no matter how devoid of anything even remotely sacred the world seems, this silence brings with it a healing balm, an awareness of the "goodness, deep down things," as Hopkins put it. We gain an awareness of the presence of the Holy, whispering to us, if only we will listen, comforting us and telling us that "all is well, all is well, and every manner of thing will be well."[4]

Not only do we become *aware* of God's presence, we learn to *enjoy* that Presence. The Holy becomes not only noticeable, but comfortable, desirable, lovely—*enjoyable*. It may be hard to discern at first, but once we do, we can lean into it; indeed we can lean *on it*.

A Mystic's Story: George Fox

George Fox was born at a house named Fenny Drayton in Leicestershire in 1624 (because, oddly, the English name their houses), and he lived his entire life in the shadow of the English Civil War. His father was a weaver and the young Fox apprenticed as a shoemaker.

He never actually went to work as one, however. In 1643, at the age of nineteen, he found himself disillusioned with the Church of England, and—like Siddhartha before him—he left his family behind, setting out on foot to find the truth. After many hardships and much soul searching, he came to a mystical awareness of God in all people, what he called "the Light within."

In 1647, he continued to roam the countryside, only this time he did so preaching, wherever he could find a crowd to hear him. He loved a good theological argument. He thought nothing of going into a church—which he pejoratively called a "steeple-house"—and inter-rupting the preacher in the middle of the sermon to contradict him and challenge him to a debate.

He was thrown out on his ear by more than one congregation, and eventually he took to preaching an "alternative" sermon directly out-side the steeple-house while the normal sermon was going on inside. For this and other disturbances he was thrown in prison, not once, but almost annually—certainly more times than we actually know about. There, he invariably bore up with good humor and often converted—or "convinced," to use his term—his jailers to his way of thinking. Slowly he gathered a small flock to his teaching—a flock that became progressively larger, much to the alarm of the English religious author-ities. He called his movement the Society of Friends.

So what were Fox's views that caused him so much trouble? First and foremost was the doctrine that the "Light of Christ" indwells every human being and that this Light is the only reliable spiritual authority.

That doesn't sound too radical, you might be saying, but in seven-teenth-century England, Fox's teachings rubbed almost everyone the wrong way. For one thing, if the Light of Christ dwelt equally in all people, then all people were of equal value in the sight of God. This meant that in Fox's teaching, men and women were held in equal esteem and granted equal power and equal rights, right from the very beginning.

This doctrine also led Fox and his followers to reject the rigid classism of his day. Again like the Buddha before him, who insisted on the equality of all people and rejected the Indian caste system, Fox refused to acknowledge the various strata in British society, and he did this chiefly by the use, or lack of use, of his hat.

In the time and place where he lived, it was customary to take off your hat in the presence of someone of higher standing than you. If a merchant and a noble approached each another on the street, the mer-chant would remove his hat and show obeisance; women would do the same to men, and children to adults. But George Fox would have none of it and kept his hat firmly on his head even when enjoying his annual audience with the Lord Protector Oliver Cromwell. This insolence gained him a reputation as arrogant, but I think this was a perception of his enemies rather than a reality known by his friends.

Another implication of this doctrine of the Inner Light was that it was the sole spiritual authority. Not bishops, not priests, not ministers, not confessions, not creeds, not churches, not nations, and not even the Bible itself were considered authorities equal to the quiet whispering of the Light of Christ in the soul of every person.

Since the Church of England was a national church and because one paid taxes to support it, Fox's denunciations of all churches, all ministers, and all bishops was nothing short of treason, not to mention heresy.

Fortunately for Fox and his followers, it was a time of great religious upheaval. The last hundred years had seen England swing from Catholic to Anglican to Catholic again, back to Anglican, to Puritan under Cromwell, and to Anglican once again under the new King. Since lots of people had differing notions of just what kind of church should be the one church in England, people were more tolerant of dissenting voices.

But then along comes George Fox, who says that no church is favored of God, and what are you going to do with that? At that time, people were convinced that there should only be one state religion and that society would fall apart if that were not upheld.

Friends got no support from Puritans or other Protestants, for Fox rejected the inerrancy of scripture. While he found scripture helpful and knew it better than most of his theological sparring partners, he believed that personal revelation of the Light within held greater authority than the Bible.

Not only did Friends not support the state church, not hold the Bible as an inerrant spiritual authority, and not recognize the obvious social strata so important to everyone around them, this doctrine of the Inner Light also moved them to become pacifists. For if God resides in everyone, how can we possibly kill one another? From the very beginning, then, Friends were countercultural.

They were also, at least in the early days, exceedingly tolerant. If one lived one's life by the Inner Light, then truly one was free of all social constraints. The story is told of a man who confronted George Fox in front of a crowd. He held his pipe out to Fox and bid him to smoke it, because he argued that those who follow the Light are free in all things. Now, understand that tobacco had much of the same social stigma in Fox's day that marijuana has in our own, so everyone was watching closely to see what Fox would do. According to the account, Fox took the pipe from the man, held it to his lips for an instant, and then returned it to the man. (Apparently George Fox, like Bill Clinton, did not inhale.)

So if Friends rejected steeple-houses, the authority of scripture, the very idea of ministers, and socially decreed stigma, then what does religious life look like for the Friends?

Friends orient themselves, and everything in their lives, in honor of the Light within. Their worship services are called "meetings." In Fox's day, a meeting consisted of a bunch of Friends sitting together in silence for an hour. If the Inner Light inspired someone to speak, they did so. But speaking at length and having more than three people speaking in any one service was frowned upon. Even today, most Friends worship consists of simply sitting in silence, listening for the gentle whisper of the Inner Light.

Just as Christians were first given that name by their enemies, Friends were called "Quakers" for the first time by Justice Bennet of Derby when Fox was hauled before him on blasphemy charges. Instead of trembling before the magistrate, Fox informed him that Friends trembled (or "quaked") only at the Word of God. It stuck, but Fox preferred Society of Friends, possibly because of Jesus's assertion at the Last Supper that he called his followers not servants, but friends.

It was a name that fit them well, because Friends have no hierarchy to speak of[5] and are fiercely antiauthoritarian. They are all simply friends, with none greater than another.

This radical egalitarianism later brought Friends to the forefront of the antislavery movement in the United States and has always moved Friends to advocate for peace, justice, and civil rights, often at the cost of their own lives.

Fox was truly an unstoppable man. Prison did not deter him, nor did inclement weather, nor his own health. Late in life he sailed to Barbados, and from there to New England, where he preached to record crowds. Finally, in 1691 at the age of sixty-six, he succumbed to poor health and what was at the time a ripe old age, dying peacefully at home, surrounded by his Friends.

Those who came after him definitely inherited his mantle, traveling far and wide and preaching the Light of Christ in the face of deadliest peril. Even during Fox's lifetime, one woman named Mary Fisher traveled to the Mediterranean, escaped the clutches of the Inquisition, gained entry into Turkey, and managed to set up an interview with the Sultan in his army headquarters. She preached to him about how the Light was common to all peoples and how Islam and Friends Christianity had much in common. Her message was well received and she returned to England in safety. Others were not so fortunate. One Friend set out to convert the pope and died at the hands of the Inquisition.

The early Friends kept voluminous journals, so their beginnings are better documented than most religious movements. One amazing story tells how a ship full of Friends set sail from Europe to America without a navigator! They were certain that the Light within would not steer them wrong, and even many of their own number in the colonies were amazed when their ship sailed into Boston Harbor in record time.

Today, there are approximately 240,000 Friends in the world; about 120,000 of these are Americans. When you remember that there are approximately six million Lutherans in the United States alone, this is a very small number, and their influence has far exceeded their size. Friends were instrumental in ending slavery in the United States and England, and though they refuse to fight in wars, the Quaker Ambulance Service has been in the thick of many of them, providing first aid and taking the wounded of either side to safety.

In the United States, Friends differ greatly. Some of them keep to the old traditions of worshiping in silence, while others have adopted many of the practices of their Protestant neighbors, hiring pastors and using hymns in their worship. Perhaps more effectively than anyone before him, George Fox taught Christians how to be mystics—by inviting them into the Quiet of Deprivation, sitting in silence, listening to the Inner Light.

Spiritual Practice: Quiet and Acquisition

On August 29, 1952, pianist David Tudor took the stage at a recital of contemporary piano music. Dressed smartly in a black tuxedo, he opened the keyboard lid and began . . . doing nothing. He sat there in complete silence for a minute or so, then closed the piano lid. Then he turned the page on his score and opened the lid again. Again, he just sat there. After another minute or so, he closed the piano lid and turned another page on the score. He opened the piano a third time and, once again, sat quietly, not touching the piano at all, only looking at a stopwatch he was holding in his hand. Finally, he closed the lid, stood to face the audience, bowed, and walked off-stage.

The audience was stunned. Some of them spluttered in indignation. Some scoffed. Some laughed nervously. And some of them smiled knowingly. In other words, some of them got it, and some of them didn't.

I am, of course, recounting the story of the first performance of one of the most famous compositions in twentieth-century experimental music, John Cage's 4'33". The point (according to those who study such things) is that because the performer is making no sound, the audience becomes aware of the profound *amount* of sound that is always there: the rustling of programs, the whine of wind, the clearing of throats, the creak of chairs—an undiscovered symphony that is always present, is always different, but which is almost always unnoticed. But in the space set aside for simply listening, these random noises become elevated, for those who have ears to hear, to a work of art in their own right.

Note that the audience has to become quiet to receive the grace of such art, and since only some of them are prepared to receive it, only some of them even *perceive* it as art. The others laugh, and why not? It *is* kind of silly, and no harm is done by laughing. But for those who are ready for it, a work of art such as this can be life changing, because afterwards no alleged "silence" will ever sound the same again. The transformed listener will forever after be attuned to the serendipitous symphony of every quiet moment.

I'm not sure what the Christian mystics would have made of Cage's première, but they certainly do have something to say about the serendipitous grace communicated by silence. In the practice of Deprivation (which we just spoke about above), we pursue a strangely paradoxical effort—we are working really hard to do as little as possible. It is an *active* pursuit, made by being assiduously *inactive*.

(A note to the wise: this is religion we are talking about here. Paradox is the norm, and it is always far weirder than the general culture will ever admit. You go forward by going backwards; when you are weak, you are strong; if you want to be straight, you have to let yourself be crooked; and so on and so on. None of it makes any *logical* sense, so just give up on that right now. All of this will be much easier if you do.)

You work really hard at doing nothing to achieve Deprivation, and then what? In Deprivation, *you* do something, but in the very next step, something happens *to you*. You've reached the tipping point, so in some ways, it is all downhill from here. From here on out, mysticism is more of a passive pursuit than an active one. Okay, that's not entirely accurate. There are efforts to be made on the second half of the journey, but the balance between active and passive pursuit certainly shifts at this point.

Deprivation gets us to the top of this hill and gives us a little push. What's on the other side? The mystics call it *the Birth of the Word in the Soul*. And it is as profound as it sounds.

Deprivation sets us up to receive this boon by stilling us to our very core. Just as we discovered that when we are busy in our outer life we are unaware of God's Presence there, we also discover that as we move inward, into more intimate and interior landscapes of our soul, we are unquiet there as well—and just as unable to notice God. The innermost soul, too, must be quieted. Only when that is accomplished is our soul quiet enough to hear the Word that God speaks into our innermost being.

And just as God, in Genesis, spoke the universe into being, when we are quiet enough to hear his whisper in our deepest and most inward part, the mystics testify that he will speak a new creation in us. And just as in the beginning the Word of God spoke order into chaos, so the Spirit of the Living God speaks a new and profound order into us.

For this Word creates in us a new being. We become like Mary, who in the stillness of her room acquiesced to the Spirit, and the Word of God became incarnate in her. Just so, the Seed of God is planted in us and we become a new creature. To use the words of St. John's Gospel, we are born again. But not in the crass way that we have come to hear those words, but in the most profound way possible, for in that tender moment between our soul and the Spirit of God, Christ is born in us.

And in that moment, we, too, become the mothers of God. In that moment, God unites himself with our souls forever. It's true we do not yet fully understand the implications or the magnitude of such union—that will happen in future stages in our journey—but we do know that some profound shift has occurred that we do not understand and cannot fully articulate.

Even the mystics struggle with this one. The Birth of the Word in the Soul is a metaphor, of course, but it points to something real—the beginning of a period of spiritual gestation in which the Word of God, Christ himself, begins to grow in us. Like Mary's body during her pregnancy, as her bones and body fat shifted, as her flesh rearranged itself to nurture and protect the new life stirring within her, so will it be with us. The Word of God has been spoken, the Seed of God has been planted, and our lives will inevitably begin to shift to make this birth possible.

But let's not get ahead of ourselves. It is enough today to rejoice in this divine fertilization. For when it happens to us, when the Word of God is spoken in the temple of our souls, we cry out like Simeon, "Lord, you now have set your servant free, to go in peace as you have promised, for mine eyes have seen the savior, whom you have prepared for all the world to see."[6]

Profound things happen then. Remember that it was only when Mohammed found his place of quiet meditating in the cave at the top of Mt. Hira that the Word of God was spoken in his soul, a Word that changed the world forever. I'm not saying that if you find your place of quiet, a Word as influential as the Koran will be spoken in you, but you never know. For, as some of the listeners to John Cage's experimental piano concerto discovered one muggy summer night in 1952, there is profound music in silence, for those who have ears to hear it.

STEP TWO: BEHOLDING THE WORLD-IN-GOD

Then some people came, bringing to him a paralyzed man, carried by four of them. And when they could not bring him to Jesus because of the crowd, they removed the roof above him; and after having dug through it, they let down the mat on which the paralytic lay. When Jesus saw their faith, he said to the paralytic, "Son, your sins are forgiven." Now some of the scribes were sitting there, questioning in their hearts, "Why does this fellow speak in this way? It is blasphemy! Who can forgive sins but God alone?" At once Jesus . . . said to them, "Why do you raise such questions in your hearts? Which is easier, to say to the paralytic, 'Your sins are forgiven,' or to say, 'Stand up and take your mat and walk'? . . . He said to the paralytic, "I say to you, stand up, take your mat and go to your home." And he stood up, and immediately took the mat and went out before all of them; so that they were all amazed and glorified God, saying, "We have never seen anything like this!"

—Mark 2:3–12

In the last ten years there has been an explosion of interest in Gnostic Christianity. Many popular writers today misrepresent the Gnostics as the warm and fuzzy misunderstood underdogs of the early Christian era, which might be great for book sales but doesn't really accurately reflect the nature of Gnostic Christianity.

Christian Gnosticism, in fact, presents a vision of an extremely dualistic universe in which the Creator is evil, the flesh is corrupt, and the world is a dark and dangerous place. Only the spiritual world has any value and the best we can hope for is to get free of these mortal bonds and escape "into the mystic" (as Van Morrison put it).

In the Gnostic system, humans are the creation of an inept and, in some writings, horribly malevolent deity, who makes the world and then fashions Adam and Eve, bringing them to life for the sole purpose of keeping them imprisoned on this earth for countless rounds of reincarnation and servitude. His mother—yes, the Creator has a mother in this story, so it *does* get better—takes pity on Adam and Eve and places within them a spark of True Divinity. It is this spark that has its home in the pure, spiritual world, and it is this spark that longs so desperately to escape the world and the flesh.

It's a bleak picture, mitigated only by the fact that there is this bit of True Divinity residing in all of us, spurring us to be more spiritual and less worldly. Unfortunately, many aspects of this curious theology actually infected the Christian Church, largely through the teaching of St. Augustine, who spent eleven years as a Manichean Gnostic before becoming a Catholic Christian. It is from this Gnostic stream of thought that we get these crazy dualistic notions that the spirit is better than the body, heaven is more important than the earth, and men are superior to women. In fact, I would venture to say that most of the things that drive us crazy about Christianity today have their origin not in the teachings of Jesus, but in the philosophy of the Gnostics.

But then here come the Valentinians to prove otherwise. The Valentinian Gnostics were those who followed the third-century teacher Valentinus, who put a major twist on the whole Gnostic cosmology. He taught that, far from the world being a separate, dualistic, misbegotten place, it, too, was enveloped within the One-Who-Is, the True God in whom all things "live and move and have their being."7

The Valentinian system was a unitive mystical cosmology in which there is only one thing in the universe—God. All that is exists within the womblike embrace of that One. Valentinus taught that the blind Creator God was indeed misguided and that his misguided actions resulted in a seeming pocket of duality within the True God. But this pocket is just an illusion, and anyone who sees through the illusion will be free of its power. Not a bad twist, eh? Valentinus came very close to becoming pope—wouldn't *that* have sent the Christian Church off on a different trajectory?

So which is it? Is this world separate from God, a place into which God shows up as an interloper, as Divine sparks inhabiting otherwise worthless bits of matter? Or are all things just God in disguise, enveloped in an ocean of divinity? These two conflicting worldviews, as evidenced by these two different kinds of Gnostics, keep showing up in mystical thought.

Chapter Four

In the Gospel of Mark, Jesus frequently walks *into* a scene, works his healing magic, and then leaves. He is the image of God, like a spark of divinity, entering into a sick and dark place and bringing a bit of light and healing. But in the story of the paralyzed man, we see a symbol of something much more profound. Jesus is filling a house with his teaching, and several men, moved by their faith and love of their paralyzed friend, cut a hole in the roof and lower their friend into the space where Jesus is holding forth. The paralytic man is like the world, not separate from the sacred place, but waking up to find himself within it, part of it, enveloped by it, and this very realization brings with it healing and salvation.

This is the very shift that awaits us in the last stage of mystical attainment of the Illuminative Way. We have worked hard to cleanse ourselves of all that is unreal in the Purgative Stages, and in the Illuminative Stages we have opened ourselves to increasing awareness of God's Presence in the world. Through the practice of quiet we have experienced the Deprivation of the Senses, becoming still enough to notice that God is there. And as we continued in this practice, we experienced an acquisition: the Birth of the Word in the Soul.

This birth ushers us into a new plane of perception in which everything we have known is turned inside out. For it is in this final stage of Illumination that we realize that God is not in the world, but that the world is *in God*. Divinity does not come into some dark and dire place as an interloper, but reveals to us that, in fact, there are no dark and dire places. In this stage, we finally break through illusions of separateness and see that there are no places, no creatures, no people that are separate from God. All is enveloped in God, all are swimming in God, just as fish are swimming in the ocean.

Such an awareness has profound implications. As Mechtild of Magdeburg said, "the day of my spiritual awakening was the day I saw—and knew that I saw—all things in God and God in all things."[8] Awakening to this reality can have powerful consequences. If all things are in God, then is anyone truly beyond redemption? If all things are in God, can anything truly be said to be unclean? If all things are in God, are there any truly evil people? If all things are in God, can suffering or hypocrisy or cruelty or illness ever truly prevail?

In the story of the paralyzed man, Jesus is not the interloper, entering a sin-sick world and forgiving a man here, a woman there in piecemeal fashion. The way I read this passage, Jesus isn't forgiving anyone anything. He is simply telling the man the truth: "Your sins are forgiven you." God holds nothing against you, never has, never will. God doesn't hold anything against anybody. Never has, never will. The only one keeping you on that mat of yours is *you*. Healing, forgiveness, and grace are not precious commodities handed out sparingly to the worthy. They are as plentiful as the water in the ocean. They are the very waves in the ocean of God that we swim in. If you were but aware of it, and if you aren't careful, you could drown in grace. It's that plentiful. It's that free.

That's the Good News. Understanding this is easy, but *experiencing* it, well that's the hard part. That is the difference between *studying* mysticism and *being* a mystic. I'm sure it pleases God that we are reading about mysticism, but I think it would send him into handstands, into ice-cream–magnitude pleasure if we actually *tried* it. Because we *can*.

We *are able* to begin to see all things in God. But it's not easy to stay in this awareness: we hit our thumb with the hammer, or get jammed up by an erroneous bank statement, or are spoken to rudely by a passing stranger, and we're instantly jolted out of the place of peace we have worked so hard to achieve. But these times of frustration and rage are exactly the times when we most need to *see* all things in God. For then their power over us is revealed to be the illusion that it is, and their power to disrupt our peace is undone. Stress and anger can make us lame. But in the Illuminative state, we have been lowered into a world filled with God, and Jesus says to us, "Get up and walk." We can, you know.

Chapter Four

A Mystic's Story: Meister Eckhart

Meister Eckhart writes about his own birth in splendid terms: "When I flowed forth from God, creatures said: 'He is a god!' This, however, did not make me blessed, for it indicates that I, too, am a creature. In bursting forth, however, when I shall be free within God's will . . . I shall be what I was once, now, and forevermore . . . for in bursting forth I discover that God and I are One."[9]

His biographers have tended toward a more mundane approach however, informing us that he was probably born just before 1260 in a little German village called Hochheim. His given name was probably John and he entered the Dominican Order as a very young man. He studied theology in Cologne and Paris, earning his master's degree, and thus his nickname Meister ("Master"), around 1294.

In 1300 he was sent back to Germany to begin his ministry proper. He must have done well in his post as Vicar of Thuringia, because three years later he was appointed the Provincial of the entire Dominican Order in one sizable province that contained more than sixty religious communities.

Eckhart was successful not only with the hierarchy, but also with the common folks, for unlike most clergymen, he felt that the spirituality of ordinary people was important; he angered many of his contemporaries by preaching and writing prolifically in common German, which was tantamount to heresy.

When challenged, he simply said, "If the ignorant are not taught they will never learn; the business of the doctor is to heal," and the people loved him for this. He taught them in their own tongue, using images and examples that they could readily understand.

He was also very supportive of alternative religious communities such as the Beguines—not nuns, but not exactly laywomen either. Beguines communities were more like religious communes for women who simply loved God. These communities of pesky, upstart women made the Christian Church and society very nervous: they were not married, so no husbands kept them in line; they were not under the authority of the church; and it simply would not do to have women who could make up their own minds about anything! But Eckhart supported and offered guidance to the Beguines, and his fame grew.

But it was not simply his style and approach to ministry that made Eckhart so beloved; it was also what he taught that was so extraordinary. In his view, the idea that there was any distinction between God and the material world was an illusion, and a dangerous one at that. God and humankind were made of the same stuff, Eckhart said, and shared one being. He is known to have said, "the eye with which I see God is the same eye with which God sees me."[10] For Eckhart, there is no distinction between God and human, between creator and creation, and he exemplified the latter stage of Illumination, seeing not God in all things, but all things *in God*.

Eckhart's vision was similar to others who favored the "negative" way in mysticism. His theology is *apophatic*, without images, because God is so far beyond anything that words or ideas or images can express that all attempts to do so are meaningless at best, and distortions or outright fictions at worst. Thus he advised against even trying: "All the creatures cannot express God. For they are not receptive of what God is. God the ineffable one has no name. . . . So, be silent and quit flapping your gums about God."[11]

To grow spiritually, Eckhart advised against the standard pious practices and advocated pure quiet. "The more you seek God, the less you will find God," he wrote. "If you do not seek God, you will find God. God does not ask anything else of you except that you let yourself go and let God be God in you."[12] In this quiet, one should allow all images, all words, all concepts to fall away, including even the idea of oneself, since that, too, is an illusion. "Bare your soul of all mind. And stay there without mind. Moreover, I advise you to let your own 'being you' sink away and melt into God's 'being God.' In this way your 'you' and God's 'his' will become a completely one 'my.'"[13]

Chapter Four

As you might guess, Eckhart's teaching did not sit well with the church hierarchy, and in 1325 a complaint against his teaching was brought before the Holy Inquisition. Eckhart delivered his protest to the Inquisition in 1327 and even offered a Declaration of Orthodoxy. Unfortunately, it was rejected.

But Eckhart had one more trick up his sleeve: timing. Before his excommunication was handed down in 1329, he had the sense to die while he was still in the good graces of the church.

So, like Origen, that other great scholar and heretic, he died in safety, in the arms of Mother Church, with the full benefits of last rights and Christian burial. By the time his excommunication was made official, Eckhart was already within the pearly gates, having the last laugh.

- *For Questions and Answers that clarify points in this chapter, turn to page 161.*
- *To read what the mystics say about Illumination, turn to page 198.*
- *To try some exercises around Illumination, turn to page 239.*

He said, "Go out and stand on the mountain before the Lord, for the Lord is about to pass by." Now there was a great wind, so strong that it was splitting mountains and breaking rocks in pieces before the Lord, but the Lord was not in the wind; and after the wind an earthquake, but the Lord was not in the earthquake; and after the earthquake a fire, but the Lord was not in the fire; and after the fire a sound of sheer silence.

—1 Kings 19:11–12

Chapter Five

Transition:
Dark Night of the Spirit

Frequently, when I am working with spiritual direction clients, it becomes clear that they have an idea—a picture—of who God is that is completely tripping them up. Often, the god that they were given as children is still in charge, pulling the strings, and often that god is . . . monstrous. You know the kind of god I'm talking about—the finger-pointing, judgmental, "you're-a-piece-of-shit" god that some minister somewhere felt morally obliged to plant in our brains.

Intellectually, these clients might realize that this god is not the "real" God, but it's still the only image they hold, so many people just give up on God altogether. Other people long for an intimate relationship with God; many people try heroically, but with this kind of monstrous image in their heads, it's difficult to feel warm and fuzzy. So even though clients might be coming to spiritual direction and might be making real effort at spiritual practice, they end up sabotaging their spiritual progress—usually unconsciously—because they really don't *want* to cozy up to this kind of god.

At this point, I usually suggest that they draw three pictures: (1) the god they were given as children; (2) the god they *wish* could be true; and (3) the god they secretly think *might* be true.[1] These pictures usually usher us onto an enlightening path of discovery. After talking through all of the pictures, listening closely to the feelings and fears and hopes of my clients, I will eventually say something like,

"So . . . why don't you fire your childhood god and hire one of the other two? Here, I'll help you fill out his pink slip right now."

For many clients, this is often the first step toward a healthy, robust spiritual life. As long as we have harmful or inadequate images of God, it's going to affect (usually negatively) how we relate to God. After all, in all of our relationships, do we ever actually relate to others? No. We are only ever relating to our internalized projections of others. I don't say "hi" to *you*, I say "hi" to the person I *think* you are. And who I *think* you are impacts how I treat you and the kind of relationship we have. This is true of all of our relationships—and it's just as true of our relationship with God.

And as we have seen, our projections of what God is like—our images of God—are inadequate. For this whole mysticism thing to run its course, these images have to go. But this isn't easy. Letting go of our images, our ideas, our understanding is painful, even traumatic. When you let go of the god you have always known, what are you left with? The old saying, "better the devil you know than the devil you don't" applies to deities, too. Familiarity is safety, even if that familiar god is hurtful or abusive or antiquated. A lot of people stay in abusive human relationships for the same reason—the abuser is less scary than the unknown.

We can consciously try to let go of our images and ideas about God—firing your old god is a good way to ritualize this. But this can only go so far. Even if you fire that god, he's still going to be kicking around in your consciousness (I suggest giving him another job to keep him busy—janitor or low-level advisor). We desperately cling to that which we know, no matter how hard we try.

In the end, we will fail, because we can only go so far. To purge us of this final idolatry, God himself has to act. We don't fire him—he quits.

In the Book of Kings, we see an example of exactly this kind of "quitting" and see that, yes, it was hard even on a hero of faith like Elijah. Elijah challenged the prophets of the false god Baal to a duel.

Elijah built a pyre and Baal's prophets built a pyre and then they both prayed for fire. Baal's prophets cut themselves and prayed loudly and long, to no effect. Then Elijah stood up, said a short prayer, and fire consumed both his pyre and the one belonging to Baal. Then Elijah went on a murderous rampage and hacked over a hundred of Baal's prophets to bits with his sword.

(Now, I'm not sure why more than one hundred able-bodied prophets stood by amiably while one elderly lunatic with a scimitar hacked through the lot of them—maybe they were simply paralyzed with shame at having lost the contest; who knows?)

What really concerns us is what happened next. Queen Jezebel, having heard that her kingdom was suddenly and inexplicably facing a horrific shortage of clergy, ordered up Elijah's head on a platter. Finally terrified of something, Elijah fled for his life into the wilderness.

It was a very dark time in Elijah's life. The Bible says that while he was hiding out in a cave, something prompted him to go out and stand on a mountain. While he was standing there, a great wind rushed by, so great that it split the mountains and broke rocks into pieces, but, the scripture says, "God was not in the wind. And after the wind there was an earthquake, but God was not in the earthquake. And after the earthquake there was a fire. But God was not in the fire."

Now, most English translations follow the King James and report that after the fire, Elijah heard a still, small voice, but the Hebrew does not actually say that. Probably the translators were trying to soften a very grim passage, because what it actually says is "and after the fire there came a sound of sheer silence." It then relates that at the sound of this—or rather, at the absence of any sound—Elijah wrapped his face in his mantle.

It may be that the King James Version translators considered it pastorally irresponsible for the people to think that God would abandon someone as powerfully connected, spiritually, as Elijah. Hacking away at a hundred prophets of another religion, no problem; but that

85

God might abandon one of his chosen? Surely a little massaging of the text was in order. In the KJV reworking, Elijah hides his face in his cloak because he is awed before the Lord. But in the literal rendering, Elijah hides his face out of despair. Powerful people are trying to kill him—not without good reason, mind you—and God has led him into the wilderness and abandoned him there.

God wasn't fired. He quit. And Elijah was left utterly alone, bereft, and uncomprehending.

"If this is how God treats his friends, I wonder what happens to his enemies?" you might exclaim.

May I remind you about the hacking with a sword bit? But yes, the point is well taken—so to speak—abandonment *is* how God treats his friends. And not just his acquaintances; this is how he treats his *best* friends.

This is the second of our dark nights: the Dark Night of the Spirit. This is the most painful of the two dark nights—and also the most rare. In our walking the mystics' path, we have been through the trials of Purgation, passed through the ambivalently uncomfortable Dark Night of the Senses, enjoyed the joys and triumphs of Illumination, seeing all things in God and God in all things, but apparently that is as far as we can go without smacking our noggins on the Dark Night of the Spirit. And this dark night is the place where those of us who have worked the hardest, sacrificed the most, and loved the most passionately are left utterly alone.

Exactly like some deadbeat Dad who impregnates us with the Word and then says, "I'm out of here," in the Dark Night of the Spirit, God is just gone. The mystics tell us that in this stage God simply removes himself from the scene. And those who have given up everything for him, who have abandoned all other pleasures, all other means of support, and sometimes even forsaken the love and comfort of other people, are left with . . . what? "The sound of sheer silence," says the scripture.

What could possibly be the meaning, the purpose, of such abusive treatment? Why in the world would God string us along so far, demand so much, and then just dump us? Of course, it feels terrible, but it is not as bad as it feels. The mystics tell us that this is a necessary step on the way to full Union. It is a horrendously painful step, yes, but necessary just the same. Why?

COVENANT

This is precisely what the Jews were asking in the World War II concentration camps. They, too, felt like God had abandoned them. They watched their people being marched out to the gas chambers and they wondered aloud how God could possibly have betrayed them so utterly. For the Jews, the terms of their covenant were very simple: they promised to worship only the true God, and God, in turn promised to protect them.

Why had God forsaken their covenant? Why did he not protect them now? A possibly apocryphal story relates that one group of prisoners decided to have a formal trial, to try God for his indifference—apparently in absentia.[2]

A judge was selected, other roles were assigned, and the trial began. Numerous possible defenses for God's abandonment were put forth—was it a punishment for straying from the Law? Was it a purification, as in the flood of Noah? Was it a sacrifice, as in the sacrifice of Isaac by Abraham? Or, like the same story of Abraham, was it all just a test of their faith? Perhaps, they reasoned, it was simply a consequence of free will. One man complained that God had never been "good." He had simply been on "our side." And now he had, apparently, made a deal with another people, the Nazis, whose banners proclaimed, "God is with us."

Eventually the arguments were exhausted and the verdict was announced: "guilty." God was guilty of breaking the covenant. The trial finished, the prisoners disassembled—and what do you think they did next? They went to pray.

Even in the midst of war, in the face of death, in the event of God's apparent abandonment, these Jews did not abandon *their* side of the covenant—they prayed. This is the primary difference between a contract and a covenant. When a contract is broken, it's broken. But in a covenant, one party can continue to hold to it even when the other drops it; the party that continues to hold hopes that the offending party will eventually come around and the relationship can be restored.

A marriage is a covenant. Just because one party is unfaithful doesn't mean the marriage is over unless both parties agree that it is so. The wronged party can remain faithful and continue to uphold the covenant, and if the cheating partner eventually comes around, the covenant can endure.

There are lots of times when we have been unfaithful to God—and yet God has not given up on us. The covenant between us endures because God has patience and is constantly waiting for us to come around and get back to the business of loving. But in the Dark Night of the Spirit, God drops his end of the bargain. If the relationship is to make it, if our covenant is to endure, we must uphold it, regardless of how heartbroken or despairing we feel.

I love the story of the trial of God because it so starkly illustrates how hard it can be. It shows that it is possible to remain faithful against odds we can hardly imagine. I would like to think that if these concentration camp inmates can do it, so can I, but I quail at the thought of it. Would I really be able to uphold such hope and courage? Or would I take the advice of Job's wife: "curse God and die"?[3]

If we are to make it through the Dark Night of the Spirit, this is what is required of us: to remain faithful even when God abandons us. It's one of those "this is for your own good" things. It's painful and seems pointless. But like so many of these things—like, say, going to the dentist—it is also vitally necessary. Because if we *can* stay faithful even when God has disappeared into darkness, into nothing, then an invitation emerges: *to follow God into that darkness.*

FOLLOWING GOD INTO DARKNESS

Going through the Dark Night of the Spirit is hard. But what is happening is really very simple: we have done what we can do to rid ourselves of our false images of God—even firing those old images—but now God must finish the job.

All of our images are illusions. So long as I am relating to God as an "other," as someone whom I can perceive as "here" or "not here," I am tied up in an illusion of duality. As long as I can even conceive of "God," then I am still worshipping a metaphor, an idol, no different from Baal. God needs to move us beyond images and idols, beyond subject and object, beyond dualities of darkness and light. So in order for that to happen, God winks out of existence—so far as the mystic is concerned. The image we held so dear—everything we thought we knew about God—disappears. Similarly, every vestigial illusion about ourselves is extinguished when we enter the darkness as well.

This is necessary because no matter how hard we work at shedding false images, there are still vestiges remaining. The only answer for these remaining bits of *maya* is surgery, and surgery is painful, even when it is the Great Physician doing the cutting.

Progress is made by a process of subtraction. By taking things *out.* First, God surgically removes himself, which precipitates the Dark Night of the Spirit. The only thing left is the mystic and his or her broken heart—covering his face in despair like Elijah. But these are all illusory things—the mystic, the broken heart, even our faces as we cover them.

At this point, the mystic has a choice: to turn from the path, to give up, to abandon the covenant, to surrender to the hardness of the task and go back to a normal life of relative ease . . . or to follow God into the darkness. This is the ultimate act of trust—to turn from the world of being and form and follow God into nothing, to become nothing ourselves.

And in this nothingness, the mystics find themselves transformed. For when you subtract everything that is not real from God, you end up with nothing. And when we subtract everything that is not real from ourselves, we end up, once again, with nothing. When we meet God in the nothing, when we experience the *nothing that we are* and the *nothing that God is* as the same nothing, *we are transformed into God.*

For in this experience, the separateness between "I" and "Thou" is snuffed out. There, beyond all two-ness, the soul enters into true union with the Divine. As Thomas Merton described it, "In its proper meaning, contemplation transcends all objects, to all 'things,' and goes beyond all 'ideas' of beauty or goodness or truth, passes beyond all speculation, all creative fervor, all charitable action, and 'rests' in the inexpressible. It lets go of everything and finds All in Nothing."[4]

Granted, this is a highly rarified and advanced state of spiritual progress that few of us will ever experience, but most of us have—or will have—the dreadful experience of feeling as if God has abandoned us. There are few emotions as desperate and painful. To be left alone, especially by the one that professes to love us so much. How are we to bear it? And why?

Far be it from me to presume to explain the ways of God, but God's logic is, at least, consistent. Painful as the lesson is, the Dark Night of the Spirit happens to teach us. I remember the words of the Anglican mystic and singer/songwriter Bruce Cockburn: "I used to feel like God was my daddy, and I was toddling along, holding onto his finger. But for the past few years, it feels like God has withdrawn his finger, and I have had to learn to walk by myself."[5] I read this statement in an interview maybe twenty years ago, and it has stuck with me and I have remembered it every time I have felt similarly alone.

Nevertheless, it is scary when Big Daddy removes his finger. My mother tells me that I was doing fine riding my bike so long as I thought Dad was holding onto the back of my banana seat. But when

I looked back and realized that he had let go a block behind me, I fell straight over.

Granted, I eventually learned to ride my bike, but that is small comfort when I am feeling abandoned and despairing. Being abandoned may be a teaching tool but it still seems unnecessarily uncomfortable and abusive. During such times, it helps to remember that these feelings are temporary, that they will pass, that God will come back, and that I will be wiser and stronger when it is over than I was before—easier to see after the fact, but that's what *faith* is for.

A MYSTIC'S STORY: ST. JOHN OF THE CROSS

One of the greatest of the Spanish mystics, John de Yepes, was born in 1542 to a poor family of weavers. Like many great people of faith, he failed miserably when he tried to do "practical" work, but excelled at study.

His family worried for him, but one night, while he was praying, he heard the voice of the Blessed Mother telling him to be at peace. She told him that he would spend his life in service to God, restoring an age-old practice of perfection.

Encouraged, he joined the Carmelites, but was disappointed by how lax their religious life was. He had expected to live in a disciplined, ascetic fashion, and the leisurely life the friars lived confused and discouraged him. He asked his superiors for permission to live according to the most primitive—and most strict—rule of the Carmelites and was granted leave to do so.

But since he desired to practice his austerity supported by his community, this was not ultimately satisfying. So he decided to leave the Carmelites for a more ascetic order, the Carthusians. Before his change was irreversible, however, he met a woman who changed his life forever. St. Teresa of Avila (more on her later) begged him to remain and help her reform the Carmelites—she, the women's order; he, the men's.

Intrigued, he accompanied her to her convent to see how her nuns were living out their austerity, and he was impressed. A couple of his brother friars came to visit and, encouraged by the reforms Teresa was making, they stayed.

Before long, John and the brothers formed the male order of Discalced Carmelites (literally, "the religious men of Mount Carmel who don't wear shoes"), and he took to calling himself John of the Cross. After this, he traveled, helping the new order to grow, and eventually he accepted a post as the confessor at St. Teresa's Incarnation convent in Avila.

Meanwhile, the "normal" Carmelites (the ones who *do* wear shoes) were not taking this reform lying down. They felt extremely threatened, and in their rage, they kidnapped John and imprisoned him. It was a cruel and horrible fate and John endured more discipline and hardship than even he might have wanted. His cell was extremely narrow and he suffered frequent lashings.

It was during this time that he suffered his dark nights. On the surface it might appear that just being in prison could facilitate a dark night of the soul, as we use the term in contemporary, common speech. But in fact, he made good use of his time in prison, and spending much time in prayer, he made speedy progress on the mystical path. He kept a diary of sorts of his experience in the two poems for which he would be famous: "The Spiritual Canticle" and "Dark Night of the Soul."

When he wrote about the second dark night, the Dark Night of the Spirit, John used terms that were both graphic and familiar to him: "The afflictions of this Dark Night are many: you feel helpless, like you are being imprisoned in a dark dungeon, hands and feet tied, not able to move, or see, or feel anything, either from heaven or from the earth. This condition continues until the spirit is humbled, softened, and purified, and it becomes so delicate, simple, and refined that it can be one with the Spirit of God. . . . To be truly effective, this night may last for years, although there are brief intervals in which this dark shadow stops attacking the soul, and you can once again experience illumination and love."[6]

Nine months into his imprisonment, John succeeded in removing the hinges from his cell door and he crawled into the room next to his own, which had a small window. It was not small enough to hinder someone as emaciated as he was, however, and he slipped through it and escaped.

Immediately he went back to work with a renewed vigor born of his spiritual advancement. He founded new monasteries in Granada, Segovia, Cordova, and many other places. He continued this good work tirelessly until Teresa, his companion in reformation, died.

Deprived of their guiding light, the Discalced Carmelites floundered, and John was soon out of favor with the new leadership. He was assigned to an impoverished community where he became very sick. Even after being moved to another monastery for treatment, he was treated poorly. But eventually, those who had been told of his willfulness and wickedness were converted by his gentle and loving manner. They began to realize that, far from being a scoundrel and a troublemaker, as they had been told, he was, in fact, a saint. He died in 1591 and was canonized a saint only thirty-five years later.

John is best remembered not only for the two poems he wrote in prison, but for the commentaries on those poems he later wrote to explain them. Almost verse by verse, these commentaries provide one of the most comprehensive accounts we have of the mystic's growth into God. And they are made more effective because, instead of being academic, they are passionate descriptions of John's own harrowing and inspiring experiences.

- *For Questions and Answers that clarify points in this chapter, turn to page 169.*
- *To read what the mystics say about the Dark Night of the Spirit, turn to page 209.*

"I am the vine, you are the branches. Those who abide in me and I in them bear much fruit, because apart from me you can do nothing."

—John 15:5

"As you, Father, are in me and I am in you, may they also be in us, so that the world may believe that you have sent me. The glory that you have given me I have given them, so that they may be one, as we are one, I in them and you in me, that they may become completely one, so that the world may know that you have sent me and have loved them even as you have loved me."

—John 17:20–23

Chapter Six

Union

As I write this, there's been a lot of hullaballoo in the press around the fiftieth anniversary of Disney's film *Pinocchio*, and I was intrigued by a report on NPR about the differences between Disney's version and the original novel. Not surprisingly, Disney's version is pretty tame, pretty linear, a neat little story. Not so, the book. Even the *Cliff's Notes* version had my head spinning. It is a mess of a narrative with no discernible plot—an endless parade of episodes in which Pinocchio gets in and miraculously out of trouble.

Not only is it nonlinear, but the characters are kind of mean. For heaven's sake, Pinocchio actually kills Jiminy Cricket with a frying pan. He also bites the paw off a cat—granted the cat *was* trying to defraud him, but that's quibbling. There is a heroic tuna, which sadly never made the Disney version, nor did the wonderful story of the snail who tells Pinocchio he will let him into his house for the night, but morning breaks before the hospitable snail ever reaches the door.

But the basic pathos of the Pinocchio story survives in Disney's version. It is still the story of a wooden puppet that desperately longs to be a real boy. In the book, Pinocchio finally achieves his aspiration when, walking into town to buy himself a new suit of clothes, he hears from his friend the snail that the Turquoise Fairy is on her deathbed. He has come to love the Turquoise Fairy like his own mother, so he forks over all the money he has in the world to assist her.

Chapter Six

That night the Turquoise Fairy visits him in his dreams and kisses him. When he wakes up, he is a real boy, and the fifty copper pennies he gave the snail for the fairy have been replaced by fifty gold coins.

Despite its rocky literary beginning, the Pinocchio story has enjoyed a lively popularity, and it makes me wonder—why? What does Pinocchio's desire to be *real* symbolize for most of us? It doesn't seem like a political aspiration or even a developmental one. It could be about psychological integrity, but that lacks the pain and longing that so powerfully permeates this story.

My theory is that it is a spiritual metaphor—that in a world full of charlatan cats, fame-obsessed folk, and lay-about donkey-boys (and who hasn't known a few?), there is a desperate desire not to end up as either the fooled or those doing the fooling. We all desire to see through the glamour of the world, to find an authentic self that can apprehend reality—that can, in fact, be *Real*.

Certainly the mystics of the Christian tradition have employed precisely this kind of language, and it is this kind of authenticity, this kind of Reality that they, in their writings and in the example of their lives, call us to.

Thus far, we have been on quite a journey: we have been through the fires of Purgation—the stripping away of all that is not real; and we have enjoyed the pleasures of Illumination—seeing God in all things, and all things in God. If the mystic can remain faithful and endure the Dark Night of the Spirit, then finally, mercifully, he or she enters into that blissful state of Union that is the goal of all mystical endeavor.

The problem is that it is impossible to describe what that experience must be like. Very few people ever achieve it and those who do aren't that interested in such mundane activities as writing. From those sources that we do have, it is clear that Union is an experience like no other—the imaginary wall between me and you, between creature and creator, between time and eternity is dissolved—and all that is, is *you*. The only time is *now*. And every image you have ever had of who God is has gone up in smoke.

It is impossible for a wooden boy to know what it is like to be a real boy. He can imagine, he can dream, and he can aspire, but the actual experience will be like nothing he's pondered.

Likewise, we cannot, in our current state of embeddedness in the illusion of the world, imagine what it would be like to be Real people, free of all illusion. But the mystics typically speak of what it is like using two metaphors: Divine Marriage and Deification.

DIVINE MARRIAGE

"Hallelujah! For the Lord our God the Almighty reigns. Let us rejoice and exult and give him the glory, for the marriage of the Lamb has come, and his bride has made herself ready; to her it has been granted to be clothed with fine linen, bright and pure"—for the fine linen is the righteous deeds of the saints. And the angel said to me, "Write this: Blessed are those who are invited to the marriage supper of the Lamb."

—Revelation 19:6–9

Not long ago, I was privileged to perform a wedding in beautiful downtown Stockton. The bride and groom were a friendly, lovely young couple and it was entertaining watching the polite but testy relations between his Chinese relatives and her Filipino family.

The rehearsal was more fun than they usually are. I asked the couple to practice their vows and coached them on speaking louder so that those in the back row could hear. "C'mon, Jeremy," I coaxed, "These folks have come a long way to hear these words." He tried again and burst out laughing. Finally, he got the right volume, but I had to instruct him further. "Jeremy, look at *her* when you're saying this. If you're not careful, you'll end up married to the flower display."

The next time he tried it, they both burst out laughing. We got through it in rehearsal . . . but then the day of the wedding arrived. The bride walked down the aisle, as radiant as any I have ever seen.

Chapter Six

The groom met her at the stairs and led her to her place. We stood during the readings. No one fainted in the heat. Then we came to the vows. "Repeat after me," I said to Jeremy.

He nodded, dutifully looked at his bride, and in a loud, even voice, began to repeat my words: "I, Jeremy, take you, Kristine, to be my wife, to have and to hold, from this day forward, for better, for worse, for richer, for poorer . . ."

He seemed to be doing fine. Except he wasn't. Watching his eyes, I saw that what was just a form to be practiced yesterday, he was saying for real now. The words were registering. Too late, perhaps, he was actually conscious of what he was saying, and I could read the panic on his face.

". . . in sickness and health, until death do us part. This is my solemn vow."

I watched him warily as he teetered back and forth, the finality of what he'd just done washing over him. He had *married* himself to this woman, and she to him. They had made a sacred vow to each other in the presence of everyone they held dear.

His moment of realization brought home to me just what a marriage vow is. Jeremy was saying "yes" to this person, not in every decision, certainly, but in every day of his life. He was saying "yes" to waking up with her, to sharing his material wealth with her, to sharing his inner life with her, to sharing his body with her, to sharing his future with her—to sharing all that he has and all that he is. That is a profound and awesome promise.

It takes a lot of preparation to get to that stage, if it is to be real. It takes a lot of maturity, a lot of compromise to do it well, a willingness to know and be known that doesn't come easy for many people. It requires both strength and vulnerability in equal measure and a great willingness to make one life out of two.

To be successful, both bride and groom must want this kind of joining, this kind of intimacy, this kind of permanence. And when all these things are present, it is a wondrous thing. A true marriage is always a mystical act, because in this process—which begins months or years before the marriage and is sealed and signified in the ceremony itself—two lives combine to create a third. Even if there is no physical offspring, there is always a mystical offspring, for the lives of two people come together and a new life begins—the life of the relationship itself.

For the rest of their marriage, the health of either one of them as an individual will be weighed against the health of this mystical third entity. The needs of either of them will be evaluated, and often sacrificed, in order to make sure this mystical third is fed, loved, cared for, and happy. When couples fight, when relationships end, it is usually because this mystical third person—the relationship itself—has not been nurtured, has not been ministered to, has not been adequately loved.

That marriage is an intrinsically mystical act should be no surprise to us, however. This intuition is so strong that scripture often uses it as a metaphor for the relationship between Israel and God, and in the New Testament, between Christ and the church. The mystics of many traditions likewise employ the symbolism of marriage to describe the intimacy between Divinity and the human soul.

This is the domain of the kataphatic mystic, employing symbols and images willy-nilly. Overwhelmingly, these mystics speak about their union with God in terms of marriage. Unlike the apophatic mystics (whom we'll discuss in a moment)—whose writings are terse and tentative—the kataphatic mystics let it all hang out. They are romantic fools. Even though the experience of union is impossible to describe, when they do write about it, it is in the most flowery, romantic, sickeningly sweet terms imaginable.

No less a heavyweight than Augustine even waxed treacly when he wrote: "O Lord, how I love you! You pounded on my heart with your Word until I loved you. . . . But what do I love when I love you? Not beautiful bodies or the loveliness of the passing seasons, not the radiance of light around us that make our eyes leap with joy, not the sweet melodies of songs, not the fragrance of flowers or perfumes or spices, not cakes or honey, not the entangled limbs of lovers. These are not the things I love when I love God. And yet, I love a light and a voice and a fragrance and a food and an embrace when I love God, who is a light, a voice, a fragrance, a food, and an embrace to my innermost self. . . . This is what I love when I love God."[1]

This kind of description is common not only in Christian mysticism, but in Hindu, Sufi, and Jewish mystical writings, among others. Sufi mystic Rabia is no less eloquent in describing her love for Allah when she writes, "My Joy—my Hunger—my Shelter—my Friend—my Food for the journey—my journey's End—You are my breath, my hope, my companion, my craving, my abundant wealth. Without You—my Life, my Love—I would never have wandered across these endless countries. You have poured out so much grace for me, done me so many favors, given me so many gifts—I look everywhere for Your love—then suddenly I am filled with it. O Captain of my Heart, Radiant Eye of Yearning in my breast, I will never be free from You, as long as I live. Be satisfied with me, Love, and I am satisfied."[2]

This is not just beautiful poetry, it is a sincere attempt to communicate something that is essentially ineffable—the union between a soul and her God. Just as a bride and groom surrender themselves to the unknowable in their vows, so too does the mystic surrender him- or herself to mystery in the act of divine union. For the mystic leaves behind forever her former, separate life, and, together with God, her beloved, they create a new life—one that she could not even imagine on her own: a new life that is the product not of either spouse alone, but of the joining of these two lives, one that must be nurtured and loved if it is to thrive.

A CALL TO COMMITMENT

If a human marriage is to work, if it is to thrive, if it is to be permanent, both parties must want it—it is no different with divine marriage. The testimonies of the mystics and of Jewish and Christian scripture is clear: God desperately desires this kind of relationship with us. God loves us and wants our love in return. God wants to surrender himself to us and wants us to surrender ourselves to him so that a new, more vibrant, more abundant life can be born.

In training spiritual directors, I hammer home that we are here for one thing and one thing only: to foster intimacy between the client and the Divine. It is our job to be matchmakers—to bring the client again and again to the dance so that she can be courted, to identify what resistance she might have to this marriage, to assist her in wooing the Divine. Spiritual directors—and ministers in general—are professional busybodies, always trying to match you up. We're Cyrano de Bergerac, helping you find the right words to woo. It's annoying, I know, but we mean well.

Because, really, all the resistance is in us humans, not in God. Scripture and the mystics clearly tell us that God already has on his tuxedo and his boutonniere. We might be having cold feet, but God is ready for the wedding. As an officiant, I usually have the best man and maid of honor sign the wedding certificates *before* the ceremony rather than after—things are crazy after a wedding and people want to celebrate, not do paperwork. Once I have their signatures, I usually nudge the groom conspiratorially, saying, "Dude, the paperwork is all done. You're legally married. You don't actually *have* to go through with the ceremony." Because men, being men, can typically take or leave the ritual stuff. But God isn't your ordinary guy. He *wants* to get married. And, annoyingly, he is popping the question *all the time*. We're just too busy with our nails and our shopping to notice.

I'm being silly of course. Even the mystics will admit that these are metaphors. But this metaphor—marriage—is the closest we humans ever get to what God wants with us. He wants to promise himself to us forever. He wants to say "yes" to us forever. He wants to merge his life with ours, to create a new life that simply wasn't possible before. *That's* what God wants.

Like a human marriage, this is a call to *commitment*—and it's a big commitment! It means your whole life has to change. But when you read the mystics, there's no question—they feel *loved*. And isn't that what we want more than anything? It's what God wants more than anything, too.

Deification

Jesus came and stood among them and said, "Peace be with you." After he said this, he showed them his hands and his side. Then the disciples rejoiced when they saw the Lord. Jesus said to them again, "Peace be with you. As the Father has sent me, so I send you." When he had said this, he breathed on them and said to them, "Receive the Holy Spirit. If you forgive the sins of any, they are forgiven them; if you retain the sins of any, they are retained."

—John 20:19–23

Sacred Marriage is how Union manifests for most kataphatic mystics—which is to say, for most mystics. However, some few mystics are apophatic—followers of the negative way—and for them this stage looks very different.

The Dark Night of the Spirit is an apophatic experience: it is the stripping away of not only everything that is not real about ourselves, but everything that is not real about God. And, when you think about it, there is nothing you can say about God that is actually accurate. Because God is all that is, any image, any description, any idea you may have of God is so incomplete as to be utterly false. The apophatic way is the way *without* images. This has always been a way that was less about relationship with God, and more about self-negating until the only reality left *is* God. It is a transformation of consciousness, becoming aware of one's essential identity with the Divine, that nevertheless feels like a transformation *into* God.

This process is called *deification*, and there's rather a lot of evidence for it in patristic sources. St. Athanasius wrote in his interminable creed that "God became human so that we might become God." And indeed, Eckhart states this even more forcefully when he says, "Our Lord says to every living soul, 'I became human for you. If you do not become God for me, you do me wrong.'"[3]

Unlike the kataphatic journey, where the mystic leaves the dark night married to a God he's basically never met (since all images have just died), the path of deification takes the mystic through the black hole of the Dark Night of the Spirit and spits nothing but God out the other side. The mystic himself has been negated; all traces of self or ego have been neutered. There is no trace of either the God or the mystic who began this journey. Where there were two on one side of the wormhole, only One emerges, and this One bears no resemblance to either of the original two.

The deified apophatic mystic still has an ego but sees through it like a shadow; it is a mere tool for navigating the illusory world— powerless to hold the person in thrall, to frighten her, or to mislead her.

We have a fine image of what this is like in the resurrection of Jesus. Jesus the man is abandoned by God on the cross and cries out, "My God, my God, why have you forsaken me?"[4] He then endures the great nothing of the grave and "descends into Hell,"[5] the ultimate Dark Night of the Spirit, and then emerges on the other side of the Resurrection transformed into divinity.

If we aspire to follow him, is this not our path as well? After all, he says that we all must take up our crosses, we all must lose our lives if we want to save them. What is he talking about if not the mystical path, the journey from illusion into Reality?

When Jesus appeared to the disciples after his resurrection, he wasn't the only one who'd had a rough weekend. The disciples had been through the wringer when all their ideas about who Jesus was were stripped away and they were left with nothing. But when Jesus came to them and breathed on them, he infused them with the Holy Spirit, as fine an image of Deification as we are ever likely to get. As the Spirit was breathed into them, they shared in his divine life, they became *enGodded,* as the German mystics put it.

In his book of Acts, St. Luke makes everyone wait for Pentecost for this moment, but St. John places this immediately after the resurrection, no doubt to draw a parallel between Jesus's mystical transformation and ours. Because *he* has been deified, we can be deified, for he promises that we will do greater things than even he accomplished in his time here on earth. It is no vain hope. It *is* possible for us to see through the veils of illusion that trap us. It *is* possible for us to wake up to our true nature. It *is* possible for us to experience our oneness with God and with all things. It *is* possible for us to be transformed from our small, separate, limited selves into divinity that is at once all things and no-thing.

This scene is never-ending; new characters come and go but we are still in the upper room. Only now *we* are the disciples—you and I. Jesus is still breathing on us, the Holy Spirit is still at work in us, nudging us, prodding us, loving us toward a wholeness that we cannot even imagine. But if we remain faithful, we might find ourselves kissed while we sleep, to awaken in the morning to discover that, like Pinocchio, we have been made real—that indeed, we always have been.

UNION AND ACTION

God is love, and those who abide in love abide in God, and God abides in them. Love has been perfected among us in this: that we may have boldness on the day of judgment, because as he is, so are we in this world. . . . We love because he first loved us. Those who say, 'I love God', and hate their brothers or sisters, are liars; for those who do not love a brother or sister whom they have seen, cannot love God whom they have not seen. The commandment we have from him is this: those who love God must love their brothers and sisters also.

—1 John 4:16–17, 19–21

Phyllis is one of the most dedicated laypeople at our church. We would not have survived the last fifteen years without her. She has kept the books, managed the building, kept the clergy in line, and generally made sure that everything and everyone is exactly where they are supposed to be. One of Phyllis's favorite Bible stories is the one about Mary and Martha, because she sees a lot of herself in Martha.

You remember the story: Jesus travels to Bethesda and stays with his friends Mary, Martha, and their brother Lazarus. Jesus and the disciples—the menfolk, basically—are reclining in the living room, discussing the mysteries of the universe, and Martha is in the kitchen making peanut butter and jelly sandwiches (a lot of them because these guys have been walking for twenty miles).

Martha is perfectly okay with this sexist arrangement, except for one thing—her sister Mary is not playing by the rules. Mary is sitting with the menfolk, gazing moonfaced up at Jesus, drinking up his every word. "Get a grip," Martha whispers to her sister, "and give me a hand here." But Mary refuses. So Martha goes over her head. She says to Jesus, "Will you please tell her to resume a gender-appropriate role and give me a hand in the kitchen?"

But to Martha's horror, Jesus sides with Mary. "Mary is choosing the better part," he tells her, "listening to the Good News is much more important than making sandwiches." And you can just see Martha's jaw hanging in disbelief.

Jesus tries to tell her that if she opens her mouth any wider weasels will wander in and try to nest, but she doesn't hear him. She just stands there, feeling betrayed and hurt.

And well she should! Where would any spiritual community be without its Marthas? Where would our congregation be without

Phyllis? Where would any spiritual community be without those people who tirelessly and selflessly give of their time, their sweat, their kindness, and their care?

We would be nowhere, meaning our communities would not exist. So is Jesus wrong? Well, in one way maybe no, in another way, maybe yes. He's certainly not wrong that listening to spellbinding theological discourse is a heck of a lot more fun than making dinner—although perhaps I am simply revealing my geeky proclivities, here. (Indulge me that one, won't you?) For some people, at least—the kind of people who read St. Augustine for fun—listening to Jesus riff *is* more compelling than making sandwiches. I imagine Jesus to be precisely that species of geek, so perhaps it's safe to assume that he thought so, too. So in that way, yeah, it's the better part.

But the mystics would disagree that it is necessarily the more *advanced* part or the *morally* best part. What they tell us is that, after all this work—after the trials of Purgation, after the ecstasy of Illumination, after the terrors of the dark nights, after the bliss of Divine Marriage or Deification—there is, *what*? I hate to break it to you, but there's more *work*.

It's *different* work though. It's no longer the ego-slaughtering work of seeing through your illusions, or the countless hours of focused concentration in meditation. At the end of Union, there is the kind that you don't mind doing, the kind that you can't help doing, the kind that is nothing but joy to do.

And what kind of work is that? It is *selfless action on behalf of others*. The way the mystics describe it is this: once you have achieved Union, once your life and God's life have merged so completely that there is no distinction between you, when your will is knit so finely to the divine will that what God wants *is* what you want, then you cannot help but to direct your every step out of love and compassion for others, for that is what God does.

The mystics in Union have surrendered their wills, their minds, and their bodies wholly and completely to God, and when God is

106

moved to compassion, the mystics are moved to compassion, and when God desires to save, to help, to love, the mystics desire the same, and act. When St. Teresa of Avila said that "Jesus has no hands on earth but ours," she was speaking specifically of this kind of "holy possession," where, in Union with the Divine, our bodies become the body of God, acting for the healing and the comfort of the world.

Scripture says, "By their fruits shall you know them," and indeed, you can tell if a mystic is blowing smoke or has actually "made it" by one test—does the mystic act out of self-interest in any way, or has he or she utterly abandoned self to the service of the hurting? Just as the image of Jesus sacrificed on the cross shows us a symbolic snapshot of a God who refuses to turn his back on us, who remains in union with flesh not out of necessity but out of love, so the mystic allows him- or herself to be sacrificed for the healing and the benefit of others.

In St. John's Gospel Jesus says, "Whoever remains in me, with me in him, bears fruit in plenty"—another symbolic image of what we are talking about. The true mystic, the one who is truly remaining in Christ, with Christ in her or him, the Divine Marriage or deification complete, *will* bring forth fruit.

They'll be fruitful not because it is a good thing to do, not out of obedience, not even out of pity, but because God's will and our will have become one will, and God, moved to compassion, desires to reach out in love to his creation, and so does it through our hands, speaking with our voice, carried by our feet, comforting by our presence, healing by our touch.

This is the end of mysticism—not warm and fuzzy feelings, not an emotional opiate, not being lost in bliss, not obedience, not even a love relationship between me and God, because it does not end there. Mary was right, the love relationship between her and Jesus is a good thing, but Martha is even more correct—if this love does not reach beyond itself, if it is not moved to compassionate action on behalf of others, it is an immature love, even an aborted love.

If love does not see beyond the immediate couple involved, if it does not see the hurt and the need that surrounds us, then it is a narcissistic, self-involved kind of love. It is, in fact, yet another illusion. The God that calls us beyond illusion, beyond narcissism, beyond a narrow concern for me and mine, ultimately, at the end of all this spirituality and religion stuff, calls us to serve one another, to love one another, to give ourselves on behalf of others. Again, it is a call to *commitment*.

One night, early in his ministry, Saint Francis realized he was being followed. He looked back and saw a man. As he looked at the man's face, he recoiled in horror; the man was a leper. At first he was angry because lepers are supposed to carry bells to warn people of their presence, so that healthy people can avoid the risk of contact with the dreaded disease. But then he was moved to pity for the disfigured man. He took the few pennies he had begged that day, and careful not to actually touch the man's skin, dropped them into the leper's hand. He then turned away, but the Spirit tugged at his heart. He knew he wasn't done.

Francis pulled the woolen blanket he had draped over his shoulders and placed it over the shoulders of the leper. He patted the man on the back (touching only the blanket, of course) and told him to go with God. But the Spirit wasn't done with him yet.

A terrible thought crossed Francis's mind. It was suicide surely, yet it seemed to be what God demanded. Once again, Francis approached the leper, and taking the man's face—covered with sores—between his palms, he drew the man's face to his own and kissed him on the lips with real tenderness and affection.

And to his great surprise, the leper vanished. And Francis realized that the leper was Christ himself, and he also knew from that moment what he should do. Never again would he be afraid to touch lepers, never again would he hesitate to risk himself on behalf of others, never again would he put his own interests above another's. In that moment, the last vestiges of his separation from the world, of self-preservation, of holding back from God were broken through, and Francis began to bear the kind of fruit that God worked so hard to plant in him.

God wants to plant that kind of fruit in us, too. For this is the true end of mysticism, this is the true end of all genuine religion, of all authentic spirituality—that we reach out in love to those who need us; that we allow our hands to be God's hands; that we let go of our selfishness and pride and begin to desire what God desires, which is only and everywhere to love, to heal, to comfort, to bring joy and justice and faith and hope and, yes, the greatest of these, love.

For if this is not our end, if all of our spiritual pursuits do not culminate in this, then we have just been chasing another illusion. And if we have learned one thing in this study, it is that we have had enough of illusions. It is Reality that we seek—and the reality is that this is a broken world with people hurting everywhere we turn. There is more ministry to do here than we can ever accomplish; there is more hunger, more injustice, more hatred than we can ever heal by ourselves.

And if we tried to do it by ourselves, it would be a useless endeavor. But we do not do it alone. We abide not alone, but in God, and God in us. And if we can truly do this abiding, if we can truly marry our life with God's, then there is no end to what we can do. Francis, as one man, could do little, and yet, abiding in God, he rebuilt the church.

And the mystics are clear on this: when God truly lives in us, we can do much more than we ever could on our own. For it isn't we who are bringing forth all this fruit. If we can just get ourselves—our fears, our illusions, our desires, our egos—out of the way, God will do it all. All we have to do is give our permission, cooperate, and, as I said, get out of the way. That's good news for people who are already run ragged, who are already tired. All we have to do is say, "Yes." God will do the rest.

Chapter Six

A MYSTIC'S STORY: ST. TERESA OF AVILA

St. Teresa's life was a study in the state of being in between. Born in between religions, her family was Jewish by ethnicity, but recently—and forcibly—converted to Catholicism. The authorities were suspicious of them, and her family was always aware that they were being watched—and judged. Her mother was anxious for Teresa to grow up a pious Catholic and often told her stories of the saints.

Teresa took these stories to heart and when she was seven years old, convinced her brother to run away with her so that they might be martyred by the Moors. (Fortunately for them—and us—their uncle caught them just outside the city walls and marched them home.)

As a very young woman Teresa again ran away from home, this time to the relative safety of a convent. Her father grieved at the loss of her but soon became reconciled to the idea and gave her his blessing.

Almost instantly she fell ill, due probably in part to the ascetic rigors of religious life, to which she was not accustomed. She eventually recovered but would vacillate in between sickness and health for the rest of her life.

However, she made good use of her down time while sick, devoting herself almost entirely to contemplative prayer. As with John of the Cross in his prison cell, the enforced quiet of her sickbed facilitated a very quick advancement in her mystical life, and she passed quickly through Purgation and Illumination, discerning the bodily (yet invisible) presence of Jesus with her at all times.

Eventually she passed into the unitive state, which culminated in an experience of ecstasy, which she described as being stabbed repeatedly through the heart by a fiery, golden lance. (The statue by Bernini, *The Ecstasy of St. Teresa,* enshrines this moment of religious breakthrough at the Santa Maria della Vittoria church in Rome.) Her friend John of the Cross described the phenomenon this way: "While the soul is inflamed with the love of God . . . it will feel that a seraphim is assailing it by means of an arrow which is all afire with love. . . . It seems to it that the entire universe is a sea of love in which it is engulfed, for, conscious of the living point or center of love within itself, it is unable to catch sight of the boundaries of this love."[6]

Even though she suffered greatly in her religious life, Teresa was so impacted by the gravity of her own sin that she desired even greater penance through austerity. The "moderate" lifestyle of the Carmelites seemed too lax to provide this, so she set out to reform the order, calling it back to its original level of ascetic discipline.

In 1562 she founded St. Joseph's Convent in Avila, espousing absolute poverty. At first, the extreme rule followed by her and the sisters who joined her scandalized the people of Avila, but they eventually came around. She had some powerful people in her corner, including the bishop and some wealthy laywomen who covered the meager expenses of the fledgling convent.

The next year she received official approval for her reform, although this was challenged many times. For the rest of her life she would vacillate in between being seen as a hero and a villain—a rogue nun and a saint.

She let nothing stop her. Although her body was feeble, she seemed indefatigable, founding convents for the new order in Medina del Campo, Malagon, Valladolid, Toledo, Pastrana, Salamanca, Alba de Tormes, Segovia, Beas de Segura, Seville, Caravaca de la Cruz, Villanueva de la Jara, Palencia, Soria, Burgos, and Granada.

Along the way she recruited John of the Cross, who founded nearly as many monasteries for the men of the new order. Altogether she founded sixteen new convents, attracting hundreds of women and men to the new, austere monasticism, largely due to the magnetic attraction of her own saintliness and zeal.

For all of her work, she never ceased in her practice of contemplative prayer. She also wrote prodigiously, contributing such classics of mystical literature as *The Interior Castle* and *The Way of Perfection*. Her descriptions of the stages of mystical attainment are practical and based on her own experiences. Most of them are reflected in the practices in this book (such as Recollection and Quiet), and the imagery of both deification and divine marriage are used by her, as she was one of those few mystics who actually seemed to occupy a space in between the negative and positive ways—being both apophatic and kataphatic in her approach, as the mood struck her.

Her zeal for reform and tireless labor in the service of God has seen few equals. "Do you know what it means to be truly spiritual?" she asked her readers. "It means becoming the slaves of Christ."[7] From her work with fellow Jewish converts to her leadership in reforming monastic life, Teresa's spirituality manifested through seemingly inexhaustible effort on behalf of her Lord. Hers was a true "mysticism in action," as it was her experience of union with God that drove her to work for the benefit of others.

Eventually, however, her frailty caught up with her. She died in 1582 at Alba de Torres, but her time of death is one of the most curious facts about her life. It seems she died on the very night when the Western world made its switch from the Julian to the Gregorian calendar, which skipped ahead nine days at midnight. Therefore, if she died before midnight, she died on October 4, but if she died after midnight, then she died on October 15. That's Teresa—always finding the in between places, even in death.

Like Teresa's life, being in Union is a curious in between experience—needing to cooperate with the illusion of separateness in order to navigate daily living, but at the same time fully united with God and aware that the separation *is* illusion. Life in Union is life in between, embracing paradox and ambiguity, committed to giving yourself utterly to others—because, indeed, every "other" is in reality God, which is to say, yourself, since you are also part of God.

Union

- *For Questions and Answers that clarify points in this chapter, turn to page 170.*
- *To read what the mystics say about Union, turn to page 214.*
- *To read what the mystics say about Union and Action, turn to page 219.*
- *To try some exercises around Union, turn to page 240.*

"To seek is as good as seeing. God wants us to search earnestly and with perseverance, without sloth and worthless sorrow. We must know that God will appear suddenly and joyfully to all lovers of God."

—Julian of Norwich

Conclusion

This Tradition Belongs to You

The Christian mystical tradition is not the sole possession of whispering saints of yore or those possessed of arcane knowledge. It does not belong to some church hierarchy or to any particular denomination. If you follow Jesus, this tradition belongs to *you*. It is yours to do with what you will. If you just want to dabble, feel free—you will go as far as you desire to go. If you want to dive in headfirst and pursue full Union with God, you can. But you won't do it because any outside authority says it's okay. You'll do it because you had an affair with God, just the two of you—you fell in love and got married (or you were deified or were impregnated with the Word—take your pick of metaphors).

That said, just as a human marriage does not take place in a vacuum, the spiritual journey, too, takes place in the context of a wider human community. In the introduction we talked about the importance of having a good spiritual director—this is essential to avoiding the pitfalls on this path. Just as important is a church community. Not because you need permission or connection to some apostolic succession, but because an authentically Christian life is always one that is lived among others. There are no successful Christian lone rangers. Even the medieval Christian mystics were held and supported by their communities—usually their fellow monks and nuns. Even Julian of Norwich had regular visitors who came to her window to fellowship with her and to receive spiritual direction.

It is in community that we learn what it really means to follow Jesus. On our own, we can be deceived by all kinds of romantic spiritual notions, but it is in the daily life of a spiritual community—as we bump against other people's prickly natures, share their joys and sorrows, rejoice and grieve, get mad, hurt each other, reconcile and forgive—that we learn what it means to be "spiritual." This is the real stuff. Church is the school where we learn to be the Community of God. St. Teresa of Avila wrote:

> People will tell you that you do not need friends on this journey, that God is enough. But to be with God's friends is a good way to keep close to God in this life. You will always draw great benefit from them. This is to love: bear with a fault and not be astonished, relieve others of their labor and take upon yourself tasks to be done; be cheerful when others have need of it; be grateful for your strength when others have need of it; show tenderness in love and sympathize with the weakness of others. Friends of God love others far more, with a truer, more ardent and more helpful love. They are always prepared to give much more readily than to receive, even to their Creator.[1]

Don't fall into the trap of saying, "I just can't find the place that feels right." There is no such thing as a perfect fit. There is only the "good enough" church, just as there are only "good enough" Christians. No Christian is perfect and neither is any Christian community. Just pick one that seems reasonably healthy and where there are a few people you like, and settle in.

You'll instantly find things you don't like—things about the people, about the liturgy, about the politics of the place. Don't run. *This is where the gold is.* Stay put and let it work on you, even as you work the practices and stages in this book. You will find that all these pieces form a coherent whole that will work on your soul and grow it into Divinity, amazingly and inexplicably. Not only that, but along the way you will find people too precious for words, lifelong friends who will support your spiritual journey and uphold you in good times and bad.

CONTEMPORARY REFRAMES OF THE CLASSICAL MODEL

I have attempted to unravel and explain, in a reader-friendly way, the labyrinth that is Christian mysticism. So as not to add to the confusion, I have used the terms most familiar to the tradition. But the terms are arcane and often confounding to people today. Scattered amidst my explanations are other terms that describe this process in a more contemporary fashion. For those wanting to understand the history and the tradition, the old terms are useful and necessary, but for those teaching people how to simply grow closer to God, I suggest a more contemporary frame. Here are a couple:

The Four Paths. Matthew Fox, in his many books on Creation Spirituality,[2] has gleaned from Meister Eckhart's writings something he calls "the Four Paths," which is a recasting of these stages of mystical growth.

His model begins with the *Via Positiva*—a revisioning of Awakening—in which an experience of wonder sets us off on our journey. One brilliant sunset is enough to kick it off, just as the close examination of a dog's paw can inspire similar wonder, or even the ecstasy found in the arms of one's beloved. All are occasions for awe. Wonder is all around us; for the goodness God proclaimed in the creation of the world is not diminished by human sin, but is made more poignantly apparent.

But just as one cannot climb a mountain without coming down, the first path inevitably gives way to the second, the *Via Negativa*—a revisioning of Purgation—the way of sinking, cooling, of darkness, pain, and letting go. The second path is harder than the first, for it teaches us that all those things that cause awe and wonder must come to an end. All things rise and fall. Joy is followed by sorrow, light by darkness, ecstasy by agony.

But Fox insists this is a necessary and holy thing. God does not wish us to live in an illusion that everything is sweetness and light. Instead of insulating ourselves from pain, Fox insists that we embrace the Negativa, enter it willingly and with courage, knowing that it is not the end of our journey, but rather the dark valley before the next rise can be approached. We must learn the lessons of the valley before the next path is possible. The Negativa has many gifts to impart: detachment, not taking ourselves too seriously, and the ability to "let go and let God," as the saying goes. Letting go and letting be is the hardest part of the spiritual journey, but without it our travels are aborted.

If we can walk through the valley, a great prize awaits us: the Via Creativa—a revisioning of Illumination—the Way of Creativity. Once we have emptied ourselves in the Negativa, we are ready to be filled. The Creativa is the result, as our pain provides the fuel for our creative expression. As we give form to our experience, our experience is transformed. In the act of creativity, God illumines our minds and souls by expressing himself through our art—singing with our mouths, drawing with our pen, dancing through our bodies. The wonder and pain of all of creation pours through us as the Spirit of God in us gives us utterance. Art, music, poetry, dance, woodworking, and cooking are ways in which sense is made of the first two paths, and God is made flesh once again.

The Via Creativa, the proclamation in art of both our joy and our sorrow, cannot help but have an effect on us and others. For as we share these experiences, as our art is heard and understood, even by ourselves, we are already embarking on the fourth and final path: the Via Transformativa—the Way of Transformation and Reformation—a revisioning of Union and Action.

In this path, we are moved by the art we produce to act in the world, to make it better, to alleviate suffering, to encourage the downtrodden, to feed the hungry and visit the sick, to challenge the powerful on behalf of the weak. The Transformativa is similar to what our Jewish brothers and sisters call *Tikkun*, the remaking of the world.

Seen in this way, spiritual growth is cyclic, not linear: Wonder ushers us into sorrow, wonder and sorrow together move us to express our inmost being, and this expression moves us and others toward social justice and communal transformation. Each time we move around this circle we deepen; we grow a bit more into God.

Fox does a great thing for us by showing us how these stages work in a cyclic fashion, and he successfully gleans from the writings of the mystics—especially Eckhart—support for this way of viewing spiritual growth.

Parallel Growth Model. In my own teaching, I have found it useful to discern contemporary terms for the primary actions of each stage of spiritual development. These not only rename the stages but reframe them, giving a slightly different emphasis to each:

Classical Terms	Contemporary Terms
Awakening	Invitation
Purgation	Discernment
Illumination	Enjoyment
Union	Commitment

While the classical model lends itself to a linear process, and Fox's reframing to a more cyclic process, the Parallel Growth frame suggests a process in which all four are happening at the same time, with different emphases. For instance, God is always inviting us into deeper communion, although this invitation is likely to be more dramatic at the beginning of the journey to get our attention, and lessen in intensity as we progress. Likewise, there is never a time when we are not discerning, although discernment will be fairly intense earlier in the process, because there will be so much to discern when we are just starting out. We are always invited to enjoy God's presence, and it is our glimpses of this while we are being invited and are discerning that continue to lure us forward in our process. (However, enjoyment certainly intensifies once our major discernment is complete, as practice gives way to a way of being.) Finally, we are being called to commitment at every stage, but it is only late in the process when it hits home for us what this really means and requires. The metaphor of Divine Marriage is especially apt near the end of this process as we enter into a true union that changes our identity in a fundamental way.

Understood through these contemporary terms, the process is not as clean and orderly as the classical model; each stage occurs simultaneously with the others, but the focus or the intensity is likely to be greater as one progresses—in a more or less linear fashion—as one stage organically gives way to another.

GOD WANTS YOU!

Regardless of how you view this process, God is holding it with grace, and it is important that we do the same. It is easy to get discouraged, to feel as if we are not making as much progress as we would like. But two steps forward, one back is still progress. It is also the way human beings grow—not perfectly, not reliably, but irregularly, in fits and starts. Cut yourself some slack and lovingly hold your imperfections, your regress as well as your progress, your mistakes as well as your triumphs—just as God does.

God never called any perfect people—because there *aren't* any perfect people. God only ever calls flawed, wounded, limited, scared, imperfect people because that's the only kind there are. So don't be discouraged—you're actually in pretty good company.

God doesn't call us to be spiritual accountants who must have everything in perfect order. God calls *lovers*. This is what God is calling you to: to *lovemaking*, to union—just as you are, in the midst of all your messiness and complications. That's part of your charm, you know. You may hate it, but God loves it. *Trust me.*

This is the Good News of Jesus: no matter who you are, no matter what you have done, no matter your background, who you love, what you believe or don't believe, God wants to embrace you and be embraced, to love and be loved, to be wedded, united, made one with you forever.

What are you waiting for?

Questions and Answers

No matter how carefully I prepare a lecture and how complete I think it is, my students invariably have questions. I knew this book would be no different, so I sent it out to students, friends, and colleagues. The questions that follow are actual questions from real people (though some of them have been edited or are composites of two similar questions). I hope you will enjoy the dialog, and if you have any questions of your own, please don't hesitate to email me at apocryphile@ me.com. Your question may be selected for the ongoing "Growing Into God" blog at http://growingintogod.wordpress.com/

QUESTIONS ABOUT THE INTRODUCTION

Where did this word mystic *come from? Is it related to* mystery?

The two are definitely related. *Mystic* comes from the Greek word *mystikos*, one who is an initiate into the mysteries.[1] *Mystery* comes from the Greek word *mysterion*, which refers to the sacred and the unknown. The word *sacrament* is a Latin translation of *mystery*. All the sacraments are mysteries, because through unknown means, they bring us closer to God.

You use the term **the church.** *What church do you mean, the Roman Catholic Church? Or the small "c" catholic church as in "all Christians"?*

When I say *the church*, I mean it in the truly universal sense: the mystical body of all those who follow Jesus, regardless of what institutional structure they attend or what denomination they belong to.

Do you think our resistance to intimacy with God is related to having a healthy ego? Or is it related to having a lot of unhealed issues?

This is a very good question, and I believe you are on to something regarding ego. Michael Washburn, in his book on Transpersonal theory, *The Ego and the Dynamic Ground*, posits that when we are born, we have an undifferentiated consciousness—the infant experiences complete immersion in the world and in the Divine (which Washburn calls the Dynamic Ground). In order to function in the world, we have to develop healthy ego boundaries, which children normally do. But at some point, usually around middle age, a rapprochement to the Dynamic Ground becomes desirable. However, so long as the Dynamic Ground is unknown, it is perceived by the conscious mind as frightening and resistance is the norm. Only when that resistance is worked through and real acquaintance with the Dynamic Ground is made does it become "known," appearing then as a benevolent presence. In chapter one, I describe an example of a frightening experience of the Dynamic Ground, an often unsettling experience Evelyn Underhill labeled "Awakening."

On the other hand, yes, many people who have been wounded experience a lot of resistance when approaching God—especially those who have experienced religious abuse. This abuse can be overt or covert—blatant or subtle—but it can still wound. People who have been raised in conservative religious homes suffer greatly and have the most trouble approaching God in a healthy way. This is often related to the fact that people are frequently given the most abominable images of God when they are children. If the God your parents gave you is a soul-sucking monster that does nothing but shame you and tell you how evil you are, and you have not dealt with that image, it is going to be very difficult to cozy up to that God. For people in this position, I highly recommend the help of a reputable spiritual director.

I consider myself to be spiritual but not religious. Isn't mysticism for people who want to become more religious?

Mysticism is for people who want to feel a greater connection to the ultimate Mystery. If you want to see through the illusion of your separate self and experience your essential oneness with all things, then you are likely to find mysticism a fruitful pursuit. Religions are traditions that arise in particular cultures and places, in part to approach this Mystery. Religions clothe that mystery in metaphor and symbol to help us access it (definitely a kataphatic approach).

Do you need to be religious? No. You don't need to buy any tradition uncritically and I would recommend against it. Should you avail yourself of the wisdom that various traditions offer for this journey? Absolutely.

I feel a mystical calling—but I don't feel called to practice any particular tradition. Are my feelings authentic? Or, if authentic, can a mystical path be traversed without a particular tradition as its foundation?

Yes, indeed your mystical tendencies are authentic. In my book *Faith Styles: Ways People Believe,*[2] I discuss six different ways that people hold faith—some of them attached to a specific tradition and some of them not. In the spiritual direction biz we say that you are the expert on your spiritual life and you should not let anyone else presume to tell you differently. About seventy percent of Americans today consider themselves "Spiritual but not Religious," which often translates to what my colleague Jurgen Schwing calls being "Spiritually Eclectic"— piecing together spirituality from several sources. An example might be someone who attends church on Christmas and Easter, but practices yoga, sits zazen less often then she would like, and reads Deepak Chopra. All good things, and this person may indeed be a budding mystic. Many of my students are Spiritual Eclectics and have deep mystical tendencies. I trust this completely.

That said, people who practice their spirituality (and their mysticism) apart from a tradition and a community are at a distinct disadvantage. Tradition gives us a roadmap for the journey, offers advice on how to avoid traps and pitfalls, gives us practices, techniques, and disciplines, provides mentors (both living and literary), and gives us an amazing gift of a spiritual community to encourage us, care for us, and correct us. As my poetic alter-ego Najat Ozkaya wrote, "Sure, it's possible to grow spiritually all by yourself, but it'll take you a lot longer to do it. A three-legged dog can certainly cover some ground, but it still only has three legs." So yes, it can be done outside of a tradition, but it's harder and more dangerous.

Besides, you don't have to be a Christian (or a Buddhist or a Hindu) to benefit from the wisdom of those traditions' mystics— including their roadmaps, advice, and even community. No spiritual community worth its salt would turn away a sincere seeker, even if you keep on seeking after years in their midst.

If friendship with God is for everyone, even me, what if I'm not Christian and I can't relate to Jesus and the saints and the mystics? I'm still feeling left out. Can you give me an example of a contemporary non-religious mystic so I know this is possible?

The Christian tradition is just one path to Divine Union; there are lots of others. Protestant mystic William Law wrote, "There is but one salvation for all mankind, and that is the Life of God in the soul . . . you have no true religion, are no worshipper of the one true God, but in and by that Spirit of Love which is God Himself living and working in you. . . . Turn therefore inwards, and all that is within you will demonstrate to you the Presence and Power of God in your soul, and make you find and feel it, with the same certainty as you find and feel your own thoughts."[3]

No Jesus necessary. There are lots of non-Christian mystics about—check out Deepak Chopra or Eckhart Tolle, for example—they'll give you lots to chew on and I recommend them if you want a tradition-free approach. There are lots of paths, and Christianity is one of them.

Are you saying that God is personal or impersonal? It seems like you are implying that God is both, depending on what tradition you follow.

Both things are true because either option in isolation is false. God is so much bigger than any of our perceptions of him; if you try to put him in a box like "personal" or "impersonal," he'll bust out of it just to spite you. So yes, I am saying that God is both personal and impersonal. Just as in physics we ask, "Is light a particle or a wave?" The answer is, "It depends on which one you're looking for." The question of whether God is personal or impersonal depends on your perspective.

In Hinduism, is the impersonal Godhead the Divine Brahman? Or is it the Divine Krishna who loves us and wants to be loved by us? The answer depends upon one's spiritual constitution, one's personality. In the Christian tradition, those who are wired to see God as an impersonal force are usually *apophatic,* while those who are wired for relationships are usually *kataphatic.*

Why do some mystics talk about God as being one with us, and some as if God were "other"? Are we separate from God, or are we "of" God? This is confusing.

It's confusing only if you are expecting it to make sense in some kind of linear, logical fashion. But that kind of "it's either this or that" thinking gets you nowhere with something as confounding as religion. The sooner you embrace paradox, ambiguity, uncertainty, and mystery, the better off you'll be with this whole mysticism thing.

The Christian mystics are maddeningly inconsistent regarding this point, so making logical sense of it is really not an option if you are looking to them for guidance. Mysticism is something you must feel your way into, not something you can do like a cookbook (although I've done my darnedest to present it as such in this book).

I've already touched on this, but let me see if I can make it clearer. In Christianity, there are three basic "positions" on the matter:

a) **mysticism = union of wills:** these mystics are clear that we and God are of different substances, and never the twain shall meet. The goal of their mysticism is a *union of wills*—becoming so intimate with God that his will and the mystic's will are in complete synch. (Some Church Fathers, Roman Catholics, and most Evangelical Protestants fall into this category.)

b) **mysticism = gradual deification:** these mystics believe that God is in the process of turning the whole of creation into himself—the church is here to assist with this task. (Most Eastern Orthodox believers and some Roman Catholics and Protestants fall into this category.)

c) **mysticism = identification with God:** these mystics insist that we and God are of the same substance, and we're just not aware of it. Mysticism for them is about gaining greater awareness of an already-existing oneness. (Many Roman Catholic mystics fall into this category.)

However, mystics are not consistent and will sometimes seem as if they are speaking from one perspective, but then they will shift mid-paragraph and begin to speak from another. Feel it, don't think it.

I'm not sure what you mean by images *of God. In the section on apophatic and kataphatic orientations, it seems you mean ideas or concepts of God, not just visual expressions. Still, can actual images (especially music and pictures) be used to express or support mystical practices? Or is this considered an obstacle to realization?*

I am a visually-oriented person and so I often speak of *images* in a visual way, when what I actually mean are ideas or mental constructs, so this is a good clarification. The world's religions are quite divided on your second question regarding whether visual images are helpful or harmful. Jews and Muslims come down firmly against them, but many forms of Hinduism and Buddhism are very image-positive.

Christianity has known its image-detractors—such as the iconoclasts in the fourth century and many of the Protestant reformers—but by and large, Christianity is also very fond of its images and considers them a help more than a hindrance. Music (especially chant) has long been used to usher people into a contemplative space, and Eastern Orthodox Christians pray regularly with icons, painted carefully with special prayers at every step along the way to aid the icon-gazer in reaching a state of mystical awareness.

Certainly, though, images can be obstacles—those Children's Bible pictures from the 1960s never evoked any feelings of devotion or mystical awe in me, and nostalgic kitsch doesn't count. Working with images works great for some people and not so well with others. That's why Christian mystics come in two varieties—*apophatic* (no words or images) and *kataphatic* (with words and images)—something for everybody.

You say people are frequently put off by reading the mystics. Do you think this is because the mystics are primarily Catholics?

It is true that the most famous of the Christian mystics are Roman Catholics, but by no means are all of them Catholic. There are plenty of Eastern Orthodox and Protestant mystics to pick from (check the lists on pages 225 and 231). Here's an example from Lutheran mystic Johann Arndt, who gives a concise summary of the very mystical map we've been discussing:

> Just as our natural life has its stages, its childhood, manhood, and old age, so too our spiritual and Christian life is set up. It has its beginning in repentance, through which a person does penance every day. A greater enlightenment follows after this like middle age, through the contemplation of divine things, through prayer, through the cross, through which all God's gifts are increased. Finally comes the perfection of old age, being established in complete union through love, which St. Paul calls . . . being a perfect man in Christ."[4]

So yes, there are non-Catholic mystics. But I would hope that just being Catholic would not be a reason *not* to read someone.

I think the reason people are often put off by reading the mystics is because they are often found in bad, musty versions that sound like they were translated by Shakespeare's grandpa. And also because they are trying—often not that skillfully—to eff the ineffable, to describe the indescribable, to put words to what is simply not speakable. So their logic is circumlocutious, their examples strained, their prose clunky, their poetry sickeningly pious. Don't be too hard on them—they are attempting the impossible. You or I would not fare any better—especially if we were read hundreds of years after our deaths, in different cultural contexts, by people with different religious assumptions.

From my perspective sports are fun, but I am not trying to make it to the Olympics. Mysticism sounds to me like trying to make it to the Olympics. In other words, it takes a lot of work—I think that I just want a little bit of it to make my life better. Do I have to become a fanatic for mysticism to help me?

Not at all. The great thing about God is that he meets us wherever we are. We get to say how much is too much. Mostly, it is we who control how close we get to God. A little bit of mysticism is going to help us a little. A lot of mysticism is going to help us a lot. But you are in control.

That said, God is always inviting us into deeper communion and greater intimacy. It really is very much like a romantic relationship. How would it sound if I recast your question in terms of human relationship? "Relationships sound to me like they take a lot of work—I think that I just want a little bit of romance. Do I have to become a fanatic to enjoy a relationship?" The question is, what is it you really want? Do you want a one night stand, a thrill? Or do you want a committed relationship that is going to last your whole life long, that is going to deepen as you grow into it, that is going to require hard work to make it succeed? As Teilhard de Chardin wrote, "Created beings must work if they would be yet further created."[5]

A lot of us (especially us men!) have issues with commitment—not to mention intimacy. There is a reason that the mystics use marriage as a metaphor for their relationship with God. It is that intimate, it is that sweet, it takes that much work, and it is that rewarding.

The phrase Union with God *sounds scary. Does this mean I will cease to be myself?*

It *is* scary. It will require a lot of loss—mostly all of your illusions about who you are and who God is. So will you cease to be yourself?

No, you will become more authentically you. But you will have to relinquish the lies you tell yourself and others about who and what you are. Is that a painful process? Yes. But remember: nothing real is ever lost. You will not be asked to give up anything authentic or genuine—only what is false and illusory.

You mention the benefit of having a spiritual director and say that it doesn't matter what religion your spiritual director is. I am not a Christian. If I go to a Christian spiritual director, won't that person subtly be pointing me toward a Christian spiritual path and Christian beliefs?

Not if that spiritual director holds an interfaith orientation (an openness to and understanding of other faiths) and is properly trained. He or she may be most familiar with the Christian tradition, and so of course examples and metaphors from his or her own tradition will leap most easily to mind. But a spiritual director's job is to help you discern *your* authentic path and to walk it with integrity. They are trained to focus on the spiritual lives of their clients and to recognize their clients as the experts on their own spiritual lives. Well-trained spiritual directors are very careful not to project their beliefs onto their clients or to see their own spiritual paths as normative for everyone.

I recommend interviewing directors to make sure you have a good "fit." You can ask how they feel about working with someone from a different religion. If they say, "I'm not comfortable with that," thank them for their time and move on. There are plenty of well-trained spiritual directors who are sensitive to interfaith issues or who have been specifically trained to work with people of different faiths. I direct one such program in Berkeley,[6] and teach for another program in Palo Alto, California.[7]

Is Christian mysticism different from Muslim mysticism or Hindu mysticism?

It is and it isn't. Christian mysticism describes union with the Divine as it has been experienced by Christians in the past 2,000 years of the Christian tradition. It views the journey from within the Christian paradigm, using Christian concepts, symbols, and metaphors.

Hindu mysticism describes union with the Divine as it has been experienced by Hindus in the past 3,000 years of the evolving Vedic and Vedantic traditions. It views the journey from within the Hindu paradigm, using Hindu concepts, symbols, and metaphors. Ditto for the Muslim (Sufi) perspective. Or the Buddhist. Or the Sikh, etc.

Is this the same journey? Yes. If you look at the stages of spiritual progress the mystic travels through, there are close parallels in most traditions. So while the images and metaphors are culture- (and religion-) specific, the *experience* of Divine union is remarkably—uncannily—similar.

QUESTIONS ABOUT AWAKENING

When you say that Julian sees herself as "orthodox," what do you mean by "orthodox"?

In Christian writing, *orthodox* is often used in two ways. The word actually means "correct teaching," so the most general meaning is teaching that conforms to what the majority of Christians believe. Of course, what is considered "orthodox" is going to change depending on who you ask. For Julian, it meant believing everything the Roman Catholic Church of her time and place taught. These days it means the teachings that all Catholics and most Protestants agree on.

The more specific meaning of the word, though, is the name of several denominations of Eastern Christianity, such as Greek Orthodox, Russian Orthodox, Armenian Orthodox, etc. So if you see *orthodox*

131

with a small *o* it means correct teaching. If you see *Orthodox* with a capital *O* it refers to the denomination.

Julian's declaration that all is already well brings up the issue of suffering and evil in the world. How can everything already be perfect with all this bad stuff going on?

Hm . . . I don't think I said everything was perfect, and I don't think Julian would, either. The idea that everything is "perfect" just as it is, is a common idea in Buddhism, but not in Christianity. Christianity affirms the reality of human sin, the brokenness of human nature, and the harm that humans do in the world. To deny this is true is (for Christians) buying into an illusion—we harm the earth, we harm ourselves, and we hurt each other. We don't always mean to—though sometimes we *do* mean to—but we do it just the same. What Julian is saying is that human sin is not sufficient to derail God's plans. Yes, human sin is bad, she says, but in the end everything is going to work out okay.

I like her approach because although she doesn't soft-pedal the reality of human sin, her trust and optimism in the love and power of God to make all things right inspires me and fills me with hope—something this world desperately needs right now. We don't need false illusions like the denial of human sin—not when injustice and evil are still wreaking havoc in the world—but we do need Julian's affirmation that evil will not have the last word, that God will eventually make "all things well."

When you say that the theologians of Julian's day placed the block to communion (between God and humanity) in God, what do you mean? Can you unpack that a little?

While most Christians agree on what Jesus saves us *from* (death), there is no consensus in Christianity on exactly *how* that salvation is effected. The favorite (but not "official") theory among Roman

Catholics was put forward by St. Anselm in the twelfth century. Anselm taught that, like a medieval monarch, God's honor must be defended. We humans are like sinful, rebellious serfs whose sin has besmirched God's honor, which has caused him to turn his face from us. God's pride has been wounded and he refuses to have anything to do with us until this pride, this honor, can be restored.

Enter Jesus, who lived a perfect human life—up to and including his death—just to show us screw-ups down here that it can be done—which also somehow magically restored God's honor. In exchange for this heroic act, God granted Jesus a boon: the gift of eternal life. But because Jesus *is* God, he did not need this gift, so he gave it to humankind to be distributed through the sacraments of the church. Thus, grace became a commercial commodity that could be exchanged, so this is called the "Commercial" Theory of the atonement.

A few centuries later, John Calvin came along and modified this theory, stating that it was not God's honor, but God's *justice* that must be maintained. Law must be upheld above all things, and because humankind is sinful, someone must pay for that sin. God's justice *must* be satisfied, and the full punishment for human sin is poured out upon Jesus on the cross. (Apparently it doesn't matter *who* gets punished just so long as there is someone to whip.) Some variation on Calvin's theory has become the accepted norm amongst almost all Protestant churches.

Notice that in both of these theories, the block to communion between humans and God resides in God, not in humans. It is *God* who cannot look upon us because his honor has been offended. It is *God* who cannot embrace us until justice is served. In both cases, God is unwilling or unable to do the very thing that Jesus insists that we do for each other: simply forgive.[8]

Why must God's honor be restored? Why must God save face and who is he saving face in front of? *Why* must God's justice be satisfied? Why can God not simply forgive as we are commanded to do? It seems a very hypocritical God who demands something of us that he is himself unable or unwilling to do. In my opinion, both of these theories completely miss the point of Jesus's teaching, distorting the Good News into—well, not Bad News exactly, but Rube-Goldberg-style Complicated and Highly Inconvenient News.

There are better theories. Abelard, a professor of theology at Paris, was a contemporary of Anselm, and he reminded Anselm and others of the atonement theory favored by the church fathers and St. Augustine, which is actually much closer to Jesus's actual teachings. Often called the "moral example" theory, it says that Jesus showed us how to live a truly human life that is pleasing to God. In this theory, God is like the father in the story of the Prodigal Son. He is always there, with his arms outstretched, eager to receive us, no matter what we've done or how far we've roamed, if only we would turn around and come home.

God is not holding us at arm's length because of our sin, as Anselm or Calvin assert. What separates us from God is the fact that we, in our shame, have turned away from him. Like Peter, we have said, "Leave me, Lord,"[9] because we don't feel worthy; we're ashamed. Julian was undoubtedly instructed in this much more ancient teaching.

Do you believe that a person has to be "born again," to accept Jesus as their personal Lord and savior?

Short answer: No. Long answer: In order to . . . what? Go to heaven? Avoid hell? Be happy? The phrase "accept Jesus as your personal Lord and savior," entered Christianity only in the past one hundred years. There's no such thing as a "personal Lord" or even "personal salvation" in any branch of Catholicism (Catholics are saved as a group, as a people). Protestants often think of themselves as being saved as individuals, but even this is a distortion of Luther's and Calvin's theologies—they'd probably have been horrified by this phrase, and with good reason.

Personally, I don't believe instantaneous conversions are very common. Awakening experiences can reorient a person, but they must still grow into faith, into increasing maturity and intimacy with God. To be "born again" doesn't necessarily mean what it has come to mean in Evangelical parlance. The notion that one can pray the Sinner's Prayer and then go automatically to heaven is an absurd distortion of the Gospel. This distortion makes salvation an act of intellectual assent—not a genuine change of life, an end to a life based on illusions, and an invitation into a new life based on what is Real.

So was Julian a universalist? Are you?

A universalist is someone who believes that no one is going to hell, that God is going to save everyone—Origen was declared a heretic for this teaching back in the third century, and a whole denomination of Universalists gained a great deal of force in the United States in the eighteenth and nineteenth centuries.

Universalism is a position that never would have occurred to Julian. It's kind of like asking, "Would Jesus wear Nike's or Hush Puppies?"—it's a chronological error. She did not deny the "orthodox" (correct) teaching that people go to hell; she's just saying she didn't see it in her vision. She's not asserting that there is no hell, but I think she's cracking the door on that idea just a bit, and she might have been open to the possibility.

Am I a universalist? That's a complicated question. I believe that most of the great world religions are salvific—that Jews and Hindus and Muslims, for instance, have valid and saving relationships with God. Also, I don't believe that God sends anyone to hell. But that's not the same as saying that hell doesn't exist.

That sounds like tap dancing. Are there mystics who don't tap dance? Are there mystics who are unafraid to dispose of hell?

You make me laugh. It's not tap dancing to respond cautiously about things we can't possibly know. I can be utterly convinced that there is no state of Nevada—and I can even convince others of it—but that doesn't change the fact that if I jump in my car and head east, before long I'll come to a large geographical area that I will have a hard time accounting for in my philosophy.

So there might be a Christian mystic somewhere who says, "There's no such place as hell," but why should I believe him—how the hell does he know, anyway?

The Christian scriptures mention several nasty places often translated "hell," and so most people in this tradition have affirmed its reality. What is not so sure, however, is whether God actually sends anyone there. Swedish mystic Emmanuel Swedenborg firmly believed in hell. He said that, while in trance, he made several journeys there. After these visits, he published his interviews with the inhabitants. But what he discovered in talking to both angels and those in hell was that God sends no one to hell—people walk there all on their own. They walk there during their earthly lifetimes, and so in the next life they simply gravitate to the place where they feel most comfortable.

Jesus said, "What you sow, you will reap," and you probably do not have to work too hard to think of someone you know who is alive and well and in hell right here on earth. When that person dies, assuming there's an afterlife, do you think that this person is going to undergo a miraculous change of attitude? Or will she simply continue to be the same miserable soul she is now? God doesn't send her anywhere. We choose to go to hell. We choose to stay there. And we can choose to leave, anytime we want.

As Lutheran mystic Jacob Boehme wrote, "We live and are in God; we have Heaven and Hell in ourselves. What we make of ourselves, that we are: if we make of ourselves an angel, and dwell in the light and love of God in Christ, we are so; but if we make of ourselves a fierce, false, and haughty devil which condemns all love and meekness in mere covetousness, greedy hunger, and thirst, then also we are so."[10]

Anglican mystic Charles Williams affirmed this way of understanding hell and asserted that anyone can turn around and walk the other way, in this life or the next. But the longer one walks in any particular direction, the harder it is to turn around. He illustrated this in several of his wonderful novels, and his friend C. S. Lewis did the same in his novel *The Great Divorce*.

Eastern Orthodox Christians believe that when they die, everyone is ushered into the presence of God. Those who have loved and been intimate with God experience this as bliss. But those who have lived their lives pursuing selfishness and illusion experience this presence as horrifying torment.[11] As Metropolitan Hierotheos of Nafpaktos wrote, "Paradise and Hell exist not in the form of a threat and a punishment on the part of God but in the form of an illness and a cure. Those who are cured and those who are purified experience the illuminating energy of divine grace, while the uncured and ill experience the caustic energy of God."[12]

Is Awakening the same as enlightenment?

If by *enlightenment* you mean what Hindus do by *moksha* or Buddhists do by *satori*, then no. Awakening experiences are extremely varied. They can be altered states of many varieties, some of which may include a temporary flash of unitive consciousness. Zen Buddhism calls this *kensho*, and like the Christian Awakening, it's a brief taste of that unitive state that serves to redirect us toward a life of serious seeking and disciplined spiritual practice.

Real enlightenment isn't temporary. It's permanent, a state in which one lives all the time. In our map, this is known as Union. Awakening can give us a brief experience of Union, but it fades quickly because we are not prepared to live there.

It sounds like having an Awakening requires having a breakdown as much as it does having a breakthrough. What's the difference between spiritual Awakening and having an emotional breakdown and recovery that's framed in religious terms? Or is there a difference?

You are quite right, sometimes Awakening experiences are traumatic. In spiritual guidance circles, we call positive Awakening experiences *spiritual emergence* and negative Awakening experiences *spiritual emergencies*. Sometimes, whether someone is having a spiritual emergence or an emergency comes down to the old drug terms, *set and setting*—whether the setting is safe and my mindset is a good one.

For instance, if I have an Awakening experience while I'm relaxing by a riverbank with a fishing pole, I may experience it in a very positive way—the setting is safe and I'm in a good, receptive mood. If I have that same experience while I'm trying to navigate rush-hour traffic or while I'm at a podium talking to five hundred people, I am going to have a very different—and very negative—reaction.

So that's one variable. But it also comes down to readiness. If a person has an orientation of love toward God and the spiritual life, this kind of experience can be perceived as ecstatic and welcome, while if I am repelled by all that God stuff, I'll be more likely to experience an Awakening as scary and threatening. Kind of like what we were saying about the Orthodox idea about heaven and hell. An Awakening experience is a moment of the unmediated Presence of God—whether that is a positive or negative experience is entirely dependent upon how you have lived your life and prepared your soul.

Many people who have spiritual emergencies go to the hospital where they are often medicated until the symptoms pass. These folks are usually relieved when the experience is over; they chalk it up to "an undigested bit of beef," as Ebenezer Scrooge did, and go back to business as usual, rejecting the invitation to a deeper, more Reality-based way of life.

Others, intuiting that something important is going on, will accept the invitation, will reject the numbing medication, and will begin to tend to their souls. Spiritual directors are invaluable in helping people through spiritual emergence and spiritual emergencies.

Having a spiritual emergency sounds like what is called hitting bottom in the terminology of the various Twelve Step programs. Is it the same thing?

There are definitely similarities, but they are not the same thing. A spiritual emergency occurs when an Awakening experience is frightening and unwelcome. Hitting bottom is usually unwelcome as well, but it happens when a person's attempts to control and rationalize his or her addiction simply fall apart. There's not usually anything mystical about it—although it is not unheard of for a person to have an Awakening experience that coincides with hitting bottom. So they can happen together, but they are not synonymous.

The two experiences do have similarities: during both experiences the lies and illusions that we have been telling ourselves are revealed to be false, and both experiences can inspire us to change the trajectory of our lives. Both can also be ignored, and both can save our lives. So, yeah—similar, but different.

Do I have to have a spiritual emergency in order to have an Awakening experience?

Not at all. Most awakening experiences are mild and many are pleasant. Spiritual emergence experiences become spiritual emergencies for one of three reasons:

1. A person is so out of touch with his or her authentic self that any contact with Reality is jarring and scary. Such people are simply not prepared for such an experience.

2. A person is in a situation where a mystical breakthrough experience is unwelcome or even dangerous.

3. A person's life trajectory is so dangerous or perilous that a divine intervention of great magnitude is required to wake a person up. This is the big stick approach to mystical awakening and is the spiritual emergence equivalent of a nightmare. All dreams come in the service of our health and wholeness,[13] but nightmares happen when we need to be yelled at in order to hear.

When I experienced what I called an Awakening, I had no desire at all to be reconciled to my old religion. Was that wrong?

We respond with the greatest degree of health we can muster at any given moment, if we're honest and sincere. So no, it wasn't wrong. It may be that you answered the face of God that speaks to you where you are right now, and that's a good thing. But just the fact that you use the word *reconciled* clues me in to the fact that you may indeed have some unfinished business with your childhood faith.

I was terribly wounded by my childhood experience of Christianity—lots of people are. People generally choose to respond to such abuse in one of two ways. Some, like me, stay put and fight for a healthy version of the faith, but many simply run. I don't judge those that run—I thought about it good and hard myself and have been sorely tempted to on several occasions.

For instance, I am really attracted to Buddhism. I think it's a great path and I feel a lot of affinity with it. And I could do all of the work needed to construct a whole new pantheon and theological system in my imagination in order to fully enter the Buddhist universe. But no matter how hard I worked at that, the old Father, Son, and Holy Spirit would still be kicking around in my subconscious—and conscious—mind, making trouble, making me neurotic, etc.

The Father, Son, and Holy Spirit are the archetypes for the Divine that loom largest in my imagination, and it simply seemed to me to be way more expedient to rehabilitate them than to build a whole new edifice and still not have banished those troublemakers from my childhood faith. I'm never going to be rid of them, so why run? Might as well face them, have it out, and establish healthy and good relationships with them.

Even if you don't end up going back to your original religion, I strongly recommend working with a spiritual director to rehabilitate your relationship to the God of your upbringing. If you don't make friends with those images left over from childhood that are still kicking around in your head, they are going to haunt you and torment you. This may or may not have anything to do with the Real God; it may just be psychological detritus, but you'll still have to deal with it if you want to have any peace at all. Ever read "The Hound of Heaven" by Francis Thompson? If not, read it and you'll see what I mean.

Both Julian of Norwich and Origen seemed to want to embrace suffering. I want to enjoy life—why would I want to embrace suffering? Is suffering necessary to become more spiritual?

The first line of M. Scott Peck's best-selling book *The Road Less Travelled* is "Life is difficult." He goes on to say, "Most do not fully see this truth that life is difficult. Instead they moan more or less incessantly, noisily or subtly, about the enormity of their problems, their burdens, and their difficulties as if life were generally easy, as if life *should* be easy."[14] Many people who turn to spirituality to escape the hardness of their lives pretend that everything is blissful and perfect just as it is—we call this *spiritual bypass* in the spiritual direction biz.

Spirituality and mysticism don't deliver us from the hardness of life—they give us a firm foundation and nourishment in order to meet the difficulties in our lives. So yes, embracing suffering is part of the mystic's path, because our experience of suffering is real. Pretending that it isn't is only buying into another illusion.

Peck also says that the delaying of gratification is the sign of maturity—the same is true of spiritual maturity. Real spiritual growth has no quick fixes, no easy ecstasy, no place for spiritual voyeurism. At every step it requires commitment, discipline, and effort. Every stage comes with its share of pain—just like real life.

Karl Rahner prayed, "Your commands are often hard because they enjoin the opposite of what my own inclinations would lead me to do, but when you bid me love you, you are ordering something that my own inclinations would never even dare to suggest: to love you, to come intimately close to you, to love your very life. You ask me to love myself in you, knowing that you will take me to your heart."[15]

So if you're looking to mysticism in order to escape suffering, you've come to the wrong place. However, if you are ready to fully embrace your humanness, your wholeness, this is going to include your suffering, your struggles, your shadow, just as much as it is your joy, liberation, and light.

The Christian tradition has always embraced suffering as the way in which God strengthens us morally and spiritually. Christians call it *soul making*, and while it isn't the ultimate answer to the question of why there is evil in the world, it is undeniably true that "what doesn't kill us makes us stronger."[16]

Can using certain substances allow the user to have a true religious Awakening? Can drugs lead us to God?

Yes, drugs can definitely trigger Awakening. They can provide temporary experiences of Illumination and unitive consciousness that in many cases have long-lasting and permanent effects on a person by reorienting life toward spiritual pursuit and discovery.

That said, I don't recommend them. There is a logic to Awakening experiences—usually they happen when you are ready for them. They are given by God as invitations, on God's own timetable (I know, I know, God's timetable sometimes seems arbitrary and ill advised—do take that up with him, won't you?). But just the same, I don't recommend doing it on *your own* timetable. I choose to trust that there's a logic to how God works, even if I rarely understand it.

There are many dangers to drugs, of course. They can lead to serious physical injury (we are more prone to accidents when under the influence). Also, using drugs to access this state is kind of "cheating," and there is very real danger in accessing a deep or advanced state of consciousness before one is prepared for it; this can lead to a psychotic break.

Particularly perilous is the danger of becoming dependent on drugs in order to access spiritual connection. One cannot pursue authenticity via artificial means. Real mysticism is the gradual building of trust, of commitment, and relationship. It's like working on a marriage. Dropping acid is like a one-night stand. Which one is more valuable?

QUESTIONS ABOUT PURGATION

Can one take baby steps? Dip a toe in?

That is how most of us do it. Of course, you mostly hear about the saints who plunge in so gung-ho that we question their sanity. But most of us must be weaned off illusion gradually. As I've noted elsewhere, this whole process can be seen as linear, overlapping, or cyclic (going deeper every time you cycle through).

So take your time; there's no hurry. Surrender what illusion you can, as you feel able. Work on your spiritual practice, up your commitment gradually, work with your spiritual director, and don't sweat it. If God is really real and in this with us, he's going to do his part, working on you from the inside out. You don't have to do it all. The Tao Te Ching says, "The journey of a thousand miles begins with one step." So say "yes" to God for that one step and worry about the next step when you get to it.

I'm a bit uncertain about this "saying Yes to God" thing. I've mostly felt either confused or carried along by something powerfully insistent, seeing more clearly only in hindsight. Are these feelings part of the mystical journey too, or a diversion?

This sounds exactly right to me. This process *is* confusing, so get used to *that*. We're stripping away illusions we've based our lives on. You're going to feel lost at sea at times, scared, and, yes, plenty confused. Relax. That only makes you normal.

And I know exactly what you mean about being "carried along." The times I've felt like I've been at my center and growing fast were times when I felt like it was happening *to* me; I wasn't doing it. And this is certainly true of both Awakening and Illuminative experiences. But if you want to sustain growth, there are the periods when we have to go under our own steam.

Don't pooh-pooh these times or think that they are "less than," because growth is still happening—it's just that different muscles are being developed. And you have to be willing to do that work. Purgation is often this kind of "roll up your sleeves" and endure the grind commitment, and not only do you have to agree to do it, you have to actually do it!

If you say, "Well, anything that doesn't come naturally and easily isn't authentic," I think you're fooling yourself. Part of having a mature spiritual practice (and maturing spiritually) is recognizing that valleys follow peaks and that God is in those valleys, too. Remember, you're not the only one on this bicycle-built-for-two that is spiritual growth. Sometimes God pedals; sometimes you do.

Instead of purging, wouldn't it be better to take an inventory? Surely there are things we need to keep as well as things we need to purge?

Absolutely. This process could just as easily be called "Discernment," because what you are doing is discerning what is Real from what is not. But what happens when you discern something that is unreal?

Eventually, if you are serious about your spiritual path, you let go of it, you purge your life of it. You keep the good stuff and you let go of the illusions. It sounds like your real difficulty is with the terminology, not the process. This is the vocabulary we have inherited. Are these the best words to describe the process? Assuredly not. But are they valuable? Yes. Do they tell us something true about the process? Yes. So, let's see . . . they're valuable but not perfect. Sounds like everything else I love in my life!

How can you tell Purgation from condemnation? How can you tell Detachment from indifference or unconcern?

Purgation doesn't ask us to condemn the world, only to discern whether something is helpful for us, whether it is authentic, whether it points to the Real or distracts us from it. Condemnation doesn't enter into it. Neither does self-recrimination or self-loathing.

Spiritual discernment is something we learn to do; it takes practice; it is sometimes subtle and difficult. And it is indispensable. Spiritual discernment happens when we think critically about faith, about our own spiritual growth, about our lives. It's discernment that helps us say, "That's nonsense" and walk away from a teaching or a community that is abusive. It's discernment that enables us to change the direction of our lives to embrace values and actions that are congruent with our authentic natures. It's discernment to tell whether an activity energizes me or depresses me, and question what that means.

Purgation is an intentional period of discernment. It asks us to look honestly and critically at every aspect of our lives and ask ourselves hard questions about them: does this activity lead me to be the kind of person I want to become? Is this what I really value, or do I value something else more? Is this who I really am, or am I supposed to be something or someone else? Jesus said, "Where your treasure is, there your heart will be also."[17] Purgation is the process by which we ask ourselves, "What is really important to me? Is the way I'm living my life congruent with that? Would you know that this is where my heart is just by looking at my life? If not, why not? What needs to go? What needs to be added? What needs to change?"

As for Detachment, if your attempts manifest as either indifference or unconcern, this is not true Detachment. One can love and care about something and still let it go. For instance, if God were to call me to pastor a church on the other side of the country—and I discerned that it was a true call—would I go? It would mean leaving behind people I love, work that I value, and Berkeley, a place that is like no other on God's green earth. Yes, I would go. Does that mean I don't love my friends or my work or my home? Of course not. It means only that I love God *more*, which is precisely as it should be. Even after I move, if one of my friends calls at three in the morning, I'm there for him. If I have to jump a plane to be with him, I'm there. But I'm still going to move to the new church, because my first love is God.

Detachment is about having one's priorities straight, not about becoming an unfeeling automaton. As Ignatius of Loyola put it, it's about making myself "available to God." It doesn't mean that I don't have a life—only that my commitment to God comes first in my life. I'm not saying I'm there. This is an ongoing discernment for all of us. *Wanting* to say "yes" to God is the first step to actually doing it.

Is not caring at all for your family similar to Buddhist detachment?

In Buddhism, detachment doesn't mean not caring—it means caring deeply, but not clutching onto things or people. Enjoy them while they are here—fully and completely—but let them go when they leave or pass away. It also doesn't mean don't grieve—let the feelings come, feel them fully, but don't wallow in them. Allow them to rise, allow them to fall. Allow people to come, allow them to go. Enjoy your life completely, but don't insist that things stay the same, don't manipulate people to keep them the way you want them. Accept that everything changes.

Similarly, Purgation invites us to love the people and things in our lives fully, but when we discern that a higher purpose is asking us to walk away from them, we should be willing to do it. Grieve but start walking.

When you say "what we thought was God, what we thought was religion, what we thought was us, has all been an illusion," what do you mean by this? Can you give an example?

Sure. I was brought up to believe that God was a punishing monster just waiting for me to step out of line so that he could crunch on my bones and toss my sorry ass into hell. When I decided to get serious about this Christianity thing, I discerned that this image of God was a gross distortion of the God that Jesus revealed. It was an illusion planted in me by pious but misguided fundamentalists, and I had to let it go.

Likewise, I was told that Christianity was about following a bunch of rules and believing a list of things. When I really investigated it, however, I found that this wasn't true. I discovered that Christianity is about freedom—freedom *from* rules, freedom *for* manifesting the love of God in the world. I also discovered that it wasn't about a list of beliefs. I don't really have a fixed set of beliefs—my beliefs are evolving all the time. Instead, Christianity is about relationship—it's about being romanced by God, and saying "yes" to his insistent and sometimes suggestive advances. If God is so naughty, why should I have to behave? I don't. I just have to love—deeply, honestly, and with all that is in me.

Likewise, who I thought *I* was is changing. I thought I was a worthless sinner. I've come to find out that I am the precious object of God's amorous attentions. So are you.

Why do you capitalize "Real"?

Because as we discover the difference between what is Real and what is illusion, it becomes clear that our entire culture is trapped in an illusion of its own making. This is, in part, what Jesus was referring to when he taught about the Kingdom. He was critiquing a mass societal delusion that held that power was the ultimate good and that those who held power got to define reality. He shocked everyone (and royally pissed off those in power) by teaching that God's favor is with the powerless, that those who have power will be pulled from their seats of privilege, and that those who have been spurned as less-than, sinful, ignorant, or unclean are the most valuable in God's eyes.

Jesus challenged the lie of consensus reality with the truth of Reality as God sees it. The Christian mystical path applies the blow-torch of that same refining fire to our lives, exposing the lies of consensus reality in our culture (curiously still power-obsessed), and revealing the Reality of the blessedness of every small thing, of our essential unity, and the connectedness of all things.

So I use a lower case r for our culture-defined consensus reality, and I capitalize "Real" to denote the universe-as-it-is when our illusions are stripped away.

When you say, "we must give up the idea that we know what we are doing," what do you mean?

God is weird. I don't understand what he's up to. And don't fool yourself, no one else does either. The mystics don't—they're just saying, "this is what happened to me." And what happened to them rarely squared with what the conventional religious wisdom of their day told them God was like, or what their faith was all about, or what their lives were supposed to be about. If you think you know what you are really here for, what your life is about, or where your spiritual life is headed, get ready for a major disruption if you decide to get real with

God, because all of those ideas are illusions that are going to go right out the window. Only God knows what he's up to or what your life is for. And you're only going to discover it as it unfolds one moment at a time. So, are you up for anything? Ready to be surprised? Ready to let go of everything you thought you were sure about? Does that scare the hell out of you? Good, it should.

What's the difference between meditation and contemplation?

In the Christian tradition, the two terms are often used interchangeably. I do this sometimes myself, but it's sloppy, because there is a difference. Meditation (or, Recollection, as the mystics sometimes call it) is the practice of quieting the mind by focusing on a single point—the breath in zazen practice or the Jesus Prayer (which is very similar to using a mantra) or the Hail Mary.

Contemplation is the quiet awareness that one is in God's presence, and relaxing into that presence. Thomas Merton described it this way:

Contemplation . . . is life itself, fully awake, fully active, fully aware that it is alive. It is spiritual wonder. It is spontaneous awe at the sacredness of being. It is a vivid realization of the fact that life and being in us proceed from an invisible, transcendent, and infinitely abundant Source. Contemplation is, above all, awareness of the reality of that Source. . . . Real contemplation is a sudden gift of awareness, an awakening to the Real within all that is real. A vivid awareness of infinite Being at the roots of our own limited being. An awareness of our contingent reality as received as a present from God, as a free gift of love. [18]

Meditation (or Recollection) is something we can do to help bring real contemplation about, but it takes time to learn to be truly contemplative. Also, it's a mixture of our own effort and a gift of grace that God works in us. Reread the section on the Practice of Quiet in the chapter on Illumination (p. 61). In short, we start with meditation so that we can eventually lead lives that are contemplative.

Seems you can't be married and have a family and be a mystic. Or, can you? Does having a family help or hurt this process? Can't a couple support each other in what God is calling each of them to do? Are there any mystics from the suburbs?

Yes, of course there are! Mysticism isn't something that only trained professionals are called to, although from reading the writings of the mystics, you might think that—most of them were full-timers. But that's not true of all of them, especially for Lucie-Christine[19] and Protestant mystics like Martin Luther and George Herbert, who seemed to find time for family and house-holding responsibilities in addition to their time spent in contemplation.

As Meister Eckhart wrote, "Spirituality is not to be learned by flight from the world, by running away from things, or by turning solitary and going apart from the world. Rather, we must learn an inner solitude wherever or with whomsoever we may be. We must learn to penetrate things and find God there."[20]

The key to making this work is balance and keeping your priorities straight. In other words, does your Real Love (God) come first? It's okay if family comes second, but that thing about God being a jealous god? True. Don't be too hard on him for that—nobody's perfect.

Someone has said that almost everything that is fun is either illegal or immoral or fattening. It looks like Purgation will take all of the fun out of my life. Why would I want that?

The purpose of Purgation is not to take all the fun out of life. As Charles Williams put it, "Eros (erotic love) need not for ever be on his knees to Agape (Divine love); he has a right to his delights; they are part of the Way. The Division is not between the Eros of the flesh and the Agape of the soul; it is between the moment of love which sinks into hell and the moment which rises to the in-godding."[21]

Indeed, Purgation is precisely about the discernment of one's appetites and whether they move one toward communion with the Divine or away from it. For most of us, there comes a time when the need for this discernment asserts itself. At some point, people wake up and realize they've been chasing their tails, that the things they've been living for are diversions, that the pleasures they've indulged in have only been serving to anaesthetize them to feelings of hopelessness and meaninglessness that have been creeping up on them.

It is usually near middle age that people suddenly stop themselves and go, "Wait, is this all there is? What is my life really about? What am I doing with the short amount of time I've got?" In other words, the Big Questions suddenly become real and the "fun" that has filled people's lives is revealed as the emptiness that it is.

This is often a literal "come to Jesus" moment—when people begin to ask hard questions of themselves, get deeply honest, start looking critically at how they've been living and spending their time and energy, and they begin to chart a more intentional and thoughtful course. This is the time when people begin to look at mysticism as more than a cheesy spiritual curiosity and find within it invaluable guidance for spiritual discernment.

So will Purgation take all the fun out of your life? No, but it will strip you of your illusions. The things you have looked to for "fun" will be revealed as potential for diversion, destruction, or nourishment. New sources of joy—Real, deep, lasting, healthy joy—will replace old habits and addictions. It's not that you can't do the things you used to enjoy—you just won't want to.

Not ready to give anything up? No problem, take your time. Have fun. Knock yourself out. Ten years from now when you wake up and say to yourself, "Hey, is this it?" maybe you'll pick this book up and give it another look. This path will still be here when you are ready to get Real. And if that time never comes in this life, don't sweat it.

Most Christians never set out on a serious mystical path—they're still good Christians, loved by God and saved by grace. As St. John Climacus wrote, "Not every person is able to achieve the highest state of transcendent soul; but it certainly is possible for everyone to find reconciliation with God, and it is this that will save them."[22]

In Mortification, how do we avoid getting attached to our plans for spiritual growth, i.e., changing the way we actually live? Every plan is another conceptual frame. It seems like it's more about giving up plans, intentions, good ideas, etc.

I think you might be over-thinking this. It's not conceptual, it's actually very much visceral. When you discover that it hurts when you touch the burner on your stove, you stop touching it. That's it. When it is revealed to us that something in our lives is an illusion, is hurting us instead of helping us, we stop doing it. That's it.

Of course, it's not always that easy. We often realize that something is hurting us long before we are willing or able to give it up. This is especially true of things we are addicted to or are otherwise dependent upon. Yet, just realizing that something is hurtful is an important first step toward stopping it.

If you see that something is no longer serving you but you're not ready to change your life, what should you do? Well, you could pray about it. After all, what God is most interested in is intimacy, not behavior. So why not pour out your pain and frustration and struggle to God in prayer? Let yourself be held and comforted by him. That's way more important than making resolutions and keeping them. Just be honest before God and let yourself be loved. *That* will change your life way more than making plans and trying to keep them ever will.

Something else to be careful of here, though, is pride in one's ascetical achievements. Our zeal for mortification can actually take us further away from God if it all becomes about Herculean effort and not about God. St. Ignatius is a good example of this: he prayed all night, sleeping little; he starved himself nearly to death; and he was ridiculously cautious about doing everything "right." Fortunately he wised up before he killed himself or gave himself an ulcer. He realized that he wasn't impressing God one little bit, and that starving himself was only feeding his ego. He realized that simply loving God and being moderate in one's appetites—including one's appetite for holiness—was best.

What's the difference between discernment and making a decision?

Discernment is information-gathering in order to see what is true. Making a decision is committing oneself to some kind of action. Mortification is actually following through on that action. So they are not synonymous, but sequential. First we discern: we ask questions as we seek to discover the truth of a situation. Based on the truth that we find, we make a decision to act in one way or another. Then we act.

Is it possible to discern without making a decision? They do kind of go hand in hand, because once you have the information, you have to do something with it. Even if you do nothing, you've made a decision to do nothing.

First you say that Purgation is something we do, then that we "allow ourselves to be cleansed." Which is it? Who does the cleansing, us or God?

Like most things on the spiritual path, it's a collaborative effort between ourselves and God. This is a romantic relationship, remember? It takes two to tango.

When we sincerely seek to discern what is Real and what is illusion in our lives, God graciously reveals it to us. The prophet Muhammad said, "If we take one step towards God, he takes ten steps towards us." As, one by one, our illusions are revealed, we are cleansed of their hold on us, their influence, and we become increasingly oriented toward the Real.

I love Meister Eckhart's take on this. He says, "The best thing about love is that it forces me to love God. On the other hand, detachment forces God to love me. . . . God can join himself to me more closely and unite himself with me better than I could unite myself with God. That detachment forces God to me I can prove by the fact that everything likes to be in its own natural place. Now God's own and natural place is unity and purity, and they come from detachment."[23] So, God's action or ours? Yes.

If we assume that death frees the soul to experience all that mystics struggle to attain while incarnate, why not enjoy our humanness knowing when it ends (i.e., we die) all will be revealed?

You could do that—and in truth, most people take this path by default. But mystics are people who have this crazy idea that human fulfillment and true happiness come from living in the presence of God. And that this presence is more full of joy, truth, and beauty than anything else the world has to offer. So you could wait, but why? Why settle for leeks and onions when you *could* eat your ice cream first?

And besides, are you so sure that at your death, "all will be revealed"? Who says? And are you really ready for the unmediated radiance of Divinity? Do you want to test that theory? I shudder at the thought, myself.

Many Christian mystics—such as Dante, Emmanuel Swedenborg, Charles Williams, and many others—tell us that if you die wrapped in illusion, that illusion will continue even after death. The notion of Purgatory in the Christian tradition speaks directly to this. In other words, you've got to do the work of Purgation sometime, so why not now?

What's with all the Hindu gods and meditation stuff? I thought this was a Christian book?

Part of the reason for bringing up other religions on occasion is personal: my doctorate is in philosophy and religion—essentially, world religions—so it's hard for me to resist noting parallels to other traditions or availing myself of their examples on occasion. Plus, because the mystical path is similar for mystics of most traditions, it makes sense at times to point out the parallels. Evelyn Underhill did the same in her book, *Mysticism*.

After all, Truth shows up wearing many cultural clothes, speaking through a variety of mythologies, communicating through a bewildering assortment of symbols and metaphors. This book is definitely written for Christians (and people curious about the Christian mystical tradition), but this isn't the middle ages where we are isolated from the riches and challenges of living with others. I'm writing for a contemporary, cosmopolitan audience that, I assume, has some familiarity with a variety of religious traditions. If I can draw on one of them for an illustration to make my point more effectively, I'm going to do that. But more than this, I think we have to be honest and acknowledge God in all of the 10,000 places that he shows up.

Recollection sounds like Zen. I already practice meditation and yoga; what do I need recollection for? What's the difference?

Not much, as far as actual practice. If you are well-practiced at zazen (sitting meditation in the Zen Buddhist tradition) or another form of meditation practice, you'll be ahead of the curve here.

The biggest difference is one of intention, of what you are trying to accomplish with your meditation. The purpose in Zen practice is to be with what is, within yourself and outside yourself—total mindfulness. Recollection is similar, but the intention is weighted slightly

155

toward discernment. You are sitting specifically for the purpose of discerning the Real.

If everything illusory must be stripped away and the mystic path can begin only when dealing with Reality with a capital R, without attachments, this sounds a lot like Buddhism. What's the difference between the Christian mystical path and a Buddhist path?

The Christian mystical path is very much like Buddhism. As I've said already, there is a lot of similarity between the mystical traditions of many religions.

Both Buddhism and Christianity have apophatic and kataphatic approaches. Apophatic mystics in both traditions honor a "negative" way of mysticism devoid of images and intimate with emptiness. Kataphatic mystics in both traditions utilize beauty and imagery and emphasize relationship and compassion.

Are there differences? Sure, significant ones. For instance, we follow the revelations of two very different men—Jesus and the Buddha— separated by time, distance, culture, and theology—both of them revered as teacher and savior by various sects of their respective traditions.

But the similarities outweigh the differences. It was only in the early 1960s that Christians began to be aware of this and to be open to dialog with practitioners of other traditions. The Roman Catholic Trappist monk and mystic Thomas Merton, especially, in his *Asian Journal* and essay collections such as *Zen and the Birds of Appetite*, significantly raised the consciousness of many Christians regarding the similarities between Christian mystical practice and Buddhist practice. Benedictine monks Henri Le Saux and Bede Griffiths did the same for Hinduism. Episcopal priest Alan Watts was a pioneering popularizer of the common ground between Eastern and Western mysticism. And of course, many people since then, such as Wayne Teasdale, have written more on this subject.

Christian-Buddhist dialog is a healthy and lively pursuit of both academics and practitioners right now, with much active sharing and comparison of both conceptual maps (such as the one you are reading about in this book) and actual experience of their practices.

So why Christianity and not Buddhism? I realize this will make me a heretic in some people's eyes, but I don't think one is better or more efficacious than the other. I love Buddhism, but I love Christianity more, because it's my home. You will have to decide for yourself where to unpack your bags.

The way you describe Purgation and Mortification, it sounds like a Twelve Step program. What's the difference between a mystical path and a Twelve Step program for the spirit? Isn't this just a self-help program with old-school religious language?

No, it isn't, although you are right that there are some definite parallels. Both Christian mysticism and Twelve Step programs employ discernment, encourage radical self-honesty, and urge practitioners toward changes in thinking and behavior that create positive results in people's lives.

But as David Sylvester has pointed out in a very insightful study,[24] the twelve steps are all about Purgation—the Twelve Step Tradition does not progress into Illumination or Union. Thus, they can only take you so far.

So while the Twelve Step programs are practical and life-saving, they are also earth-bound and limited. Mysticism, on the other hand, is concerned with ultimate things—specifically with a profound and intimate relationship with God, which is limitless. Twelve Step programs are deep, yes, but mysticism's well is *infinitely* deep.

All your quotes seem to be from medieval saints, nuns, and monks. Do you think any modern people have ever said anything useful about knowing God?

It's true that many of my quotations and stories are from the early church and the Middle Ages—those seemed to be the halcyon days for Christian mysticism. But more than that, these are the folks that have stood the test of time. The tradition has discerned that their revelations are true and authentic, their maps are accurate, their voices are trustworthy.

But there have been mystics in every age of the church, right up to the present day. If you look closely, you'll see some twentieth-century mystics scattered among the other twenty-one centuries of Christian experience. Only time will tell if we will still be honoring them 500 years from now, but you are right that it is important to include them.

QUESTIONS ABOUT THE DARK NIGHT OF THE SENSES

Is it just me, or does this dark night stuff sound suspiciously like clinical depression? What kinds of questions and self-reflection could help someone make this distinction?

This is a very important distinction. There are many similarities between depression and the Dark Night of the Senses, but they are not the same.

If I had a spiritual direction client who said, "I'm just not enjoying my life right now," one thing I would look for is a history of depression or other form of mental illness. If a person is prone to depression, then it is most likely a resurgence of that old "noonday demon," and I would recommend that he do therapy in addition to spiritual direction.

But let's say our client has no history of depression; what then? I'd ask her to discern if there were anything she *were* enjoying right now:

How was her prayer? What was it like going to church right now? Her other spiritual practices? During the active phase of the Dark Night of the Senses, her anhedonia would manifest mostly around mundane, secular activities, while sacred activities would still be life-giving and energizing. If she has not yet entered the Illuminative state, this is most likely what is happening.

If, however, she has been enjoying the consolations of Illumination and her disaffection includes not just mundane activities but sacred activities as well, she is most likely in the grips of the passive stage of the Dark Night of the Senses, and an experienced spiritual guide will know to counsel her not to give up, or "backslide," but to remain faithful and throw herself upon the mercy of God and God alone, no longer trusting in the consolations of her sacred activities.

On the other hand, such symptoms may not indicate a dark night specifically, but they might still be a valuable invitation to discernment. If a person is feeling depressed, it may be a manifestation of what St. Ignatius called "a spirit of desolation," an emotion packed with information to help us discern something true about ourselves or the state of our souls.

We can value depression as a spiritual experience, an indicator that we have been going down the wrong path or betraying our calling. When a person doesn't want to do the things he "should" want to do or has committed himself to doing, this can be seen as a positive thing, an invitation to discernment and course-correction.[25]

There is also the possibility that a person is experiencing both a dark night experience and clinical depression.[26] They are not the same thing, but that doesn't mean that a person cannot be experiencing both simultaneously. Indeed, the onset of a dark night may exacerbate a mystic's latent depression—and in people who are prone to depression, how could it not?

In such a case, it is imperative for the mystic to be cared for both by an experienced spiritual director and a psychotherapist or psychiatrist. Ideally, these two should know about each other, and wise clients will suggest a waiver so that they can consult with each other. In extreme cases, medication may be needed to control the deleterious effects of the depression, but caution is required, because the more heavily medicated a person is, the slower spiritual growth will usually be and the more difficult it may be to achieve (because one's feelings and intuitions are often more difficult to access).

Is it possible to be a mystic or go on the mystic's journey without having an emotional breakdown? Most of the saints' stories you recount seem to have one, you tell yours, but I don't have a story like that. Is a deep relationship with God only for people who have gone to "the depths" or who have "been there"?

We tell stories because they are dramatic. The stories that get passed on are the ones that have a great deal of dramatic conflict. But most stories have a short shelf life because, well, there's no "gosh wow" factor there. We're still talking about the drama of Abraham Lincoln's life, but Jack Smith down the street lived his life and died in obscurity. Was his life valuable? Absolutely. But few people are going to tell his story.

Your experience is valuable, too, even if there's no high drama. Drama is overrated—it's scary when you're going through it, it's dangerous, and the trauma of the event echoes for a long time. If your story is quieter, that's one reason to be grateful, in my opinion. It doesn't mean that your experience isn't authentic or important; just that it doesn't have a lot of drama. So what?

Count your blessings—this path is a long one and you have no idea what adventures are waiting for you around the next bend. You may receive the gift of drama yet and it might not be that welcome.

QUESTIONS ABOUT ILLUMINATION

I have to admit that, as I read about the steps in the mystic's journey, I am concerned that my "knowing" will become an obstacle and I will believe that I have achieved one of the stages. What are some ways to avoid this?

I don't think there's a problem with knowing when you've entered a stage. I think the danger is in taking pride in it, going on an ego trip because of your spiritual accomplishments. This is a very real danger and it's one reason that being in community is so important.

It's hard to have a swelled head in community because you are surrounded by fellow travelers—some of them more advanced, some of them less. You're being mentored by some, while at the same time you're mentoring others. If it's a real community—by which I mean filled with people who have been through hard times together and have emerged intact—you will be in the company of people who love you enough to tell you when you are being an ass, when you're being arrogant, or when you're about to make a mistake.

Community keeps you human. You can be describing the ecstasies of your latest prayer experience in your Wednesday evening small group meeting and you are likely to get two responses: "That's wonderful!" and "Can you take out the trash?" Both are valuable.

I can't tell you how grateful I am for my community. They have saved my soul on more than one occasion—just by being brave enough to say, "Whoa, there, cowboy. Think this through a little more." Everyone needs friends like that, especially on the spiritual journey.

But it seems like, upon Illumination, the mystic does not have community or spiritual direction on the journey. Is this true? Is community necessary? If so, what could community look like (e.g., "hanging out" with others on the same path)?

I wonder where you get that impression. Is it because Quiet is such a solitary activity? It needn't be, because, as George Fox so clearly demonstrated, Quiet with others can be just as profound as Quiet by oneself.

Indeed, I would say that the mystic in Illumination had better have a community! First, Illumination is almost impossible to achieve without one (we need support and advice). Second, it is within community that God is found. The doctrine of the Trinity speaks directly to the fact that God is found *in* community because God *is* community.

I have already expanded on this in the Conclusion, but it bears repeating: there are no such things as lone rangers in the Christian tradition. *Community is salvific.* We are saved *by* community, *in* community, *for* community. Even monks and nuns in the strictest monastic orders are in community with one another. Even hermits must assemble for corporate worship and accountability. No person is an island, and the Orthodox, Catholic, and Mainline Protestant theologies are in agreement that no one is saved alone. There's no such thing as "me and Jesus," only "us and Jesus."

As you can read in the section on Union in Action (p. 104), the ultimate end of mysticism isn't absorption into the Godhead and annihilation of one's individuality; rather, it is a realization of one's true identity and true humanness—freedom from selfish illusion so that we have freedom for service of others. We aren't primarily saved *from ourselves*, but *for others*.

A community of mystics looks like pretty much any other community—replete with both beauty and warts—except that you are surrounding yourself with people who are intentional about their spiritual journeys and are encouraging one another as they walk together toward God.

Isn't there also a downside to community? You can waste a lot of time wrestling with egos and politics. Yes, it can grow you but it can also cost you—just like staying too long in a bad marriage. The research on religious community illustrates this well.

There are no downsides to community. Every healthy community is filled with people who are easy to get along with, as well as people who are difficult. Both are valuable. Both help you grow. It takes all kinds of people to help us grow into our wholeness, to round out our rough edges, to reveal to us parts of ourselves that require Purgation.

But you are right in the sense that there are unhealthy communities—lots of them. There are communities that are ego-driven, poisoned by politics, abusive, distorted by dysfunction, woundedness, and hate. And like a bad marriage, those kinds of communities are sometimes beyond saving and any sane person would get out.

But this is where discernment is important. Conflict in community is essential to the creation of authentic community, so you shouldn't necessarily jump ship at the first sign of trouble. M. Scott Peck writes about this in his terrific book *The Different Drum: Community Making and Peace*,[27] where he draws a distinction between false community and real community.

A false community is one that is untested—everyone is polite and friendly, they have not faced danger, everyone's dark side is safely tucked away in their respective closets. A real community, however, has been to hell and back and is still together. In the midst of their trials, the fangs have been bared, the claws have come out, arguments have been had, names have been called, everyone's worst side has been revealed, and in spite of it all, love, forgiveness, and healing has somehow prevailed. Sure, they may have lost people along the way, but they've picked up others, and the core of the community has endured, love has deepened, and souls have grown.

Your take on Christianity is not something that I've ever heard of, and certainly not something I've seen. Where can I find a church that is open-minded enough to discuss things in this book the way you talk about them?

There are plenty of them. They just don't advertise, "Hey! We're mystics!" But you won't go wrong doing some church shopping. The United Church of Christ is probably the most liberal of all Christian denominations, and they would love to talk mysticism with you, although finding a contemplative practice group at a UCC church is rare.

Such groups are very common in the Episcopal Church, however, and they are also very open-minded, although you must keep in mind that every congregation is different. Likewise, you may find mystically-minded folks at an Orthodox or Roman Catholic parish, a United Methodist church, or among the Presbyterians or ELCA Lutherans. Many people in the Evangelical Emerging Church movement are rediscovering the Christian mystical tradition and are opening themselves to discovering God through ritual, tradition, and contemplative practice.

Or you might go to your local Catholic Worker house, volunteer to serve the poor with them, and talk to your fellow volunteers—find out where they go to church and tag along. Of course, there are mystics aplenty among the Swedenborgians and the Quakers, as well as several of the small independent catholic groups.

Go and explore—you'll have a good time, and eventually you will walk into the place that just feels like home. It may not be full of mystics, but hey, why not start a *lectio divina* group yourself? It may be the very reason God led you there.

Questions about Illumination

Do you have to go through the Purgative state first, in order to enjoy Illumination?

Mostly, yes. Of course, you can have Illuminative experiences without going through Purgation—those are Awakening experiences—but they are fleeting and unpredictable. We can also have Illuminative experiences while we are going through Purgation (thank God—a little carrot with my stick is always a welcome relief). As I say in the conclusion, I believe we are experiencing all the stages simultaneously; it's just that the emphases differ, and the emphases progress in a more or less linear fashion.

In true Illumination, we are gradually able to access the Illuminative state more often and more easily than ever before. It is a journey into a life fully lived "in God," moving toward a state in which God lives his life "in us."

What's the difference between "having too much to do" and being "too busy"?

Ideally, we all have "too much to do." This is the state of the world—it needs more help than we can possibly give it ourselves. Partly, this is why we work together. But this is also what drives us as Christians—compassion and a desire to manifest God's love in the world. Ultimately, this is what drives us as mystics, too.

Being too busy is different. You can be too busy and not do a single useful thing. Being busy isn't about having more to do than you can possibly accomplish, it's about compulsively occupying yourself so that you don't have to face the painful things in your life—your illusions, your sins, your emptiness. Note that, usually, when you are this busy, you also can't experience the joy, peace, and love in your life. Busy-ness shuts down our ability to discern, effectively shutting out (or shouting down) the voice of the Spirit—an effective form of spiritual resistance if there ever was one.

There's nothing wrong with having "too much to do"—that's the human condition. But we should be constantly on our guard against being "too busy."

This "divinized" idea of the world seems to clash with the idea of original sin. How do you harmonize these concepts?

That depends upon what you mean by "original sin." The oldest and most authentic doctrine of original sin comes to us from the Orthodox Christian tradition, which says that we are actually born clean of sin—but that we are very quickly corrupted by human culture. We learn hatred, selfishness, and prejudice at our parents' knees, and in our turn, we teach it to our children.

Thus, original sin is not a genetic defect, but more like a virus. We are born healthy, but we catch the disease pretty early on. Sin isn't inherent in creation, but a pollution caused by humans. Divinization recognizes the "freshness deep down things,"[28] as Hopkins put it. Jesus's Resurrection halted the corrupting effects of human sin on creation and reversed creation's slide into chaos—now all things are evolving into divinity—growing into God. It is the job of the church to help undo the deleterious effects of human sin, to help people "unlearn" destructive attitudes and behaviors, and to assist God in the work of the divinization all things.

Western Christianity has, however, been influenced by St. Augustine's unfortunate doctrine that sin is a genetic defect passed down through the father's semen. Baptism undoes this defect and renders a person capable of communion with God.

In no theology, however, is human sin so egregious that it taints the whole of the universe. We may be poisoning the earth, but to think that our sin is infecting the moons of Jupiter or the goodness of a distant planet is outrageous hubris.

Questions about Illumination

Is illumination about learning to understand that everything isn't "all about me?"

Actually, *Purgation* is learning to understand that everything isn't "all about me." Illumination is where it is revealed to us what everything actually *is* about.

I feel stupid trying to pray like Brother Lawrence. Is it wrong to give up that practice for another? Or does that make me a whiner?

Is there something wrong with feeling stupid? If so, there's something wrong with me every day. Most people feel stupid when they start to Practice the Presence of God the way that Brother Lawrence recommends. But as with all spiritual practices, sooner or later we break through our discomfort and discover something quite profound. So I guess it depends on how much effort you've really given it.

Did you make three attempts, each for a full hour? If so, and you didn't break through and have an awesome discussion with God or a heightened experience of his presence, well, then this practice may not be for you, and you should probably try the Jesus Prayer or the rosary or *lectio divina*.

On the other hand, did you just try it for ten minutes, say, "I feel stupid," and give it up? If that's the case, then yes, you might want to look into that whole "whiner" thing.

You're right, I don't like quiet and silence. Does that mean I can't get close to God? Aren't there active spiritual practices I can use, things that don't require so much silence, or does it have to be silence? There are different learning styles; can't there be different prayer styles?

This is a great question. First of all, noticing that "I don't like quiet and silence" is an excellent opportunity for discernment. I recommend taking this to your spiritual director. It might be fruitful to ask, "What is it about silence that I don't like?" "What is it about quiet that makes me uncomfortable?" You may find some really valuable insights there. You may also discover that you are less disciplined than you thought you were, and trying to get quiet just highlights how atrophied your attention muscles have become.

On the other hand, though, your intuition is right on—the Christian tradition provides contemplative practices for people of all personality persuasions. For instance, if you love quiet, apophatic prayer might be your thing, or centering prayer. If you need more activity, saying the Jesus Prayer or the Hail Mary while counting off beads on a rosary might be perfect. Need more motion? How about walking meditation on a labyrinth or taking a stroll in nature, or doing the dishes Practicing the Presence of God like Brother Lawrence? If you are of more of an intellectual bent, try *lectio divina* or reading theology or the mystics, and taking the insights you find into prayer. Liturgical prayer is also active, whether it's saying the Daily Office in your bedroom or worshipping in community.

All of these things are contemplative practices, and all of them can lead you to God. Find what works for you and commit to it on a regular, disciplined basis. Consult with your spiritual director regularly on how things are going, and lean on those in your spiritual community for everything else that you need. You'll do fine.

Mysticism seems more and more like a secret club. I feel like I ask questions, but I don't get any answers. You use the word paradox *and you say that mysticism is just something that* happens to you. *Just how do I know what I'm doing and what's happening, anyway?*

It's a sad truth that mysticism has been seen as a secret club. People have this idea that it's just a collection of arcane and opaque secrets, and that you have to spend a whole lifetime studying in order to make sense of it. And there are a lot of people—especially people drawn to occult knowledge—that *like* this view of mysticism and pad their egos by cultivating romantic visions of themselves as brilliant but misunderstood mystics.

In part, I wrote this book precisely in order to dispel such kooky notions. Mysticism isn't a secret club. It's about cultivating a relationship with God. That's all. Nothing arcane or occult about it. But you are right in that it is hard to understand, and the reason for this is partly cultural. We are inheritors of the Enlightenment tradition that emerged from Europe during the Renaissance. This tradition says that everything in the universe is orderly and explainable and that through the scientific method we can take everything apart and understand exactly how it all works.

Romanticism was the backlash to the Enlightenment tradition, saying, "No, there is still mystery in the world. The heart and the spirit have their own logic and they cannot be circumscribed or explained by science." The Romantic movement was full of mystics, such as poets William Blake and John Milton.

The Christian mystical tradition has more in common with the Romantics. There may be ultimate truth in the universe, but it is not likely that we shall ever comprehend it. The best we can do is to acknowledge that there is Mystery and to enter into relationship with it.

As to knowing what you are doing and what is happening, that is why we read the mystics, even so many years after their deaths. The terrain of Mystery may not be mappable, but there are those who have found a trail through it, and they know where the quicksand is. This book is an introduction to them.

QUESTIONS ABOUT THE DARK NIGHT OF THE SPIRIT

Does God really abandon us, or is that just the mystic's perception?

That is just the mystic's perception.

It sounds like the Dark Night of Spirit is a time when, after doing a lot spiritual work, it feels like God disappears. Why on earth would I want to experience that?

No one wants to go through the Dark Night of the Spirit—just like no lover wants to get dumped. But getting dumped is an important part of learning to be an adult, and it happens to all of us. We hate it while we're going through it, but if we're honest with ourselves, we can later admit that we learned a lot about ourselves from the experience.

To use another analogy, nobody wants to go to the dentist, but if you want to have healthy teeth, you still need to go. Likewise, nobody wants to go through the Dark Night of the Spirit, but it's necessary if we want to experience the true union that our soul aches for. It's not pleasant, but it *is* necessary.

QUESTIONS ABOUT UNION

The metaphor of marriage works for me to a point. And yet, it smacks of the desperate need to understand things in human terms— the same urge that leads people to anthropomorphize God. Isn't marriage as human a concept as ever there was? How can something as big as God fit into our limited definitions of relationship?

Can we possibly understand God in any other way? As Spinoza wrote, "If a triangle could speak, it would say . . . that God is eminently triangular, while a circle would say that the divine nature is eminently circular. Thus each would ascribe to God its own attributes, would assume itself to be like God, and look on everything else as ill-shaped."[29] Spinoza was arguing that God is not human but that it is human nature to view God in this way.

And I think that's the important distinction to make. Look, I don't see you as you really are. I see you through the lens of my own limited understanding, prejudices, preconceived notions, hurt feelings,

170

loving feelings, etc., all of which distort my perceptions of you. We do the same to God. We are relating to the projections of him that we hold in our heads. We project a human form and we relate to that.

Is that wrong? Only if we believe the projection. If we take it for real, and preach it as real, and worship it as real, we are idolaters. For truly, it is an idol—a false image that we wrongly take to be God. But if we know that our perception is skewed and our comprehension only partial, that our conceptions of God are convenient metaphors rather than Truth, then they become useful tools for us.

Just like language. The word *dog* is not a dog. It is a metaphor that all English speakers agree represents the canine species. The word *dog* will not greet me when I walk in the door or wag its tail, for the word has no tail. Likewise, our metaphors for God are not God, but they represent God, and as such they are useful. As the Buddha said, "My teachings are a finger pointing to the moon." Don't confuse the finger with the moon.

Emanuel Swedenborg wrote, "No one can believe in a God, and love a God, whom he cannot have a conception of under some form."[30] We need our metaphors in order to interact. We need language to navigate our relationships with one another. We need images of God in order to enter into relationship with Mystery. Later on, if we are of an apophatic bent, we can lose those images, because why not? They're not real, after all. But we don't have to.

William Blake understood this when he wrote:

> *To Mercy, Pity, Peace, and Love*
> *All pray in their distress . . .*
> *For Mercy has a human heart,*
> *Pity a human face,*
> *And Love, the human form divine,*
> *And Peace, the human dress.*
> *Then every man, of every clime,*
> *That prays in his distress,*

Prays to the human form divine,
Love, Mercy, Pity, Peace.
And all must love the human form,
In heathen, Turk, or Jew;
Where Mercy, Love, and Pity dwell
There God is dwelling too.[31]

Can we be so sure that our human concept of union is anything like what God wants?

We can't be sure of anything. But if we are following a tradition, we do well to trust that tradition (note I am not saying "accept the tradition uncritically"). Both the Jewish and Christian scriptures depict God himself likening the kind of relationship he wants to have with us in marital terms.[32]

Isaiah wrote, "Your husband is your Maker—His name is Yahweh of Hosts."[33] Jeremiah, too, uses marital imagery,[34] as does Ezekiel.[35] The prophet Hosea, especially, uses the marriage between God and the people of Israel as the foundational metaphor throughout his book—depicting a rocky relationship, indeed. The Jewish tradition has long understood the Song of Solomon to be an erotic love poem that metaphorically depicts the romance between God and Israel. Similarly, in the Christian scriptures, Jesus is depicted as the bridegroom, and his disciples—the Church—as his bride.[36]

Plus, it is the testimony of many, many mystics that this is the closest analogy they know of, and it seems natural to them to speak of it in this way. Now if it were just one or two mystics, we could quibble. But the tendency is nearly universal (this is true of non-Christian mystics, too). And if you've been courted by God, if you've succumbed to the rapture of mystical ecstasy, well . . . it sure *feels* like love.

So if you're afraid that God will be offended by such imagery, hey, he's been compared to worse. On the other hand, if you're afraid that

God won't want to go out with you, relax. Haven't you heard? Jesus *loves* you.

I find that a lot of my life has been focused on "selfless action on behalf of others" (though, admittedly, not perfectly or always without agenda). But I have not been on the full mystic's journey. Do we also sort of "pop in and out" of these experiences "out of sequence"?

Doing something good for someone doesn't mean a person has "skipped ahead" to full Union. It isn't necessary to be in full Union to do something compassionate, thank God, because the number of people who have "gone all the way" with God is paltry, and there's a lot of work to be done. I'm grateful that people reach out in compassion no matter where they are on their spiritual journeys.

Also, as you suggest, people doing their Purgation discernment or enjoying Illumination may reach out in love and help others, but they are usually driven by a mixture of compassion and self-interest. It may be that I get a certain satisfaction out of helping others. Well, what's wrong with that? It's not a pure motivation, but if it gets me out there and helping people, that's not so bad, is it?

But someone who has achieved full Union has no agenda, other than to simply provide the hands and feet for God to do his work, without regard for him- or herself in any way. Will they walk into danger and spend their one precious life in the service of another without a moment's thought or hesitation? Yep.

Would you or I? Right. That's the difference.

Do I have to perform great works now—like kiss a leper or live like Mother Teresa?

You don't have to do anything. God loves you just as you are. You don't even have to kiss your sister, let alone a leper. You can keep your condo. Say it with me: "None of this is compulsory." God's way is persuasive, not coercive.

That said, why not love the people around you a little more than you do now? Why not do the things that Jesus told us to do, like feed the hungry, befriend the stranger, clothe the naked, take care of the sick, visit those in prison?[37]

Do what you can, but don't knock yourself out. Make it manageable. It won't make you a mystic, but it will make you a kind person, and it will make you the kind of person that Jesus said he hopes we will become—and that's not nothin'.

If in unity, everything we think or feel affects the whole, then even cloistered monks are affecting the world without any action in the larger society, aren't they?

There's no one way to serve God or others. There are as many ways as there are people. The Hindu faith outlines four broad ways of getting close to God: Devotion, Study, Meditation, and Service. Everyone has a talent for one of these over the others, and our natural inclinations are going to determine both our spirituality and how we live that out. Makarios the Great affirmed this diversity when he wrote, "So varied are the ways that grace affects such a person and leads the soul in so many different paths, refreshing it in accord with the will of God. Grace exercises the soul differently in order to restore it to the heavenly Father perfect and faultless and pure."[38]

So yes, a person's service for the world might take the form of "heroic" prayer. I once visited a Benedictine monastery at the height of the cold war and marveled at the monks' prayer for the survival of the earth—it made me wonder if the world was still in one piece only because there were eighteen men on their knees in the San Bernardino Mountains. It wouldn't surprise me.

Doesn't all this "heroic doing" just feed the ego?

If the ego is involved in the mystic's motivation, the mystic has not achieved Union. That's what all this uncomfortable Purgation and dark night nonsense has been about—purging the ego, stripping it of its power and the illusions of its sovereignty and even its reality.

However, if you have not achieved full Union and you are engaged in compassionate action, spiritual pride is something to be constantly on guard against. I can reach rare heights of self-satisfaction and self-righteousness all on the basis of forty-five minutes of labor in a soup kitchen. This is self-delusion to the extreme! But it creeps up on us and we do have to be careful.

For the mystic who has achieved full Union, this is rarely a problem because hard work has disabused the mystic of any self-absorbed pretentions.

How do you tell the difference between sacrificing yourself because you are truly in Union with God, and "sacrificing" yourself by doing so much for other people that you become resentful or ill?

If you are truly in full Union, you will know it. However, lots of people delude themselves that they are in full Union when they may not have even made an honest start on the path. (The history of the world's religions is filled with spiritual "leaders" who fall into this category.) If you become resentful, that is a good sign that you are not in full Union, because your ego is still in charge enough to want "the good life."

Mystics in full Union may indeed become ill and may even die because of their loving service for others. This will not concern them terribly as they have realized that their contingent existence is expendable, and so long as their illness or death will advance God's project, they will be fine with it.

Okay, I can already hear you asking, "Why would I want that?" I think that's the ego talking. Self-preservation is not really a concern of the mystic in full Union.

Do we get what we expect we'll get? Your book outlines what Christian mystics have experienced as the path to Union with God. How do expectations affect this process, or is this process of "one-ing" with God preordained?

People who have been through this process describe amazingly similar experiences—and I'm not talking just about Christians. If you examine the literature of Buddhists and Hindus describing their own "maps" of spiritual development, their metaphors and symbols are very different, but the experiences are strikingly similar.

That said, when we are on *this* side of these experiences (not having had them), reading the words of those on *that* side of the experiences (those who *have* had them), we realize how tragically inept words are. We imagine what it will be like, but when we actually do go through these experiences, they are *nothing* like what we expect.

It's kind of like reading a travel memoir by someone who has visited London. Reading it, you get all kinds of images, but when you actually *go* to London, you do indeed see everything the writer described, but it looks *nothing* like the images you had in your head.

Even so, the writings of the mystics are most helpful when we are on the other side of an experience, trying to sort out the confusing stuff that is happening to us. That's when we go, "Oh, *that's* what St. John meant by that." But reading it beforehand didn't really prepare us for the reality—it just helped us make sense of it while we were going through it, or soon after the experience was complete and our heads were still spinning.

So is it different for everyone? Yes and no. We are all seeing everything through the lenses of our own experiences and assumptions, so it's going to feel different for everyone. Also, our theologies and religious metaphors are going to color the experiences for us. But is it similar for everyone, too? Yes, because we all go through the same process—Christian, Sufi, Buddhist, you name it. Theologies and metaphors may change, but the Divine Romance is pretty much a human constant. God is courting all of us, regardless of the clothes we insist he wear.

While the Catholic Church embraces the mystics, why doesn't its doctrine reflect their revelations? There continues to be a focus on sin, hell, etc., instead of the love of the Divine. Somehow the ecstatic is lost.

The Catholic Church has always had a bit of a love/hate relationship with its mystics. On the one hand, the mystics are speaking about an authentic experience of God promised in the church's teaching and sacramental system, but on the other hand the church is suspicious of them, because they are wild cards—often teetering dangerously close to heresy (remember Julian and Meister Eckhart?) and in danger of individualistic tendencies that could too easily be misunderstood as being outside the authority or control of the hierarchy. Most mystics would protest that Mother Church is absolutely central to their spirituality and that their progress would be impossible without the sacraments and the community she provides, but the hierarchy has always been a notoriously paranoid group.

And often with good reason, because while we have been focused in this book on the "authentic" mystics—those whom the church agrees are legitimate—in every age, there have been an awful lot of lone ranger, renegade mystics preaching every sort of deviation from the received doctrine. Are their experiences authentic? Hard to say. That discernment has to be done on a case-by-case basis, and it is not always possible for us to make a fair accounting due to the remove of history. Also, who are we to judge? But it's a fair bet that some of them have deluded themselves, just as many would-be mystics do today.

Rebelling against the authority or the doctrine or the boundaries of the orthodox community might be the sign of a clear-seeing mystic who rejects whatever dogmatic nonsense might actually be a hindrance to real growth. On the other hand, just as many people have refused the discipline and accountability found within the orthodox community precisely because they want to take the easy way out, refuse to surrender their egos, and live in an illusory spiritual palace of their own construction.

How do you tell which is which? This is where a good spiritual director and careful discernment comes in.

Protestants are at a greater disadvantage here for a couple of reasons. A Protestant can usually find a group that agrees with whatever "whim of doctrine" seems right to him or her, providing an easy "out" rather than forcing the seeker to truly wrestle with the theological and personal ramifications of a particular doctrine. Also, Protestantism is a child of the Enlightenment and has historically valued reason over ecstasy. Protestants are much more suspicious of mysticism than Catholic or Orthodox Christians are, even though there have been many Protestant mystics in the church's history. "Reason and good order" are the hallmarks of Reformed faith, and ecstatic or emotional or mystical experiences are often publically frowned upon and may even be preached against. Even in the Southern Baptist environment of my childhood, "emotionalism" was decried and always to be avoided.

The obvious exception to this, of course, is the Charismatic movement, through which emotionalism, ecstasy, and mysticism have rushed back into the Christian mainstream with a vengeance. You can't keep the Spirit at bay too long—she will always reassert herself, although again, she may not look anything like what you expect.

It seems that a sound mind is required to enter the mystical path. Is mental health necessary to even choose the mystical path?

Mental health is optimal, but has not always been the norm. Many of the saints—including some of the mystics—were nutty as fruitcakes. And sometimes craziness helps. After all, deviating from the cultural norm always looks like madness, doesn't it? Was St. Francis nuts or was he, in fact, the only sane person alive? You can make a fine case either way.

As I tell my spiritual direction students, you cannot assume that God is not at work in someone who is not mature, sober, or sane. God is wooing *everyone*.

Can a mystic be both apophatic and kataphatic?

A person can go through cycles of both kinds of experience. The Christian tradition is heavily weighted toward the kataphatic approach, utilizing as it does so much imagery and story. This makes sense when you consider that the foundation of the faith is the incarnation of Christ in Jesus of Nazareth. Our God is embodied, is visible, and so of course we avail ourselves of visible, visual means to approach him. Most Christians, therefore, begin their journey toward God using visual, imaginal practices and tools. And most of us continue in that vein.

But along the way some people discover a latent tendency toward apophatic spirituality within them, and it is this kind of prayer, this way of *being* with God (and *being one* with God) that becomes most fulfilling to them. But still, their practice will probably be mixed, because even though their private spiritual practice may be heavily weighted toward the apophatic, their corporate prayer (church services) will still be kataphatic—the stained glass, statuary, art, vestments, incense, music, words, ceremony, all of these will continue to work their magic, even on a devoted apophatic person.

Likewise, people with strong kataphatic leanings may have powerful, genuine experiences of apophatic prayer. Several mystics, like Teresa of Avila, clearly evidence both tendencies, and for some reason Protestant mystics seem more prone to a dialectical, both/and approach.[39] There is no disloyalty in this, no one is keeping score, no one will be upset at anyone for "changing sides." It's kind of like there are people who prefer sweet tastes and those who prefer savory. That doesn't mean that sweet-types don't enjoy potato chips on occasion, or savory-types don't enjoy ice cream now and then. We're talking about tendencies and preferences, not black-and-white distinctions. Most people will come down on one side or the other, but most people will have some experience of both.

If the mystical path seeks to culminate in love, might love help us be mystics? Can a life of service and love replace Purgation and dark nights and Illumination and Union?

The very fact that you seek to avoid these stages smacks of a spiritual bypass that just wants everything to be sweetness and light. This is not realistic—human life is hard, made even harder by our inculturated blindness, selfishness, and delusion. As the Egyptian Fathers put it, "Always to want your own way, becoming accustomed to having it, always to seek the easy path—all this leads to depression. But love, quietness, and the contemplation of the inner life cleanse our hearts."[40]

Before Real Love can be known, the dirty windows of our perception must be cleaned, the hate we have been taught must be unlearned, the lies we have told ourselves must be uncovered. If we attempt a shortcut, we just compound our illusions. "If we say we have no sin, the Truth is not in us," St. John wrote.[41] Mechtild is insistent that while it is Love that draws us, we must also prepare our hearts before Love can be fully known: "Love transforms. Love makes empty hearts overflow. This happens even more when we have to struggle through without assurance, all unready for the play of Love."[42]

But you are right that it is Love that assists us in becoming mystics—it is Love that helps us at every step along the way. It is Love that woos us in our Awakening experience. It is our desire for Love that compels us through the hardships of Purgation and the dark nights, it is the touch of Love that draws us near in Illumination, it is the fire of pure Love in which we are engulfed in Union, and it is Love that reaches out through us to those in darkness and despair. It is Love—working in us and upon us—that is acting at every stage of the mystical journey.

The Mystics,
in Their Own Words

WHAT THE MYSTICS SAY ABOUT AWAKENING

"When one is looking for something and sees no sign that it is where he is searching, he will keep on looking there only with painful reluctance. If, however, he begins to find traces of it, then he will hunt gladly, gaily, and in earnest. . . . It is like that with people who ought to be seeking God. If they get no taste of the divine sweetness, they drag; but if a man lies in wait until he does catch the taste of the divine, ever afterward he is a glad seeker of God." —*Meister Eckhart*[1]

"One day when I had been walking solitary abroad and was come home, I was taken up in the love of God, so that I could not but admire the greatness of his love. And while I was in that condition, it was opened up to me by the eternal light and power, and I therein clearly saw that all was done and was to be done in and by Christ . . . and that all these troubles were good for me and temptations for the trial of my faith which Christ had given me." —*George Fox*[2]

"All things were new; and all the creation gave another smell unto me than before, beyond what words can utter. . . . The creation was opened to me; and it was showed me how all things had their names given them, according to their nature and virtue." —*George Fox*[3]

183

"Behold, a clear light appeared on high, and raising my eyes toward it, I see the window above me full of brightness, and from out of that brightness there appeared One, in aspect, indeed, similar to a man, but in his splendor truly God. His countenance shone exceedingly, yet could human eyes gaze at it, for it caused not terror; rather had it a loveliness such as I had never seen in the world." —*John Amos Komensky*[4]

"Do you wish to know my meaning? Then lie down in the Fire. See and taste the Flowing Godhead through your being. Feel the Holy Spirit moving and compelling you within the flowing Fire and Light of God." —*Mechtild of Magdeburg*[5]

"The deepest level of communication is not communication, but communion. It is wordless. It is beyond words, and it is beyond speech, and it is beyond concept. Not that we discover a new unity. We discover an older unity. My dear brothers and sisters, we are already one. But we imagine that we are not. And what we have to recover is our original unity. What we have to be is what we are." —*Thomas Merton*[6]

"Wisdom burning in all things allures us with a certain foretaste of its sweetness, only to be swept toward it with a wonderful desire. Thus, wonder is the reason we seek to know any reality whatsoever." —*Nicholas of Cusa*[7]

"Love such as this wills to possess You as You are. Love wants You as You are." —*Karl Rahner*[8]

"Then we experience something which is inescapable (even when suppressed) in life and which is offered to our freedom with the question whether we want to accept it or whether we want to shut ourselves up in a hell of freedom by trying to barricade ourselves against it." —*Karl Rahner*[9]

"At 4:30 a.m. I saw something of which I had no idea at all previously. In the room where I was praying I saw a great light. I thought the place was on fire. I looked round, but could find nothing. Then the thought came to me that this might be an answer God had sent me. Then as I prayed and looked into the light, I saw the form of the Lord Jesus Christ. . . . The thought then came to me, Jesus Christ is not dead but living and it must be he himself. So I fell at his feet and got this wonderful peace which I could not get anywhere else." —*Sadhu Sundar Singh*[10]

"Love then came, as it desired, and as under the appearance of a cloud luminously it swooped down on me; completely on my head I saw it settle; and it made me cry out, for I was in terror. Nevertheless, after having then flown away, Love left me alone, and while I arduously searched for it then suddenly, completely it was in me in a conscious manner in the center of my heat; like a truly heavenly body, I saw it like the solar disc . . . it separated me from the visible and attached me to the invisible and granted me the grace to see the uncreated, and to rejoice." —*St. Symeon the New Theologian*[11]

"God here speaks to souls through words uttered by pious people, by sermons or good books, and in many other such ways. Sometimes he calls souls by means of sickness or troubles, or by some truth he teaches them during prayer, for tepid as they may be in seeking him, yet God holds them very dear." —*Teresa of Avila*[12]

"[The soul] aspires to its origin, to Life in its most intense manifestation: hence all its instincts urge it to that activity which it feels to be inseparable from life. It knows itself a member of that mighty family in which the stars are numbered: the family of the sons of God, who, free and creative, sharing the rapture of a living, striving Cosmos shout for joy." —*Evelyn Underhill*[13]

WHAT THE MYSTICS SAY ABOUT PURGATION

"Mortification subjects the body to the spirit, and the spirit to God. It does this by interfering with the tendencies of our senses, which are normally at odds with the Divine. By messing with the body in this way, the excessive love of the self and one's own will are avoided and eventually done away with (since these poison our spirits); and in their place the Divine Love and Divine Will enter and possess the soul." —*Augustine Baker*[14]

"I found within myself a powerful pull against the Good—namely, the desires of my own flesh and blood. I began then a difficult battle within myself. . . . While I was wrestling and fighting I was helped by God, and a wonderful light arose within my soul. It was a light entirely alien to me, completely unlike my own unruly nature. But I recognized that it was the true nature of both God and humankind—and of the relationship between them. I had never understood this before, and would never even have thought to look for it." —*Jacob Boehme*[15]

"Antoinette . . . used to pray fervently, 'When will I be completely yours, God?' And it seemed to her that he answered, 'When you possess nothing and die to yourself.' 'Where do you want me to do that, Lord?' she asked. 'In the desert,' he answered. . . . She disguised herself as a hermit and at four in the morning she set out on her own, with only a single penny to her name. And as she was going out, a voice said to her, 'Where is your faith? Is it in a penny?' And so she threw the penny away, and set out by herself completely free of the heavy burdens of the world." —*Antoinette Bourignan*[16]

"As [Catherine] knelt before [her confessor], her heart was wounded by the immeasurable Love of God. In that moment she saw clearly her own sufferings and her own failings, and how very good God was to her, and she was so moved that she nearly collapsed. The feelings of infinite love overwhelmed her, and she was drawn by a purifying impulse to remove herself from the world, crying out, 'No more world! No more sin!' Even if she had possessed a thousand worlds, she would have thrown all of them away." —*Catherine of Genoa*[17]

"It is like an object with a covering over it. It cannot receive the rays of the sun, not because the sun is not shining—it is always shining—but because the covering is in the way and blocks the sun. Destroy the covering, and the object will receive the sunlight again! . . . In the same way souls are covered by rust—by sin—which is gradually burned away by the fire of Purgation. . . . When this happens the human instinct to seek happiness in God increases, and grows through the fire of love, which seeks its goal so resolutely and violently that nothing can stand in its way. The clearer the vision is, the more painful it is as well." —*Catherine of Genoa*[18]

"Do not be surprised that you fall every day; do not give up, but stand your ground courageously. And assuredly the angel who guards you will honor your patience." —*St. John Climacus*[19]

"Remembrance of wrongs is an interpreter of Scripture of the kind that adjusts the words of the Spirit to its own views. Let it be put to shame by the Prayer of Jesus which cannot be said with it." —*St. John Climacus*[20]

"Be concentrated without self-display, withdrawn into your heart. For the demons fear concentration as thieves fear dogs." —*St. John Climacus*[21]

"It is right that you should know that to be empty of all creatures is to be full of God, and to be full of all creatures is to be empty of God.

You should also know that in this immovable detachment God has dwelt eternally and he still dwells in it." —*Meister Eckhart*[22]

"I dreamt that I . . . was pregnant and full with Nothingness like a woman who is with child. And that out of this Nothingness God was born." —*Meister Eckhart*[23]

"When your spirit withdraws, as it were, little by little from the flesh because of your ardent longing for God, and turns away from every thought that derives from sensibility or memory or temperament and is filled with reverence and joy at the same time, then you can be sure that you are drawing near that country whose name is prayer." —*Evagrius Ponticus*[24]

"A man in chains cannot run. Nor can the mind that is enslaved to passion see the place of spiritual prayer. It is dragged along and tossed by these passion-filled thoughts and cannot stand firm and tranquil." —*Evagrius Ponticus*[25]

"Just as it is hardly of a benefit to a man with bad eyes to stand gazing at the midday sun, when it is hottest, with fixed attention and uncovered eyes, so also is it of no avail at all for an impure spirit, still subject to passions, to counterfeit that awesome and surpassing prayer in spirit and truth. On the contrary, it stirs up the resentment of God against itself." —*Evagrius Ponticus*[26]

"When attention seeks prayer it finds it. For if there is anything that marches in the train of attention it is prayer; and so it must be cultivated." —*Evagrius Ponticus*[27]

"I saw all the world could do me no good. If I had had a king's diet, palace, and attendance, all would have been as nothing, for nothing gave me comfort but the Lord by his power. At another time I saw the great love of God and was filled with admiration at the infiniteness of it." —*George Fox*[28]

"Just as snow will not produce a flame, or water a fire, or the thorn-bush a fig, so a person's heart will not be freed from demonic thoughts, words, and actions until it has first purified itself inwardly, uniting watchfulness with the Jesus Prayer, attaining humility and stillness of soul, and eagerly pressing forward on its path. . . . The soul's true peace lies in the gentle name of Jesus and in its emptying itself of impassioned thoughts." —*St. Hesychios the Priest*[29]

"If you really wish to cover your evil thoughts with shame, to be still and calm, and to watch over your heart without hindrance, let the Jesus Prayer cleave to your breath, and in a few days you will find that this is possible." —*St. Hesychios the Priest*[30]

"If we purify ourselves of wickedness, then we will come to see invisible realities. But there is no point, while we are still blind, in asking why it is we cannot see the light, no point in stuffing our ears and then asking why it is we cannot hear anything." —*John of Apamea*[31]

"Learn to be empty of all things (. . . inwardly and outwardly) and you will see that I am God." —*John of the Cross*[32]

"Clinging to things will make the mind dark, the will weak, and the memory dull and disordered. . . . Not to let go is like planting a seed in untilled soil or trying to see with a cataract in the eye. In clinging to things and accomplishments one becomes unhappy with self, cold towards neighbors, sluggish and slothful in the things of God. It makes no difference whether a bird is tied by a thin thread or a cord. Still it cannot fly." —*John of the Cross*[33]

"As long as the desire endures for things discernible by the senses, the soul is not empty. But when there is no desire for things the soul will become empty and free, even if a person has many possessions." —*John of the Cross*[34]

"Cleanse the mirror of your soul and the single light will merge with you, manifesting itself to you as trinity. Then take the light down into your heart, and there you will see the Living God." —*John of Dalyatha*[35]

"I did not see sin: for I believe that it has no kind of substance nor any part of being nor could it be known except by the pain it causes. And this pain purges us and makes us know ourselves and to ask compassion." —*Julian of Norwich*[36]

"For in order to love and have God who is uncreated, we must have knowledge of the smallness of creatures and empty ourselves of all that is created." —*Julian of Norwich*[37]

"Love is a holy state of the soul, disposing it to value knowledge of God above all created things. We cannot attain lasting possession of such love while we are still attached to anything worldly." —*Maximos the Confessor*[38]

"When a sparrow tied by the leg tries to fly, it is held back by the string and pulled down to the earth. Similarly, when the intellect that has not yet attained dispassion flies up towards heavenly knowledge, it is held back by the passions and pulled down to earth." —*Maximos the Confessor*[39]

"The whole purpose of the Savior's commandments is to free the intellect from dissipation and hatred, and to lead it to the love of him and one's neighbor. From this love springs the light of active holy knowledge." —*Maximos the Confessor*[40]

"The savior . . . is hidden in the hearts of those who believe in him. They shall see him and the riches that are in him when they have purified themselves through love and self-control; and the greater their purity, the more they will see." —*Maximos the Confessor*[41]

"A soul can never attain the knowledge of God unless God himself in his condescension takes hold of it and raises it up to himself. For the human intellect lacks the power to ascend and to participate in divine illumination, unless God himself draws it up—in so far as this is possible for the human intellect—and illumines it with rays of divine light." —*Maximos the Confessor*[42]

"God has given me the power to change my ways." —*Mechtild of Magdeburg*[43]

"Love the nothing, flee the self. Stand alone. Seek help from no one. Let your being be quiet, be free from the bondage of all things. Free those who are bound, give exhortation to the free. Care for the sick but dwell alone. When you drink the waters of sorrow you shall kindle the fire of love with the match of perseverance. This is the way to dwell in the desert." —*Mechtild of Magdeburg*[44]

"All sin starts from the assumption that my false self, the self that exists only in my egocentric desires, is the fundamental reality of life to which everything else in the universe is ordered. Thus I use up my life in the desire for pleasures and the thirst for experiences, honor, knowledge, and love . . . and cover myself with pleasures and glory like bandages in order to make myself perceptible. . . . But there is no substance under the things with which I am clothed. I am hollow, and my structure of pleasures and ambitions has no foundation." —*Thomas Merton*[45]

"The things we really need come to us only as gifts, and in order to receive them as gifts we have to be open. In order to be open we have to renounce ourselves, in a sense we have to die to our image of ourselves, our autonomy, our fixation upon our self-willed identity. We have to be able to relax the psychic and spiritual cramp which knots us in the painful, vulnerable, helpless 'I' that is all we know as ourselves." —*Thomas Merton*[46]

"At the center of our being is a point of nothingness which is untouched by sin and by illusion, a point of pure truth, a point or spark which belongs entirely to God. . . . This little point of nothingness and of absolute poverty is the pure glory of God in us. . . . It is in everybody, and if we could see it we would see these billions of points of light coming together in the face and blaze of a sun that would make all the darkness and cruelty of life vanish completely." —*Thomas Merton*[47]

"Eternal wisdom will not be obtained unless the possessor owns nothing. The spirit of wisdom dwells in a pure field, in a wisdom-pure field." —*Nicholas of Cusa*[48]

"The essence of purgation is self-simplification." —*Richard of St. Victor*[49]

"Blessed is that soul whose eye has been cleansed of all the sorrows of this present age—those dark storm clouds—and which has been rendered simple and lucid so that it can discern the Lord wrapped in a cloud of light." —*Sahdona the Syrian*[50]

"There are three stages on the spiritual path: the purgative, the illuminative and finally the mystical, through which we are perfected. The first pertains to beginners, the second to those in the intermediate stage, and the third to the perfect. It is through these three consecutive stages that we ascend, growing in stature according to Christ and attaining 'mature manhood, the measure of the stature of the fullness of Christ.'" —*Niketas Stethatos*[51]

"Because the Lord is to be adored, worshipped, and glorified, it is believed that he loves adoration, worship, and glory, for his own sake; but he loves them for humanity's sake, because by means of them people come into such a state that the Divine can flow into them and be perceived; for by means of them people remove that which prevents the influx and reception of divine love." —*Emanuel Swedenborg*[52]

"The mystic finds a joy no words can describe in feeling that through his active obedience (which is a very different thing from the passive acceptance that first satisfied him) he endlessly adheres more closely to the encompassing Godhead. Endlessly, the more perfect an instrument he becomes the more does he become one with the creative Act." —*Pierre Teilhard de Chardin*[53]

"Through seeking the development of his own nature, he has found the rapture of feeling that suffering is dissolving his being, drop by drop, and replacing it with God." —*Pierre Teilhard de Chardin*[54]

"As for us creatures, of ourselves we are but emptiness and obscurity. But you, my God, are the inmost depths, the stability of that eternal milieu, without duration or space, in which our cosmos emerges gradually into being and grows gradually to its final completeness, as it loses boundaries which to our eyes seem so immense. Everything is being; everywhere there is being and nothing but being, save in the fragmention of creatures and the clash of their atoms." —*Pierre Teilhard de Chardin*[55]

"Like the Quietist I allow myself with delight to be cradled in the divine fantasy: but at the same time I know that the divine will shall only be revealed to me at each moment if I exert myself to the utmost. I shall only touch God in the world of matter, when, like Jacob, I have been vanquished by him." —*Pierre Teilhard de Chardin*[56]

"They think about their souls every now and then; although very busy, they pray a few times a month, with minds generally filled with a thousand other matters, for where their treasure is, there is their heart also." —*Teresa of Avila*[57]

"To journey into this interior world within, love must already be awakened. For love to awaken in us: let go, let be, be silent, be still in gentle peace, be aware of opposites, learn mindfulness and forgetfulness." —*Teresa of Avila*[58]

"First, in this work of the Spirit, the one who thinks less and has less desire to act does more. What we must do is to beg like the needy poor before a rich and great emperor, and then lower our eyes and wait with humility." —*Teresa of Avila*[59]

"The Lord doesn't want you to hold on to anything, for if you avoid doing so, you will be able to enjoy the favors we are speaking of. Whether you have little or much, the Lord wants everything; and in conformity with what you know you have given, you will receive greater or lesser favors." —*Teresa of Avila*[60]

"I believe we shall never learn to know ourselves except by endeavoring to know God, for, beholding his greatness we are struck by our own baseness, his purity shows our foulness, and by meditating on his humility we find how very far we are from being humble." —*Teresa of Avila*[61]

"Desire for material wealth must not lodge in the souls of those pursuing the spiritual way. For a mind with many possessions is an over-laden ship, driven by the storm of cares and sinking in the deep waters of distress. Love of riches begets many passions, and has aptly been called 'the root of all evil.'" —*St. Theodoros the Great Ascetic*[62]

"We see a sham world because we live a sham life."
—*Evelyn Underhill*[63]

"Purgation is . . . the slow and painful completion of Conversion. It is the drastic turning of the self from the unreal to the real life: a setting of her house in order, an orientation of the mind to Truth. Its business is the getting rid, first of self-love; and secondly of all those foolish interests in which the surface-consciousness is steeped." —*Evelyn Underhill*[64]

"Accept Poverty . . . demolish ownership, the verb "to have" in every mood and tense, and . . . the cosmos belongs to you, and you to it. You escape the heresy of separateness, are made one, and merged in the greater life of All. Then a free spirit in a free world, the self moves upon its true orbit; undistracted by the largely self-imposed needs and demands of everyday existence." —*Evelyn Underhill*[65]

"Poverty . . . prepared man's spirit for that union with God to which it aspires. She strips off the clothing which he so often mistakes for himself, transvaluates all his values, and shows him things as they are. . . . Poverty . . . consists in a breaking down of man's inveterate habit of trying to rest in, or take seriously, things which are less than God."
—*Evelyn Underhill*[66]

"I recited Our Father in Greek every day before work . . . with absolute attention. If during the recitation my attention wanders or goes to sleep, in the minutest degree, I begin again. . . . At times the very first words tear my thoughts from my body and transport it to a place outside space where there is neither perspective nor point of view. . . . Sometimes, also, during this recitation or at other moments, Christ is present with me in person, but his presence is infinitely more real, more moving, more clear, than on that first occasion when he took possession of me." —*Simone Weil*[67]

WHAT THE MYSTICS SAY ABOUT THE DARK NIGHT OF THE SENSES

"You cannot write on wax unless you have first expunged the letters written on it." —*Basil the Great*[68]

"The soul, led by God and drawn on by the love of God, goes forward into the dark night, enflamed with love. This is the purgation and the deprivation of all sense desires for the things of this world, the pleasures of carnal life, and the gratification of one's own will." —*John of the Cross*[69]

"When the soul denies itself the pleasure that is sweet to the ear, its hearing is 'in darkness,' having nothing to do. When it denies itself all that is inviting to the eye, its sight is 'in darkness.' . . . The soul that has spurned gratification from all things—by disciplining its desire for them—can be said to live in the darkness of night, which is simply being empty of all things." —*John of the Cross*[70]

"This is the lot of beginners at the time God commences to introduce them to a state of contemplation. . . . God often withdraws sensory delight so souls might set the eyes of faith upon the invisible grace God gives in communion." —*John of the Cross*[71]

"We call this detachment the Night of the Soul because we are talking about the absence of things—absence is not detachment, if there is still desire. Instead, detachment consists of suppressing one's desires and avoiding pleasure. This is what sets the soul free, even though one may still own possessions. It is not things of this world that occupy or injure the soul, for they do not enter into it—instead it is desire for them that is harmful." —*John of the Cross*[72]

"There are signs indicating that the darkness is from God . . . these souls do not get satisfaction or consolation from the things of God, they do not get any from creatures either. God does not allow the soul to find sweetness or light in anything." —*John of the Cross*[73]

"It may happen that for a certain time a man is illumined and refreshed by God's grace, and then this grace is withdrawn. This makes him inwardly confused and he starts to grumble; instead of seeking through steadfast prayer to recover his assurance of salvation, he loses patience and gives up. He is like a beggar who receives alms from the palace, and feels put out because he was not asked inside to dine with the king." —*St. John of Karpathos*[74]

"God didn't say, 'You won't be buffeted about by storms, you won't toil, you won't suffer.' Instead, he said, 'You won't be defeated.'" —*Julian of Norwich*[75]

"By nature, our faith is a light for us, bracing us against the night. The light is responsible for our life, while the night is the cause of all our pain and woe. But they both nourish us and cause us to give thanks to God. For with mercy and grace we stand fast in our belief in the light, going forth with wisdom and might. And when woe is at its end, suddenly our eyes shall be opened, and in the clear light our sight will be full." —*Julian of Norwich*[76]

"O happy famine, which leaves you not so much as the husk of one human comfort to feed upon! For this is the time and place for all that is good and life and salvation to happen to you, which happened to the Prodigal Son. Your way is as short and your success as certain as his was. You have no more to do than he had; you need not call out for books or methods of devotion; for in your present state much reading and borrowed prayers are not your best method. All that you are to offer to God, all that is to help you find Him to be your Savior and Redeemer, is best taught and expressed by the distressed state of your heart." —*William Law*[77]

"Let us therefore take this body and make an altar of sacrifice, and let us place on it all our desires and let us beg the Lord that he would send down from Heaven the invisible and mighty fire and consume the altar and everything on it." —*Makarios the Great*[78]

"Leave the soul in God's hands. Let God do whatever God wants with it, with the greatest disinterest as possible about your own benefits and the greatest resignation to the will of God." —*Teresa of Avila*[79]

WHAT THE MYSTICS SAY ABOUT ILLUMINATION

"My soul's eyes were opened, and I saw the generosity of God. I beheld the whole world, both here and beyond the sea, to its very depths! And in all these things I saw nothing but divine power, which I cannot even begin to describe. It was so great that my soul was overwhelmed with wonder and cried out saying, 'The whole world is full of God!' I then realized how very small the whole world really was, and how great was the power of God that filled it." —*Angela of Foligno*[80]

"By this deep trust and heartfelt assent, man gives his heart completely and utterly to God, rests in God alone, gives himself over to God, clings to God alone, unites himself with God, is a participant of all that which is God and Christ, becomes one spirit with God, receives from him new power, new life, new consolation, peace and joy, rest of soul, righteousness and holiness, and also, from God through faith, man is newborn. Where new faith is, there is Christ with all his righteousness, holiness, redemption, merit, grace, forgiveness of sins, childhood of God, inheritance of eternal life. This is the new birth that comes from faith in Christ." —*Johann Arndt*[81]

"By a process of subtraction you led me into the secret chamber of my soul. I could only do this because you helped me. I went in, and with the mysterious eye of my soul I saw the Light that never changes, the eye above my soul, beyond the power of my comprehension. . . . Whoever knows the truth knows that Light, and whoever knows it knows eternity. Love knows it." —*Augustine of Hippo*[82]

"I but open my eyes, and perfection, no more and no less, in the kind I imagined full-fronts me, and God is seen God in the star, in the stone, in the flesh, in the soul and the clod." —*Robert Browning*[83]

"When we have been made ready, we begin to long sincerely for this gift of contemplative vision, for it is full of beauty, frees us from every worldly care, and nourishes the intellect with divine truth in the radiance of inexpressible light. In brief, it is the gift that, through the help of the holy prophets, unites the deiform soul with God in unbreakable communion." —*St. Diadochos of Photiki*[84]

"Apprehend God in all things, for God is in all things." —*Meister Eckhart*[85]

"Every single creature is full of God and is a book about God. Every creature is a word of God." —*Meister Eckhart*[86]

"Earth cannot get away from heaven: let the earth drop downward or rise upward, heaven still penetrates it, imbuing it with strength and making it fruitful, whether it will or no. That is how God treats man: when he thinks to escape God, he runs into God's bosom, for every hideout is open to him." —*Meister Eckhart*[87]

"Being is God's circle and in this circle all creatures exist. Everything that is in God is God." —*Meister Eckhart*[88]

"You will not be able to pray purely if you are all involved with material affairs and agitated with unremitting concerns. For prayer is the rejection of concepts." —*Evagrius Ponticus*[89]

"The proof of *apatheia* is when the spirit begins to see its own light, when it remains in a state of tranquility in the presence of the images it has during sleep and when it maintains its calm as it beholds the affairs of life." —*Evagrius Ponticus*[90]

"We seek after virtues for the sake of attaining to the inner meaning of created things. We pursue the latter, that is to say the inner meanings of what is created, for the sake of attaining to the Lord who has created them. It is in the state of prayer that he is accustomed to manifest himself." —*Evagrius Ponticus*[91]

"If you pray in all truth you will come upon a deep sense of confidence. Then the angels will walk with you and enlighten you concerning the meaning of created things." —*Evagrius Ponticus*[92]

"Let us sit still and keep our attention fixed within ourselves, so that we advance in holiness and resist vice more strongly. Awakened in this way to spiritual knowledge, we shall acquire contemplative insight into many things; and ascending still higher, we shall receive a clearer vision of the light of our savior." —*Evagrius Ponticus*[93]

"It is more important to remember God than it is to remember to breathe." —*Gregory of Nazianzus*[94]

"Teach me, my God and King, In all things Thee to see, And what I do in any thing To do it as for Thee." —*George Herbert*[95]

"When the heart has acquired stillness it will perceive the heights and depths of knowledge; and the ear of the intellect will be made to hear marvelous things from God." —*St. Hesychios the Priest*[96]

"The soul that is full of wisdom is saturated with the spray of a bubbling fountain—God himself." —*Hildegard of Bingen*[97]

"The world is charged with the grandeur of God. It will flame out, like shining from shook foil, It gathers to a greatness like the ooze of oil Crushed. Why do men then now not reck His rod?" —*Gerard Manly Hopkins*[98]

"There lives the dearest freshness deep down things; And though the last light from the black west went, Oh, morning at the brown brink eastward springs—Because the Holy Ghost over the bent World broods with warm breast, and with, ah, bright wings." —*Gerard Manly Hopkins*[99]

"My soul wells up and my mind is illumined, my heart is on fire, and all of my desires have become gentle and kind. I don't know where I am, I just know that my Love has embraced me. And because my Love has surrounded me I now possess something I never had before. I don't know what it is, but I hope I never lose it. . . . Was this, finally, my Beloved? . . . It is indeed your Beloved who visits you, but he comes in an invisible form. He comes disguised, beyond comprehension. . . . He comes to arouse you, not to be understood by you. He comes not to give himself to you completely, but just to give you a taste, not to fulfill your desire, but to lead you and your affections on." —*Hugh of St. Victor*[100]

"Those who see light are within light and share the brilliance of the light. Just so, those who see God are within God and receive of his splendor, a radiance of the vision of God that gives us life." —*Iranaeus of Lyons*[101]

"It seems to the soul that the entire universe is a sea of love in which it is engulfed, for conscious of the living point or center of love within itself, it is unable to catch sight of the boundaries of this love." —*John of the Cross*[102]

"For as the body is clad in the cloth, and the flesh in the skin, and the bones in the flesh, and the heart in the whole, so are we, soul and body, clad in the Goodness of God, and enclosed." —*Julian of Norwich*[103]

"Here's what I understood: I saw God in a Point, by which I saw that he is in all things. . . . He is in the center of all things, and all that is done is done by him." —*Julian of Norwich*[104]

"Our Lord Jesus oftentimes said: 'This I am. This I am. I am what you love. I am what you enjoy. I am what you serve. I am what you long for. I am what you desire. I am what you intend. I am all that is.'" —*Julian of Norwich*[105]

"The fullness of joy is to behold God in everything." —*Julian of Norwich*[106]

"I saw no difference between God and our substance. It was as if all were God, and yet I understood that our substance is *in* God: that is to say, that God is God, and our substance is a creature in God." —*Julian of Norwich*[107]

"Jesus is our real mother in whom we are forever carried, and out of whom we shall never come." —*Julian of Norwich*[108]

"At first the practice of inward prayer is a process of alternation of attention between outer things and the Inner Light. Preoccupation with either brings the loss of the other. Yet what is sought is not alternation, but simultaneity, worship undergirding every moment, living prayer, the continuous current and background of all moments of life. Long practice indeed is needed before alternation yields to concurrent immersion in both levels at once." —*Thomas Kelly*[109]

"For the past few days I have been experimenting in a more complete surrender than ever before. I am taking, by deliberate act of will, enough time from each hour to give God much thought. Yesterday and today I have made a new adventure, which is not easy to express. I am feeling God in each movement, by an act of will—willing that He shall direct these fingers that now strike this typewriter—willing that He shall pour through my steps as I walk—willing that He shall direct my words as I speak, and my very jaws as I eat! You will object to this intense introspection. Do not try it, unless you feel unsatisfied with your own relationship with God, but at least allow me to realize all the leadership of God I can. I am disgusted with the pettiness and futility of my unled self. If the way out is not more perfect slavery to God, then what is the way out? I am trying to be utterly free from everybody, free from my own self, but completely enslaved to the will of God every moment of this day." —*Frank Laubach*[110]

"We believe that Christ, according to his human nature, is put over all creatures and fills all things, as Paul says in Eph. 4[:10]. Not only to his divine nature, but also according to his human nature, he is a lord of all things, has all things in his hand, and is present everywhere. . . . Heaven and earth are his sack; as wheat fills the sack, so he fills all things." —*Martin Luther*[111]

"Although he is present in all creatures, and I might find him in stone, in fire, in water, or even in a rope, for he certainly is there, yet he does not wish that I seek him there apart from the Word, and cast myself into the fire or the water, or hang myself on the rope. He is present everywhere, but he does not wish that you grope for him everywhere. Grope rather where the Word is, and there you will lay hold of him in the right way." —*Martin Luther*[112]

"My imagination takes to itself wings and flies to some wilderness, where I can talk to God alone. . . . What is this world, what is religious community, what is anything to me without God? They become a jostling crowd when I lose sight of him. The most dreary wilderness would seem like Paradise with just a little of his presence. . . . I need to be alone with God so much. . . . It sometimes seems astonishing that people who feel as I do, who have bodies just like mine—people who are in every way like me—see and know nothing of that blessed and adorable being in whom my soul finds all its happiness." —*Henry Martyn*[113]

"Blessed is the intellect that transcends all sensible objects and ceaselessly delights in divine beauty." —*St. Maximos the Confessor*[114]

"You ask me where God dwells. I will tell you. There is no lord in the whole world who lives in all his dwellings at once except God alone." —*Mechtild of Magdeburg*[115]

"God says: Now is the time to tell you where I am and where I will be. I am in Myself, in all places in all things as I ever have been without beginning." —*Mechtild of Magdeburg*[116]

"In this fashion we learn the power and the strength of silence. We learn to go into the world as still as a mouse in the depths of our heart." —*Mechtild of Magdeburg*[117]

"Our lady, the soul, has slept since childhood. Now she has awakened in the light of open love. In this light she looks around herself to discover who that is who reveals himself to her, and what that is that one is saying to her. Thus does she see truly and understand how God is all things in all things." —*Mechtild of Magdeburg*[118]

"There is in my heart this great thirst to recognize totally the nothingness of all that is not God. My prayer is then a kind of praise rising up out of the center of Nothing and Silence. If I am still present 'myself' this I recognize as an obstacle about which I can do nothing unless he himself removes the obstacle. If he wills he can then make the Nothingness into a total clarity. If he does not will, then the Nothingness seems to itself to be an object and remains an obstacle. Such is my ordinary way of prayer, or meditation. It is not 'thinking about' anything, but a direct seeking of the Face of the Invisible, which cannot be found unless we become lost in him who is Invisible." —*Thomas Merton*[119]

"The whole thing boils down to giving ourselves in prayer a chance to realize that we have what we seek. We don't have to rush after it. It is there all the time, and if we give it time, it will make itself known to us." —*Thomas Merton*[120]

"There remains to suppress the apparent division between empirical self and real or inner self. There is no such division. There is only the Void which is I, covered over by an apparent I. And when the apparent I is seen to be void, it no longer needs to be rejected, for it is I. How wonderful it is to be alive in such a world of craziness and simplicity!" —*Thomas Merton*[121]

"Divinity is the enfolding and unfolding of everything that is. Divinity is in all things in such a way that all things are in divinity. Mind itself supposing itself to encompass, survey, and comprehend all

things thus concludes that it is in everything and everything is in it."
—*Nicholas of Cusa*[122]

"The illuminative stage pertains to those who as a result of their struggles have attained the first level of dispassion. It is characterized by the spiritual knowledge of created beings, the contemplation of their inner essences and communion of the Holy Spirit." —*Niketas Stethatos*[123]

"When you become aware of the increasing fire of your love for God and inner faith in him, then you should realize that you are bringing Christ to birth within your soul. . . . When you experience your heart filled with joy and consumed with yearning for God's ineffable blessings, then know that the divine Spirit is working within you. When you feel your intellect filled with ineffable light and spiritual understandings of transcendent wisdom, then recognize that the Holy Spirit is actively present in your soul, uncovering the treasures of the Kingdom of Heaven that live hidden within it." —*Niketas Stethatos*[124]

"[Illumination] involves the intellect's purification by divine fire, the noetic opening of the eyes of the heart, and the birth of the Logos accompanied by sublime intellections of spiritual knowledge. Its final goal is . . . insight into divine and human affairs, and the revelation of the mysteries of the kingdom of heaven." —*Niketas Stethatos*[125]

"Do not therefore try and speculate upon the mysteries of God nor his relations with man but talk continually to him. . . . All the religions of the world cannot give us union with God: we must find it for ourselves." —*Pierre Poiret*[126]

"But when I love you, when I manage to break out of the narrow circle of self and leave behind the restless agony of unanswered questions, when my blinded eyes no longer look merely from afar and from the outside upon your unapproachable brightness, and much more when you yourself, O Incomprehensible One, have become through love the inmost center of my life, then I can bury myself entirely in you, O mysterious God, and with myself all my questions." —*Karl Rahner*[127]

"Often when I come out of ecstasy I think the whole world must be blind not to see what I see, everything is so near and so clear. . . . There is not language which will express the things which I see and hear in the spiritual world." —*Sadhu Sundar Singh*[128]

"The created universe . . . is so full of wisdom from love that it may be said all things in the complex are wisdom itself; for things innumerable are in such order, successive and simultaneous, that together they constitute one. It is from this, and no otherwise, that they can be held together and perpetually preserved." —*Emanuel Swedenborg*[129]

"I plunge into the all-inclusive One; but the One is so perfect that as it receives me and I love myself in it I can find in it the ultimate perfection of my own individuality." —*Teilhard de Chardin*[130]

"I felt my body, my soul, and even my spirit pass into the ethereal tint, unreal in its freshness, that caressed my eyes. Serene and iridescent, its color bathed more than my senses; it in some way impregnated my affections and thoughts. I melted away in it, lost in a stranger yearning to attain some individuality vaster and simpler than mine—as though I had become pure light." —*Teilhard de Chardin*[131]

"Lord, it is you who, through the imperceptible goadings of sense-beauty, penetrated my heart in order to make its life flow out into yourself. . . . You unfurled your immensity before my eyes and displayed yourself to me as Universal Being." —*Teilhard de Chardin*[132]

"If, then, a man is to build up in himself, for God, the structure of a sublime love, he must first of all sharpen his sensibility. By a familiar contact, prudent but untiring, with the most deeply emotive realities, he must carefully foster in himself his feeling for, his perception of, his zest for the Omnipresent which haloes everything in nature."
—*Teilhard de Chardin*[133]

"The way it happened, I was ignorant of one thing—I did not know that God was in all things. I thought it was impossible that He should be so near. It was not in my power not to believe that he was present, for it was evident that he was there." —*Teresa of Avila*[134]

"As long as union with God is sensible, the communication is only made through the senses. I find myself so weak and destitute, that with regard to myself, I would rather write nothing respecting the state of my soul. But it is nevertheless true, that I occasionally seem to experience something of a divine communication, which is exceedingly precious, but which lasts only a few moments." —*Gerhard Tersteegen*[135]

"The intellect freed from the passions becomes like light, unceasingly illumined by the contemplation of created beings." —*St. Thalassios the Libyan*[136]

"Each soul must learn to stand up in its own right and live. How blissful to lean upon another, to seek a sense of everlasting arms expressed in the vitality of a friend! We walk a part of the way together, but on the upper reaches of life, each path takes its own way to the heights— alone. Ultimately, I am alone, so vastly alone that in my aloneness is all the life of the universe. Stripped to the literal substance of myself, there is nothing left but naked soul, the irreducible ground of individual being, which becomes at once the quickening throb of God. At such moments of profound awareness I seem to be all that there

is in the world, and all that there is in the world seems to be myself."
—*Howard Thurman*[137]

"O Heavenly Joy! O great and sacred blessedness Which I possess! So great a joy Who did into my arms convey? From God above Being sent, the Heavens me enflame: To praise his Name The stars do move The burning sun doth shew His love." —*Thomas Traherne*[138]

"The barrier between human and non-human life, which makes man a stranger on earth as well as in heaven, is done away. Life now whispers to his life: all things are his intimates, and respond to his fraternal sympathy." —*Evelyn Underhill*[139]

"Leave off doing, that you may be." —*Evelyn Underhill*[140]

WHAT THE MYSTICS SAY ABOUT THE DARK NIGHT OF THE SPIRIT

"God is in such perfect harmony with the soul that when he sees it in its original purity—just as he made it—he gives to it an attracting impulse of his burning love, enough to seemingly annihilate it. . . . This is how God transforms the soul into himself, so that it sees in itself nothing but God, who goes on attracting it and inflaming it until he has brought it to the same state of spotless purity it was created in."
—*Catherine of Genoa*[141]

"God acts as if there were a wall erected between him and us."
—*Meister Eckhart*[142]

"And so, the more completely you are able to draw in your powers to a unity and forget all those things and their images which you have absorbed, and the further you can get from creatures and their images, the nearer you are to this and the readier to receive it." —*Meister Eckhart*[143]

"God works without means and without images, and the freer you are from images, the more receptive you are for his inward working, and the more introverted and self-forgetful, the nearer you are to this." —*Meister Eckhart*[144]

"The Father gives birth to his Son in eternity, equal to himself. . . . Yet I say more: he has given birth to him in my soul. Not only is the soul with him and he equal with it, but he is in it, and the Father gives his Son birth in the soul in the same way as he gives him birth in eternity and not otherwise. . . . The Father gives birth to his Son without ceasing; and I say more: He gives birth not only to me, his Son, but he gives birth to me as himself and himself as me and to me as his being and nature." —*Meister Eckhart*[145]

"When you are praying do not fancy the Divinity like some image formed within yourself. Avoid also allowing your spirit to be impressed with the seal of some particular shape, but rather, free from all matter, draw near the immaterial Being and you will attain to understanding." —*Evagrius Ponticus*[146]

"Because every thought enters the heart in the form of a mental image of some sensible object, the blessed light of the Divinity will illumine the heart only when the heart is completely empty of everything and so free from all form. Indeed, this light reveals itself to the pure intellect in the measure to which the intellect is purged of all concepts." —*St. Hesychios the Priest*[147]

"One learns that the way to the experience and vision of the power of God does not consist in ideas and meditations about God, but that it embodies one's inability to grasp God with ideas or to walk by means of discursive, imaginative meditation." —*John of the Cross*[148]

"God takes a person by the hand and guides the soul in darkness, as though blind, to an unknown place. Past knowledge cannot serve as a guide to reach a new and unknown land and to travel unknown roads. Faith darkens and empties the intellect of all its natural understanding and thereby prepares it for union with the divine wisdom. Hope empties and withdraws the memory from all creature possessions. Charity empties and annihilates the affections and appetites of the will of whatever is not God and centers them on God alone." —*John of the Cross*[149]

"Blessed . . . are those who, when grace is withdrawn, find no consolation in themselves, but only continuing tribulation and thick darkness, and yet do not despair; but, strengthened by faith, they endure courageously, convinced that they do indeed see him who is invisible." —*St. John of Karpathos*[150]

"Where all reasoning fails, where the soul is so troubled that she could not even explain that which troubles her, there the Divine Presence appears and suddenly the dizziness ceases, and peace is reborn with light." —*Lucie-Christine*[151]

"Let us therefore take this body and make an altar of sacrifice, and let us place on it all our desires and let us beg the Lord that he would send down from Heaven the invisible and mighty fire and consume the altar and everything on it." —*Makarios the Great*[152]

"There comes a time when both body and soul enter into such a vast darkness that one loses light and consciousness and knows nothing more of God's intimacy." —*Mechtild of Magdeburg*[153]

"At such a time when the light in the lantern burns out the beauty of the lantern can no longer be seen. With longing and distress we are reminded of our nothingness." —*Mechtild of Magdeburg*[154]

"God has wounded me close unto death. If God leaves me unanointed I could never recover. Even if all the hills flowed with healing oils, and all the waters contained healing powers, and all the flowers and all the trees dripped with healing ointments, still, I could never recover." —*Mechtild of Magdeburg*[155]

"Remember this: That when our Lord releases the soul it sinks down and gives him thanks, even for this." —*Mechtild of Magdeburg*[156]

"The union of the simple light of God with the simple light of human spirit, in love, is contemplation. The two simplicities are one. They form, as it were, an emptiness in which there is no addition but rather the taking away of names, of forms, of content, of subject matter, of identities. In this meeting there is not so much a fusion of identities as a disappearance of identities." —*Thomas Merton*[157]

"There are three kinds of silence; the first is of words, the second of desires, and the third of thoughts. The first is perfect; the second more perfect; and the third most perfect. In the first, that is, of words, virtue is acquired; in the second, to wit of desires, quietness is attained; in the third, that of thoughts, internal recollection is gained. By not speaking, not desiring, and not thinking, one arrives at the true and perfect mystical silence, wherein God speaks with the soul, communicates himself to her, and in the abyss of her own depth, teaches her the most perfect and exalted wisdom." —*Miguel de* **Molinos**[158]

"Where the leap into the darkness of death is accepted as the beginning of everlasting promise . . . where one dares to pray into a silent darkness and knows that one is heard, although no answer seems to come back about which one might argue and rationalize, where one lets oneself go unconditionally and experiences this capitulation as true victory . . . where a man entrusts all his knowledge and all his questions to the silent and all-inclusive mystery which is loved more than all our individual knowledge which makes us such small people . . . *there* is God and his liberating grace." —*Karl Rahner*[159]

"In short, there is no other remedy in such a tempest except to wait for the mercy of God, who, unexpectedly, by some casual word or unforeseen circumstance, suddenly dispels all these sorrows; then every cloud of trouble disappears and the mind is left full of light and far happier than before." —*Teresa of Avila*[160]

"He entered my room and said, 'Poor creature, you who understand nothing, who know nothing. Come with me and I will teach you things which you do not suspect.' I followed him. . . . One day he said to me: 'Now go.' I fell down before him, I clasped his knees, I implored him not to drive me away. But he threw me out on the stairs. I went down unconscious of anything, my heart as it were in shreds." —*Simone Weil*[161]

"It is one of the Dark Lights. . . . You are precisely not in hell; hell is final loss. You are not cut off, though it may seem, smell, and taste like it. . . . 'In the midst of this confusion and amazement . . . a voice was formed and uttered in me, as from the center of boundless darkness: "thy will, O God, be done: if this be thy act alone, and not my own, I yield my soul to thee."' So [says Quaker writer] Mr. Thomas Storey . . . you will remark his method is not to try to move it—the grim, eternal death—but to push into it. 'Press into it; it is there the thing yields.'" —*Charles Williams*[162]

WHAT THE MYSTICS SAY ABOUT UNION

"Sometimes the soul is kindled into love for God and, free from all fantasy and image, moves untroubled by doubt towards him; and it draws, as it were, the body with it into the depths of that ineffable love. . . . When we experience things in this manner, we can be sure that it is the energy of the Holy Spirit within us." —*St. Diadochos of Photiki*[163]

"The Light . . . wants to go into the simple ground, into the quiet desert, into which distinction has never gazed, not the Father, nor the Son, nor the Holy Spirit. In that innermost part, where no one dwells, there is contentment for that light, and there it is more inward than it can be to itself, for the ground is a simple silence, in itself immovable, and by this immovability all things are moved." —*Meister Eckhart*[164]

"A heart that has been completely emptied of mental images gives birth to divine, mysterious intellections that sport within it like fish and dolphins in a calm sea." —*St. Hesychios the Priest*[165]

"I compare the great love of Creator and creation to the same love and fidelity with which God binds woman and man together. This is so that together they might be creatively fruitful." —*Hildegard of Bingen*[166]

"The soul is kissed by God in its innermost regions. With interior yearning, grace and blessing are bestowed. It is a yearning to take on God's gentle yoke, it is a yearning to give one's self to God's way." —*Hildegard of Bingen*[167]

"The spiritual marriage is . . . a total transformation in the Beloved in which each surrenders the entire possession of self to the other with a certain consummation of the union of love. The soul thereby becomes divine, becomes God through participation, insofar as is possible in this life." —*John of the Cross*[168]

"For truly our Lover desires that our soul cleave to him with all its might, and that we forevermore cleave to his Goodness." —*Julian of Norwich*[169]

"Until I am substantially oned to God, I may never completely rest nor have true bliss: that is to say, until I am so fastened to him that there is nothing between my God and me." —*Julian of Norwich*[170]

"Prayer ones the soul to God. For though the soul is ever like God in kind and substance, restored by grace, it is often unlike in condition, because of human sin. That is when prayer is a witness that the soul wills what God wills; it comforts the conscience and gives us grace." —*Julian of Norwich*[171]

"We will all enter our Lord, fully aware of and fully possessing God. This will last forever. We will truly see, fully feel, spiritually hear, delectably breathe in, and sweetly drink God." —*Julian of Norwich*[172]

"God feels great delight to be our Father and God feels great delight to be our Mother and God feels great delight to be our true Spouse and our soul the loved Wife. Christ feels great delight that He is our Brother and Jesus feels great delight that He is our Liberator. These are five great joys that God wants us to enjoy." —*Julian of Norwich*[173]

"God made us all at once; and in our making he knit us and oned us to Himself. By this oneing we are kept as clear and as noble as we were made. By the virtue of the same precious oneing, we love our maker and seek him, praise Him and thank Him, and endlessly enjoy Him." —*Julian of Norwich*[174]

"God wants to be thought of as our Lover. I must see myself so bound in love as if everything that has been done has been done for me. That is to say, the Love of God makes such a unity in us that when we see this unity no one is able to separate oneself from another." —*Julian of Norwich*[175]

"This brings us soonest to the union with and conformity to the Will of God: so that resignation to, the union with, and the change of our wills into the Will of God—after many vicissitudes, trials, and purifying in and after this life—we shall find ourselves so settled and established that we shall not find any more self-love in us, but that we will only what God wills, and the Will of God is become wholly our will." —*Johannes Kelpius*[176]

"My soul lives on God, by a glance of love between him and herself. By this glance God gives himself to me, and I give myself to him. This is my habitual state, that in which God has placed me. I neither can nor should turn myself from it on account of suffering. This I accept as inseparable from love here below." —*Lucie-Christine*[177]

"I am plunged in God. I see him so intensely that my soul is more certain and more possessed by the sight than my bodily eyes by the light of day; and at the same time he is in me, he is one with me, penetrates me, is closer to me than the air I breathe, is more united to me than the soul is united to the body which lives by it; I am absorbed by him. I no longer know by what existence I exist, it seems to me that I am transported into another life, a region that is no more this earth; and this detachment is ineffable, it is a rapture and inebriation." —*Lucie-Christine*[178]

"For the soul that has been considered worthy through its consuming desire, expectation, faith, and love to receive from on high that power, the heavenly love of the Spirit, and has obtained the heavenly fire of eternal life, is one that is being stripped of every worldly affection and freed from every bond of evil." —*Makarios the Great*[179]

"How lovely it is when a spiritual person consecrates himself totally to the Lord and clings to him alone. He walks in his commands, never forgetting. Reverently honoring the overshadowing presence of the Spirit of Christ, he becomes one spirit with him and one being." —*Makarios the Great*[180]

"For God desired to have fellowship with the human soul and espoused it to himself as the spouse of the King, and he purified it from sordidness." —*Makarios the Great*[181]

"I who am Divine am truly in you. I can never be sundered from you; however far we be parted never can we be separated. I am in you and you are in me, we could not be any closer. We two are fused into one, poured into a single mould. Thus, unwearied, we shall remain forever." —*Mechtild of Magdeburg*[182]

"God takes such delight in the human person that Divinity sings this song to our soul: O lovely rose on the thorn, O hovering bee in the honey, O pure dove in your being, O glorious sun in your setting, O full moon in your course, from you your God will never turn away." —*Mechtild of Magdeburg*[183]

"If you seek after God with all your heart and all your strength, then the virtues of your soul and body will turn you into a mirror of the image of God within. You will be so merged in God, and God so merged in you, that each will endlessly repose in the other." —*Niketas Stethatos*[184]

"What is your boundless mercy, Savior? How have you deigned to make me a member of your body, me, the impure, the prodigal, the

prostitute? How have you clothed me with the brilliant garment, vivid with the splendor of immortality, which changes all my members into light? For your body, your immaculate body divine is all vivid with the fire of your divinity to which it is ineffably mingled and united; and this is the favor that you have bestowed upon me also, my God."
—*St. Symeon the New Theologian*[185]

"I see the beauty, I consider the brightness, I reflect the light of your grace, and I contemplate with amazement this inexpressive splendor, and I am beyond myself thinking what I was, what I have become— O marvel! I am attentive, I experience within me a respect, a reverence, a fear, as if in your presence, and I do not know what to do, having become all timid; where to sit down, whom to approach, and where to place these members which are yours." —*St. Symeon the New Theologian*[186]

"He heard my cry. From unimaginable heights, he leaned over and saw me. He had pity on me and again he who is invisible to all made me worthy to see him as far as it is possible for man to see him. On seeing him, I was struck with awe, as I sat locked into my house and enclosed in my jar, in the midst of so much darkness, I mean between Heaven and earth. . . . I saw him again inside my house, inside my jar. He was suddenly completely there, united with me in an ineffable manner, joined to me in an unspeakable way and immersed in me without mixing as the fire melds one with iron, and the light with the crystal. And he made me as though I were all fire. And he showed me myself as light." —*St. Symeon the New Theologian*[187]

"What seeks to be effected is more than a simple union; it is a transformation." —*Teilhard de Chardin*[188]

"Hitherto, Lord, my attitude toward your gifts has been that of a man who, feeling that he is not alone, tries to distinguish what influence is acting upon him in the darkness. Now that I have found the transparent consistence in which we are all held, I realize that the mystical effort to see must give way to the effort to feel and to surrender myself. This is the phase of communion. . . ." —*Teilhard de Chardin*[189]

"The perception of God present in all things presupposed in the mystic an intense zest for *the Real*. A little later, adherence to God active in all things forced him to develop as wide a consciousness as possible, *again of the Real*. And now that he is making his way farther into the immanent God, he is tied, as a person, to an unremitting *fulfillment*, once again, of *the Real*." —*Teilhard de Chardin*[190]

"One can say no more than the spirit is made one with God. God has desired to be so joined with the creature. Just as those who are married cannot be separated, God doesn't want to be separated from the soul." —*Teresa of Avila*[191]

"But spiritual marriage is like rain falling from heaven into a river or stream, becoming one and the same liquid, so that the river and rainwater cannot be divided; or it resembles a streamlet flowing into the ocean, which cannot afterwards be disunited from it. This marriage may also be likened to a room into which a bright light enters through two windows—though divided when it enters, the light becomes one and the same." —*Teresa of Avila*[192]

WHAT THE MYSTICS SAY ABOUT UNION AND ACTION

"It is not enough to know God's Word: one must also practice it in a living, active manner. Many think that theology is a mere science or rhetoric, whereas it is living experience and practice." —*Johann Arndt*[193]

"The soul is made into a temple of God, into a seat of wisdom, into a dwelling place of chastity, into a receiver of the covenant, into a tabernacle of holiness, into a chamber of the bridegroom, into a spiritual heaven, into a blessed land, into a house of mysteries, into a dear bride, into a dear garden, into a room and chamber of the marriage, and into a Paradise garden sweet-smelling and strewn with many beautiful flowers of virtue to which the Lord of all angels and the King of honor goes, so that he might marry the deeply beloved bride who is sick with love, adorn her with the flower of holy desire, bedeck her with the apples of virtue, and wait upon his dearly beloved when he comes in his adornment." —*Johann Arndt*[194]

"A person who does not bestow on others spiritual things and the joy that is in them has in fact never been spiritual. People are not to receive and keep gifts for themselves alone, but should share themselves and pour forth everything they possess whether in their bodies or their souls as much as possible." —*Meister Eckhart*[195]

"A person works in a stable. That person has a Breakthrough. What does he do? He returns to work in the stable." —*Meister Eckhart*[196]

"Just as I can do almost nothing without God, so too God can accomplish nothing apart from me." —*Meister Eckhart*[197]

"We are fellow-helpers with God, co-creators in everything we do. When Word and work are returned to their source and origin then all work is accomplished divinely in God. And there too the soul loses itself in a wonderful enchantment." —*Meister Eckhart*[198]

"If a person were in a rapture . . . and learned that her neighbor were in need of a cup of soup, it would be best to withdraw from the rapture and give the person the soup she needs." —*Meister Eckhart*[199]

"Do you wish to pray? Then banish the things of this world. Have heaven for your homeland and live there constantly—not in mere word but in actions that imitate the angels and in a more godlike knowledge." —*Evagrius Ponticus*[200]

"God be praised in his handiwork: humankind. And so, humankind full of all creative possibilities, is God's work. Humankind alone is called to assist God." —*Hildegard of Bingen*[201]

"Be not lax in celebrating. Be not lazy in the festive service of God. Be ablaze with enthusiasm. Let us be an alive, burning offering before the altar of God!" —*Hildegard of Bingen*[202]

"The air, with its penetrating strength, characterizes the victorious banner that is trust. It gives light to the fire's flame and sprinkles the imagination of believers with the dew of hope. Thus does trust show the way. Those who breathe this dew long for heavenly things. They carry within refreshing, fulfilling, greening love, with which they hasten to the aid of all. With the passion of heavenly yearning, they produce rich fruit." —*Hildegard of Bingen*[203]

"Spiritual directors should explain how one act done in charity is more precious in God's sight than all these visions and communications." —*John of the Cross*[204]

"Our soul has two duties: first, that we reverently marvel, the other that we suffer meekly, all the time enjoying God. We often fail to see God, and frequently we fall into ourselves, and then we find no feeling of rightness. . . . We are pained and buffeted by our sense of sin, suffering in both spirit and body in this life. But our good Lord the Holy Ghost, who is endless life dwelling in our soul, keeps us safe, and works in us peace, brings it forth easily by grace, making it flexible and pleasing to God." —*Julian of Norwich*[205]

"One who has found and possesses within himself the heavenly treasure of the Spirit fulfills all the commands justly and practices all the virtues without blame, purely without forcing and with a certain ease." —*Makarios the Great*[206]

"The soul from which the veil of darkness has been removed by the power of the Holy Spirit and whose spiritual eyes have been enlightened by the heavenly light and whose soul has been perfectly set free from the passions of shame and has been made pure through grace, how much more does this soul serve the Lord completely in Heaven in the Spirit and serve him completely in the body. Such a person finds himself so expanded in consciousness as to be everywhere, where and when he wishes to serve Christ." —*Makarios the Great*[207]

"As soon as the soul begins to grow, the dust of sin falls away and the soul becomes a god with God. Then, what God wills the soul wills. Otherwise, God and soul would not be united in so beautiful a union." —*Mechtild of Magdeburg*[208]

"When are we like God? I will tell you. In so far as we love compassion and practice it steadfastly, to that extent do we resemble the heavenly Creator who practices these things ceaselessly in us." —*Mechtild of Magdeburg*[209]

"Half of our good works and virtuous acts is a gift from God. Half belongs to ourselves." —*Mechtild of Magdeburg*[210]

"Heal the broken with comforting words of God. Cheer them gently with earthly joys. Be merry and laugh with the broken and carry their secret needs in the deepest silence of your heart." —*Mechtild of Magdeburg*[211]

"The essence of spiritual love is to do good to others, not for the sake of self, but for their sake. Infinitely more is this the essence of Divine love. It is like the love of parents for their children, in that they do them good from love to them, not for the sake of themselves, but for their sakes." —*Emanuel Swedenborg*[212]

"I pray you, divine milieu, already decked with the spoils of quantity and space, show yourself to me as the focus of all energies; and that you may do so, make yourself known to me in your true essence, which is Creative Action. . . ." —*Teilhard de Chardin*[213]

"Radiant Word, blazing Power, you who mould the manifold so as to breathe your life into it; I pray you, lay on us those your hands . . . which plunge into the depths and the totality, present and past, of things so as to reach us simultaneously through all that is most immense and most inward within us and around us. May the might of those invincible hands direct and transfigure for the great world you have in mind that earthly travail which I have gathered into my heart and now offer you in its entirety. Remould it, rectify it, recast it down to the depths from whence it springs." —*Teilhard de Chardin*[214]

"It seems clear to me that in some way we must unite our wills with God's will. But it is in the effects and deeds following afterwards that one discerns the true value of prayer. There is no better crucible for testing prayer than compassion." —*Teresa of Avila*[215]

"We cannot know whether we love God although there may be strong reasons for thinking so, but there can be no doubt about whether we love our neighbor or no. Be sure that in proportion as you advance in fraternal charity, you are increasing in your love of God, for his

Majesty bears so tender an affection for us that I cannot doubt he will repay our love for others by augmenting, in a thousand different ways, that which we bear for him." —*Teresa of Avila*[216]

"When we fail to love our neighbor we are lost. May it please the Lord that this will never be so. For if you do not fail, I tell you that you shall receive from God the Union that God promised. When you see yourselves lacking in this love, even though you have devotion and gratifying experiences that make you think you have reached this stage, and you experience some suspension in the prayer of quiet, believe me, you have not reached Union." —*Teresa of Avila*[217]

"An all-embracing and intense longing for God binds those who experience it both to God and to one another." —*St. Thalassios the Libyan*[218]

"I saw a mass of matter of a dull gloomy color, between the South and the East, and was informed that this mass was human beings, in as great misery as they could be, and live; and that I was mixed in with them, and henceforth I might not consider myself as a distinct or separate being." —*John Woolman*[219]

ABOUT THE MYSTICS CITED

Patristic and Orthodox Mystics

Basil the Great (330–379) was bishop of Caesarea Mazaca in Cappadocia. A monastic, he was involved in the Nicene controversy and was famous in his own day for his work with the poor.

Climacus, John (seventh century) was a monk at Mt. Sinai. His name means "John of the Ladder," referring to his book *Ladder of Divine Ascent,* one of the earliest books on Christian mysticism.

Diadochos of Photiki (fifth century) was a Greek ascetic and writer whose book *On the Contemplative Life* had a great influence in the Christian East. His writings are included in the *Philokalia.*

Egyptian Fathers (third century), also known as the Desert Fathers and Mothers, were among the earliest of the Christian ascetics, and the beginning of Christian monasticism.

Evagrius Ponticus (345–399), also known as Evagrius of Pontus or Evagrius the Solitary, was a monk and ascetic in Jerusalem. A very gifted man, he struggled with pride but ultimately influenced many in the Christian tradition.

Gregory of Nazianzus (329–390), also known as Gregory the Theologian, was the Archbishop of Constantinople. A great advocate for the doctrine of the Trinity, he brought Greek sophistication and learning to the Byzantine Church.

Hesychios the Priest (dates unknown) was a priest and monk at Mt. Sinai. Little is known about his life, but his writings are included in the *Philokalia.*

Iranaeus of Lyons (second century) was a bishop in Gaul (modern-day France), one of the earliest theologians of the church. He wrote extensively against various heresies.

John of Apamea (sixth century), also known as John the Solitary, was a hermit in Syria and author of "Dialogue on the Soul."

John of Karpathos (seventh century) was a Greek monk who participated in the sixth Oecumenical Synod. He is best known for his *Consolations to the Monks in India.*

Makarios the Great (fourth century) was an Egyptian smuggler who fled to the desert to escape charges of fornication. There he met Anthony the Great and was converted to monastic life. He was briefly banished by the Emperor Valens over the Nicene controversy.

Maximos the Confessor (seventh century) was a Byzantine monk and theologian. Due to Christological disputes, he was tortured and exiled. He wrote the earliest biography of Mary, the mother of Jesus.

Sahdona the Syrian (seventh century) was a Persian monk, cast out of the Nestorian church because of his doctrine of Christ. He is remembered for his *Book of Perfection.*

Stethatos, Niketas (eleventh century) was an ascetic near Constantinople, a student of St. Symeon the New Theologian. He was an advocate of hesychastic prayer.

Symeon the New Theologian (eleventh century) was a Byzantine monk and abbot of a monastery near Constantinople. He is known for his writings on mysticism and hesychastic prayer.

Thalassios the Libyan (seventh century) was a monk in the Libyan desert and friend of Maximos the Confessor. His writings are included in the *Philokalia*.

Theodoros the Great Ascetic (ninth century), also known as Theodore of Edessa, was a Syrian monk who later became bishop of Edessa. He is known for converting and baptizing the Muslim king Mauwid. His writings are preserved in the *Philokalia*.

Roman Catholic Mystics

Angela of Foligno (1248–1309) was an Italian mystic, converted after she saw a vision of St. Francis. She became a Third Order Franciscan and founded an order of Third Order sisters that were not cloistered. She is the author of the *Book of Visions and Instructions*.

Augustine of Hippo (354–430) was a philosopher, theologian, and bishop. Heavily influenced by neo-Platonism and Manichaeism, he is the single most important theological influence on Western Christianity. (His influence on the Eastern Church is negligible.)

Baker, Augustine (1575–1641) was an English Benedictine priest. Although he was raised Anglican, his family was secretly Roman Catholic. After some years of agnosticism, he formally joined the Roman Church and entered the Benedictine Order. He is best known for his mystical writings, collected posthumously.

Catherine of Genoa (1447–1510) was an Italian laywoman and mystic. Forced into a loveless marriage, she experienced a profound spiritual awakening when she was twenty-six, and ever after she gave herself tirelessly in service to the poor.

Eckhart, Meister (1260–1327) was a German theologian and mystic, and provincial of the Dominican Order in Saxony. He taught theology at Paris and Cologne, where he was accused of heresy. He was posthumously excommunicated, yet his writings are still cherished and exert profound influence.

Hildegard of Bingen (1098–1179) was a German Abbess and polymath. She excelled at everything she put her hand to, and advanced numerous fields, including theology, spirituality, medicine, and music. She was extraordinarily brave and spoke prophetically and even recklessly to powerful people, often successfully.

Hopkins, Gerard Manly (1844–1889) was a British Jesuit and poet. Born into a devout Anglican family, he was received into Roman Catholicism by Archbishop Newman. A true eccentric, he wasn't a terribly successful pastor or teacher, and he struggled with depression and poor health. His poetry, however, is universally acclaimed for its mystical insight and its startling form.

Hugh of St. Victor (1096–1141) was a French theologian and philosopher who managed to be both innovative and orthodox in his writing. He was both a mystic and a scholar of mysticism.

John of the Cross (1542–1591) was a Spanish Carmelite friar and one of the greatest mystical poets in the Christian tradition. Disillusioned with the laxity of religious orders in his day, he was heavily influenced by Teresa of Avila's reforms. Imprisoned for his reforming efforts, he wrote *The Spiritual Canticle* and other classics of mystical verse. He coined the term "Dark Night of the Soul."

Julian of Norwich (1342–1416) was the first woman to write a book in English. We don't know her actual name, but she was an anchoress and spiritual director at St. Julian's Church in Norwich. During an illness she beheld several visions, which she wrote about extensively. She is perhaps the most important and profound of all the English mystics.

Lucie-Christine (1844–1908), also known as Mathilde Bertrand, was a French laywoman, who enjoyed both a deep mysticism and a fulfilling family life. About the same time she experienced her mystical awakening, her husband began a slide into madness. She experienced much hardship, but much consolation from her faith as well.

Mechtild of Magdeburg (1207–1282/1294) was a German Beguine who had her first mystical vision at the age of twelve. When she published her beautiful and profound *Flowing Light of the Godhead*, she aroused suspicion and threats. She later became a nun in order to avoid persecution by church authorities.

Merton, Thomas (1915–1968) was an American Trappist monk in Kentucky. The author of more than seventy books, Merton is one of the most notable authors of the twentieth century. His writings include memoir, confession, social justice, comparative religion, and mysticism.

Miguel de Molinos (1628–1697) was a Spanish priest whose mysticism (known as "Quietism") emphasized a mystic's direct access to God. This doctrine led him to be persecuted by the Inquisition—partly for political reasons. He died in prison.

Nicholas of Cusa (1401–1464) was a German cardinal and a genius who made contributions in philosophy, theology, law, astronomy, and mathematics. He was also a fearless reformer within the church and was imprisoned for some of his efforts.

About The Mystics Cited

Rahner, Karl (1904–1984) was a German Jesuit, one of the most influential theologians of the twentieth century. His approach was creative, philosophical, and rigorous, earning him enemies amongst conservatives (who were suspicious of what he was *really* getting at) and admirers amongst religious and nonreligious alike who appreciated his talent for bringing Catholic theology into the modern era in a way that was both faithful to tradition and philosophically tenable.

Richard of St. Victor (twelfth century) was a Scotsman who became prior of the Abbey of St. Victor in Paris. His approach to theology was amazingly psychological, and his writings on the practice of contemplation were particularly influential.

Teilhard de Chardin, Pierre (1881–1955) was a French Jesuit, a philosopher, geologist, and paleontologist. One of the discoverers of Peking Man, Teilhard saw the theory of evolution as the hermeneutical key to understanding Christian theology and history—past, present, and future. His deeply mystical perspective has much in common with Process Theology. His work was officially condemned, and he was forbidden to publish during his life. Friends published his work after his death, and he is now much beloved in Roman Catholic circles, enjoying a vigorous cult following amongst Christians of all denominations.

Teresa of Avila (1515–1582) was a Spanish nun and a tireless reformer of the Carmelite order. Frail in health, she spent much time in prayer, and her book *The Interior Castle* is one of the most beloved guides to Christian mysticism ever published. After her death she was canonized as a saint. She was the first woman to be named a Doctor of the Church.

Weil, Simone (1909–1943) was a French philosopher who converted from Judaism to Catholicism. She suffered poor health and an extreme awkwardness in social situations that led others to think her eccentric. She was an ardent socialist, anarchist, and pacifist, and was

230

most well known in her own time for her writings on these themes. She experienced a spiritual awakening in Assisi and was increasingly drawn to mystical prayer.

Protestant Mystics[220]

Arndt, Johann (1555–1621) was a German Lutheran and author. His books were reformed presentations of mystical devotional literature so popular in Catholicism. He was a chief influence on the later Pietist movement.

Boehme, Jacob (1575–1624) was a German Lutheran theologian. As a young man he had a mystical vision that propelled him to study and wrestle with both his faith and philosophy. Although he was undoubtedly sincere in his piety, his work takes many novel and even heretical turns, and he has been very influential in groups on the fringes of the Christian mainstream, such as the Rosicrucians and the Martinists.

Bourignon, Antoinette (1616–1680) was a Flemish laywoman. Born to a Catholic family, she began a correctional institution, from which she had to flee when one of her charges died. She later started a commune, renounced all sectarianism, and proclaimed herself the "new Eve."

Browning, Robert (1812–1889) was an English poet and diplomat. Though Browning was only a nominal Anglican, his poetry is filled with mystical insight, proclaiming an imminent Divinity intimately bound up with earthly affairs.

Fox, George (1624–1691) rejected the Church of England and began instead a Society of Friends (later called "Quakers"). He rejected war and violence and insisted on the equality of all people, including gender equality. He taught that the ultimate authority in Christian life was not scripture or tradition, but the "Inner Light" of Christ.

Herbert, George (1593–1633) was an Anglican priest and a profoundly gifted poet. After a brief stint in Parliament, he spent most of his life as pastor of a small country church, where he was much beloved for his kindness. His poetry is inventive, deeply pious, and inspiring.

Jones, Rufus (1863–1948) was an American Quaker historian, philosopher, and theologian. Helping to found the American Friends Service Committee, he had deep concern for missionaries abroad and their humanitarian work. He was one of the foremost scholars of Christian mysticism.

Kelly, Thomas (1893–1941) was an American Quaker, philosopher, and scholar of mysticism, having been mentored by Rufus Jones. He is best known for his devotional essays, published posthumously.

Kelpius, Johannes (1667–1708) was a German Pietist, musician, and utopian visionary. Born in Transylvania, he came to Pennsylvania in order to set up an ideal Christian society based in part on his reading of the Book of Revelation.

Komensky, John Amos (1592–1670) was a Czech teacher and a Moravian bishop. Heavily influenced by Jacob Boehme, he was given to mystical visions and speculative scriptural interpretation. He was also an ardent proponent of universal education, far ahead of its time.

Laubach, Frank (1884–1970) was an Evangelical missionary, nicknamed "the apostle to the illiterates." Spending much of his time in the Philippines, he worked tirelessly on behalf of the poor, advocating for justice and developing literacy programs. His writings presented a Brother Lawrence-style practice for becoming aware of God's presence.

Law, William (1686–1761) was an Anglican priest, controversial for his "high church" views. Influenced by Jacob Boehme, he wrote about "practical mysticism." The Wesley brothers knew him and were mentored by him, although this was before his mystical tendencies became pronounced.

Luther, Martin (1483–1546) was a fearless reformer who led the German church to sever its ties to the Roman Catholic Church. Luther's primary theological innovation was a doctrine of salvation by grace through faith, and he insisted on the Bible as the sole spiritual authority. He was deeply influenced by the mysticism of the anonymous *Theologia Germanica*.

Martyn, Henry (1781–1812) was an Anglican priest and missionary, much influenced by John Wesley. He was ascetic by nature, and his journal reveals a deep spiritual maturity. An advocate of enculturation, he later travelled to Persia, where he was influenced by the Sufis, whom he called, "the Methodists of the East."

Novalis (1772–1801), also known as Friedrich von Hardenberg, was a pioneer of the German Romantic Movement in poetry and philosophy. He had strong mystical leanings and many of his poems were adapted into Lutheran hymnody.

Poiret, Pierre (1646–1719) was a French Reformed pastor, influenced by Antoinette Bourignon and the *Theologia Germanica*. He decried loyalty to various churches, insisting that a unification of Christendom was possible through a scientific approach to faith.

Singh, Sadhu Sundar (1889–1929) was born into a Sikh family but converted to Anglicanism following a dramatic vision of Jesus. He spent the remainder of his life as a missionary in India and Tibet.

Swedenborg, Emanuel (1688–1772) was the greatest scientist of his day. A Swedish Lutheran, Swedenborg excelled at every science known in his day, working diligently for the Royal Mines. At fifty-three he had a mystical vision that usurped his energies for the rest of his life. In this vision he travelled to heaven and hell; subsequently, he wrote more than thirty volumes that include astral travelogues, conversations with angels, and creative biblical interpretation often reminiscent of C. G. Jung's perspective. After his death, devotees began a Swedenborgian Church, of which there are now two main branches.

Tersteegen, Gerhard (1697–1769) was a German Reformed writer much influenced by Pietism. He translated many mystical texts and contributed some of his own, including his correspondence, sermons, hymns, and poetry.

Thurman, Howard (1899–1981) was a Baptist minister from the American South who served as chaplain at Howard University and Boston University. He was a staunch advocate for nonviolence in the struggle for civil rights, and his writings deeply influenced Martin Luther King, Jr.

Traherne, Thomas (1636–1674) was an Anglican priest and poet. His writing, almost lost to us, but discovered several hundred years after his death, is deeply mystical and betrays a bucolic sublimity and an unusual affection for the natural world.

Underhill, Evelyn (1875–1941) was an English poet, novelist, and scholar. She was deeply mystical Anglo-Catholic, and her study *Mysticism* has been the primary textbook for the serious study of mysticism since its publication in 1911.

Williams, Charles (1886–1945) was a British poet, novelist, and theologian. Earning his bread as an editor for the Oxford University Press,

Williams dabbled in the occult in his early life but became a devout Anglo-Catholic in his maturity. As a member of the Inklings, he was intimate friends with both J. R. R. Tolkien and C. S. Lewis, and had a profound impact on the latter's theology. His seven novels are occult thrillers, gripping treatises on mysticism in their own right.

Woolman, John (1720–1772) was an American Quaker preacher. Through kindness and persuasion, he influenced many fellow Quakers to free their slaves, and he deeply influenced Quaker attitudes on the subject. He recognized the Universal Spirit in Native Americans in his work with them, and his journal conveys a deep love of nature.

Spiritual Practices

Practice Awakening

1. **Remember:** Journal about an Awakening experience you have had. Maybe it was an experience of wonder or spiritual insight. How did it change you? If it scared you, did you run the other way, or did it leave you wanting more? How did it change your ideas about spirituality or about God? Did you do anything differently in your spiritual life after your experience?

2. **Ask yourself truthfully:** Do you want more of this kind of experience? Do you really want to *know* your true nature? Do you really want to know how much of your life is illusion? It's like that moment in the movie *The Matrix* when Morpheus offers Neo the red pill or the blue pill. You can shut this book and go back to your ordinary life and be none the worse for wear. *Or* you can pray for an experience of Awakening, as Julian did—a glimpse of a God-drenched universe in which everything is related and cherished and has its ultimate end in Divinity. But I warn you, if you do, if you really mean it, when your Awakening comes, your world will end. So be careful what you ask for. So if you want an experience—or another experience—like this, ask for it. Pray for such an experience, as Julian did.

3. **Spend some time alone or in church:** Give yourself opportunities to receive such experiences by spending some quiet time alone in nature or in church. Take time to pray and to contemplate what you

see. Awakening experiences often happen when we least expect them, so do not think that you can summon them just by being quiet. But you can *invite* them, and provide space and quiet to hear the voice of the Spirit.

PRACTICE PURGATION

1. *To practice Recollection,* try the same form of meditation that is recommended in *The Way of the Pilgrim*: hesychastic prayer. This practice goes all the way back to the Desert Fathers and Mothers. Sit and let your head hang so that your gaze is directed toward your heart. Carefully control your breath, using a mantra of sorts as you breathe in and out. Traditionally the words are "Lord Jesus Christ, have mercy on me" (or try the long version: "Lord Jesus Christ, Son of the living God, have mercy on me, a sinner"). I encourage you to try this, as it is one of the most ancient and revered prayers in the Christian tradition. Breathing in, say, "Lord Jesus Christ . . . " Breathing out, say, "Have mercy on me."

A similar method for Recollection is Centering Prayer, which has been recently popularized through the ministry of Fr. Thomas Keating and others. To do this form of prayer, pick a sacred word to focus your attention on, like *Jesus*, or *Maranatha* (Aramaic for "Come, Lord") or *Abba* (Aramaic for "Daddy") or *Shalom* (Hebrew for "peace") or any other sacred word or short phrase that has meaning for you. Sit comfortably with your eyes closed and see yourself sitting in the presence of God. Say your sacred word, focusing your attention on it until the mind becomes quiet. There is no need to keep repeating the word once you are enjoying God's presence—just use it as a tool to help you return there when your mind wanders.

Whichever form you choose—hesychastic prayer or Centering Prayer—practice it for fifteen minutes and write a few paragraphs about the experience.

2. *To practice Detachment:* Make a list of the ten things that matter to you most. Ask yourself: What are you willing to let go of? What are you not willing to let go of? Divide this list into two lists: those things you can let go of and those you can't. Pray those two lists, holding both before God, telling him what you can give to him and what you can't. Don't be afraid to ask for help or to tell God how you are feeling.

3. *To practice Mortification:* Give up something you really love for four weeks—it doesn't matter if it is Lent or not. Fast anyway. Remember that it must be something you will miss. Journal about the experience at the end of every week. Take your journal into prayer and share what is happening with God.

PRACTICE ILLUMINATION

1. *Practice the Presence of God.* As Brother Lawrence did, take an hour and do housework—garden, vacuum, fold clothes, do dishes, etc. But the entire time, speak aloud to God your thoughts. Tell him about your fears, your doubts, how stupid it feels to be talking out loud to the air, the things that make you crazy, what you hope for, what you long for in your deepest being. Tell him what you want, how you feel, ask for the things you need and things you want. In other words, just chat. The whole time. For an hour. Then journal about the experience. Do this a couple of times until you begin to feel comfortable with the practice.

2. *Active praying of the Jesus Prayer.* While the Jesus Prayer works well as a form of sitting meditation, it can help us to become aware of God's presence during more active times as well. As you do your daily activities, such as cleaning house or walking the dog, quiet your mind and repeat, "Lord Jesus Christ, have mercy on me," as you breathe in and out. This can be said at any time, during almost any activity (if

driving, be careful not to drift off into a dangerously meditative bliss). You may want to use an Orthodox prayer rope or a rosary to mark the number or repetitions. A spin around the rosary doing the Jesus Prayer a few times a day is a marvelous, active prayer practice.

3. *Get quiet with a friend and by yourself.* Ask a friend to go out into nature with you, and sit together for an hour in silence. Notice how it feels to be sitting with your friend without speaking. Notice how you can feel his or her presence even when you are not looking at him or her. Go for a walk and discuss what you noticed. A day or two later go out again and sit for the same amount of time by yourself. This time, however, focus on the fact that you are sitting with God, and keep your awareness focused on God's presence.

4. *Practice seeing God in All Things.* The Hindus have a wonderful practice: they point to everything they see and recite *Tat Tvam Asi*, which means, "Thou art that." When you are walking down the street, try it. Look at every little thing and say to yourself, "That is you, God." Look at the mailbox, the police car, the mangy cat next door, the shining sun, the dog poop, the bistro on the corner, the laughing child. What this reveals is that there is nothing we can behold, or even conceive of, that is not brimming with God, including us.

5. *Pray for the birth of the Word in your soul.* This is not something that we can accomplish, but only something that God can do *in us*. We can "prepare him room" by Purgation and by the Practice of Quiet, and it is in quiet that this gift is given. Ask for this gift, and expect to receive it in time.

PRACTICE UNION

There's nothing you can do to achieve Union, not without working out the previous stages. You can, however, contemplate that ineffable state and feel your way into it intuitively, to get a sense of what it might be like. These exercises will help you do that.

1. ***Take a walk and imagine that you are God.*** How do you view the things you are seeing? Journal about this when you get home.

2. ***Meditate on marriage.*** What if you and God really *did* get married? What would your vows be? What would *his* vows be? Write them out. Then pray them.

3. ***Do what Jesus told us to do.*** Here is a list of ten things that Jesus told us to do. Try working your way down this list, doing each one, and paying attention to your motivations and feelings as you do them:

- feed the hungry (Matt. 25:35)
- befriend the stranger (Matt. 25:35)
- clothe the naked (Matt. 25:36)
- take care of the sick (Matt. 25:36)
- visit those in prison (Matt. 25:36)
- if someone asks you for your coat, give him your shirt, too (Matt. 5:40)
- do good to others when they do evil toward you (Luke 6:27–28)
- wash each other's feet (John 13:14)
- be whole, as God is whole (Matt. 5:48)
- sell what you have and give the money to the poor (Matt. 19:21)

Imagine that the people you are serving *are* Jesus. (You may get to the point where you realize that this is not your imagination, but that they *actually are*.) Share with a friend about what happened and what you learned.

The Mystic's Journey in Liturgy and Tradition

AWAKENING

The Christian year begins with an Awakening. The Gospel reading for the first Sunday of Advent proclaims a chilling vision: "But in those days, after that suffering, the sun will be darkened, and the moon will not give its light, and the stars will be falling from heaven, and the powers in the heavens will be shaken. Then they will see 'the Son of Man coming in clouds' with great power and glory."[1] It's a momentary vision of glory, a vision of the Son of Man, but it brings with it untellable destruction, the end of the world as we know it.

Advent marks the beginning of our spiritual journey through the year, and it is appropriate that it both shows us a vision of the Real and begins the dismantling of the illusory reality that we have always known. Because we cycle around to this scenario every year, it also points to a cyclic understanding of spiritual growth. Every time we come to this part of the year, we come as changed, different people. Each time we contemplate the world ending, it is a different world. Each time we set out on a path toward God, we hopefully do it with greater depth and with more wisdom.

Awakening also manifests itself liturgically in our first experiences with the church and its traditions. When I first stumbled upon St.

Michael's Episcopal Church in college, I didn't know a kneeler from a thurible. Everything was new, strange, and charged with power, and I was warmed by the genuineness of the community that I found. (Many grateful thanks to my church family at St. George's Episcopal Church in Riverside, where I eventually ended up.) They gave me a glimpse of a different and more glorious world than I had known, and I wanted more of it.

I am not alone in my experience. Many people have stumbled upon a spiritual community and found a whole new reality with different rules, language, and sometimes, it seems, even different laws of physics. This can lead us to greater explorations, to new friends, to a new way of being.

This is one way that conversion happens. The "born again" experiences that so many people talk about are often a result of Awakening experiences that change the trajectory of their lives. Sometimes conversion is sudden; usually it is gradual; sometimes it happens when a person is alone; but it most often comes as a result of contact with a spiritual community whose ways are strange but whose worship radiates the beauty of holiness in such a visceral way that it cannot be ignored or denied.

Purgation

A very biblical image for this process of Purgation is baptism. Baptism is an ancient ritual that symbolizes cleansing—specifically the cleansing of the soul through the symbolic washing of the body. What is washed away might be sin (however we conceive of that), or selfishness, or illusion, or misconceptions, or all that separates us from walking with God the way we desire to.

John baptized for the remission of sins in the Judean desert, and Jesus commanded his disciples to continue this practice. Western Christians since Augustine have seen it as a ritual that removes the stain of original sin.

Augustine saw original sin as something genetic. Orthodox Christians believe that people are born with a clean slate but that they are born into a society that is steeped in sin and teaches it to children from an early age. The source of sin, therefore, is cultural, not genetic.

Orthodox Christians baptize their children, but it is more of a "Welcome to the church" ceremony than a cleansing ceremony. When adults join the church, however, the symbolism comes to life, as the sin of the culture is washed from them and they enter a new and spotless culture, the Kingdom of God in the life of the church. This view of things has a lot of appeal to more liberal Western Christians these days.

With this view, baptism represents the Purgation stage of spiritual growth handsomely. A person has an encounter with the living God (Awakening) that leads him or her to the church. There, he or she begins instruction in holy living and recognizes that a lot of things in life are illusory, superfluous, or just plain not helpful to Christian living and must be let go. Baptism dramatically represents being cleansed from these illusory and unnecessary aspects of life.

The problem is that sin and illusion are chronic conditions, not something you can take a sacramental pill and be done with. It takes constant effort to keep such moral clutter at bay. For this reason, the church, in its wisdom, instituted two periods of reflection and moral examination: the penitential seasons of Advent and Lent.

Advent is focused on Detachment, as is appropriate for a winter season. In Advent we reflect on the fact that Christ is coming and we take a hard look at ourselves to discern what we need to do in order to be ready for his arrival. What in our lives is getting in the way of our intimacy with God? What would we be ashamed to hold before Jesus when he gets here? Baptism and cleansing imagery abound in Advent, and the cleansing of the soul in preparation for the nativity and the second coming is emphasized.

Lent is a more intense penitential season, focused more on Mortification. During Lent we also make a scrupulous moral inventory, but we are invited to actually change our behavior in some dramatic way through the traditional Lenten fast. People are encouraged to give up something that they dearly love for the duration of the season. It would make no sense to swear off broccoli if we never ate broccoli in the first place. But if we really enjoy a good glass of wine with dinner, drinking water instead is a fine practice during Lent.

The Lenten fast is a small thing, usually, but it points to a larger invitation: to change our lives in a tangible, visible way in order to more closely conform to the Vision that has been granted to us during our Awakening.

This is an ongoing process, though, and Advent and Lent come but once a year. But the Christian tradition wants us to have ample opportunity for Purgation, so this stage is forever enshrined in our weekly liturgies. The Mass begins with a confession of sin and an absolution. The first thing that happens to us in our Sunday services, then, is a Purgation.

Roman Catholics have traditionally intensified this purgative process by requiring people to physically go weekly to confession before attending Mass. This practice has lessened since Vatican II, and these days Roman Catholics, like Anglicans, are most likely to go for confession only when they have grievously sinned and want to cleanse their consciences.

Even our devotional prayer practices begin with an examination of conscience and confession. If you have ever prayed Evening Prayer or Compline either at church or at home alone, you may have noticed that it begins by inviting us to review our day and to offer up to God those things we are not proud of in our thoughts, words, and deeds.

ILLUMINATION

Illumination is enshrined in the church calendar in the Feast of the Epiphany, the celebration in which Christ is revealed to the nations. It is a feast that acknowledges that, previously, salvation has been for only a select minority—specifically, the Jewish people. But in the Epiphany event, Gentile wise men recognize the mystery of the Incarnation and offer worship to the Christ child.

This symbolizes the fact that, in Christ, God's salvation has been offered not just to the Jewish people, but to the world. It breaks from a view of the world in which grace is rare and found only in select places into a vision of life as it really is—where grace is abundant and available to all. It is a God-drenched world in which divinity may be recognized on earth, in humanity, everywhere, and available to everyone.

Liturgically, Illumination is represented in the Mass by the Liturgy of the Word, specifically the reading of the scriptures and the preaching of the sermon. Just as the Orthodox cry before the Gospel reading, "Attend to Wisdom!" the scripture and the sermon offer Illumination (or at least the opportunity for Illumination) in every service of Morning or Evening Prayer or Holy Eucharist.

UNION

Union is seen in different ways during the two great feasts of the Christian year, at Christmas and Easter. At Christmas, we celebrate the Incarnation, that particular time in history when God wedded himself to creation for all time by being born human. God entered into creation, becoming one with creation, and made it a part of himself by condescending to dwell in it. In becoming one with nature, God made common cause with nature and all that it suffers—becoming part of it, he likewise became one with strife, illness, and death. In the Incarnation, God committed himself to creation by sharing nature's lot.

But this was no mere act of solidarity or compassion. In becoming human, God became one with death. The fuse was lit. In the Easter event, the powder keg went off and the power of sin and death and hell were destroyed forever. In Jesus's Resurrection, evil was arrested and overcome.

Appendix A

Eastern Orthodox theology emphasizes this point more than Western Christians do. In Orthodox theology, sin and death are evidence of the devolution of the universe into chaos, begun by Adam's sin and passed down through human culture, gaining strength as it goes (like a snowball rolling downhill). In the Resurrection, Jesus halted this devolution and reversed it; now all of creation is evolving into divinity—growing into God.

This is the divinization of the universe, begun by Christ's Resurrection and continued through the work of the church. It will not stop until every person, every creature, every grain of sand is wholly and completely united with God. Easter is the down payment on the mystical purchase of the universe that God is even now bringing about. Your reading this book is part of this process. By growing into God, you are participating in the redemption of creation and the healing of all things. In your own Union, you will go forth to heal as Jesus healed and facilitate even more Union. That is the mystery of redemption, the power of God's love, and the mission of the church: Union.

We celebrate this mystery every week in our worship. The Liturgy of the Table, the Eucharist, the Mass, the Great Thanksgiving, the Lord's Supper—it has many names and many expressions, but the actions are the same: bread is taken, broken, and shared. Wine is poured, blessed, and shared. And in that sharing, a marvelous mystery occurs—the transignified elements mythically become Christ—and we take Christ into us physically, becoming one with him, flesh of his flesh, blood of his blood. In so doing, we become one substance with him, share with him his divinity, his *godness*, and his mission of reconciliation for the world.

Some Christians take this more literally than others. For some it is a magical act in which the elements physically morph into flesh and blood, while for others it is an act of imagination, having no less power. Still others see it as a mystical act that cannot be explained or understood.

For some, this is just an intellectual exercise—they believe that the Eucharist makes them one with God, but they do not experience it. Others feel this union profoundly each time they approach the table, and their desire for the meal manifests in a spiritual hunger that rivals their interest in regular food.[2]

The most visible sign of union with God, however, is our participation in the life of our local congregation. In John's Gospel, Jesus speaks repeatedly of his union with God being the same as his union with us, and our union with one another.[3] If we are all "in God" as the mystics—including John's mystical Jesus—teach us, then of course we are all one with one another, with Christ, and with God by the very fact of our being. Participating in the local church community is a way of celebrating and experiencing that union as we worship together, play together, and work together for the healing of the world.

The Mystic's Journey and Spiritual Development Theory

James Fowler, in his groundbreaking book *Stages of Faith,*[1] sees the spiritual journey as a progression of seven stages. The first, which he calls *Stage Zero: Primal or Undifferentiated* faith, occurs between a person's birth and two years of age and is mostly concerned with an infant's learning to feel secure in his or her environment. A child then proceeds to *Stage One: Intuitive-Projective* faith. Between the ages of three and seven, a child's imagination runs wild, not subject to logic. It is the time when a child learns a culture's taboos and beliefs. In *Stage Two: Mythic-Literal Faith*, children begin to internalize stories and symbols, drawing on them for direction and meaning.

In adolescence, a person usually enters *Stage Three: Synthetic-Conventional* faith. Most people make their home here for life, so, spiritually, this is usually the end of the line. This is the place where one finds one's identity in a larger group—one's spiritual community, in this case. A person usually just accepts the answers and beliefs that are handed out, thinking uncritically about matters of faith—after all, they are matters of *faith* and asking too many questions is often frowned upon.

AWAKENING

Stage Three is usually where people find themselves when an Awakening experience happens. An Awakening breaks into the safe and orderly world, turning it upside down. It challenges all of the easy answers and is often the catalyst for a person to turn from Stage Three toward the questioning and questing of *Stage Four: Individual-Reflective* faith, where we begin to deconstruct the faith as it was handed down, thinking critically about spiritual matters and asking the hard questions.

Stage Four is often a very painful process because it involves a lot of loss as one lets go of long-cherished ideas, sentimental interpretations, and byzantine practices that are no longer helpful.

PURGATION

What is happening here is nothing short of Purgation, as the person who is growing through Stage Four is purging those things that no longer serve, taking responsibility for spiritual life—perhaps for the first time—and jettisoning from it those things that make no sense, are illusory, or actually are a barrier to intimacy with God.

This is also a painful place because the people around us often do not understand what we are going through. Because most people will stay comfortably ensconced in Stage Three, when someone moves into Stage Four, it looks an awful lot like doubt or backsliding or even apostasy. Loved ones don't understand that it is, in fact, a form of faithfulness; but often the person going through it doesn't understand that yet, either.

This is often a very lonely and scary time, and a person going through this Stage would do well to read Fowler's book on this stage, as it will help normalize the experience and make him or her feel less alone. Also, the services of a qualified spiritual director are invaluable during this time, as a good director will be a faithful companion through this wild and forbidding territory of the soul.

ILLUMINATION

While Stage Four is a period of deconstruction and disillusionment, *Stage Five: Conjunctive* faith, is a period of re-enchantment and re-sacralization. In Stage Five, the seeker recognizes the paradoxes inherent in spirituality and is delighted and embracing of them (whereas the Stage Three reaction to these is usually discomfort and denial).

Whereas in Stage Four a person goes on an iconoclastic rampage, tearing down everything that was once held sacred, in Stage Five one dusts that same stuff off and props it back up. However, one's relationship to it has changed. The Stage Five person recognizes that the elements of his or her faith are not literal realities but symbols and metaphors that point to a deeper, ineffable reality beyond the culture-bound elements of one particular religious tradition. As Meister Eckhart puts it, "In my flowing-out I entered creation, in my Breakthrough I re-enter God. Only those who have dared to let go can dare to re-enter."[2]

Stage Five people will return to the images, stories, rituals, and prayers of their former traditions but will see these things in a completely different way. Instead of ends in themselves—a proprietary faith that is the sole possession of one particular sect or nation—they will recognize their faith as a feeble attempt to approach a divine reality that is the inheritance of all peoples, of every faith, in every place.

For Stage Five people, the world is re-sacralized, brimming with Divinity that cannot be contained by ethnicity or borders or creed. This is a giddy stage because of the enormity of the sky that opens up for the seeker. The vision of the God-drunk universe is so vast that the mind reels and struggles to assimilate it. The Stage Five person opens his or her heart to the wideness of Divinity only to find the very next day that the actual magnitude of that wideness is a hundredfold what he or she thought just the day before. It is a delirious encounter with infinity and with infinite grace.

Appendix B

UNION

While in Fowler's Stage Five, people may glimpse—and even briefly experience—Union, but those who move into *Stage Six: Universalizing* faith pass a point of no return that utterly transforms them. A Stage Five person may see where all this is leading, intellectually, but will still hold back due to vestiges of selfishness or a reflex toward self-preservation. But once one enters into Stage Six, all caution is thrown to the wind. For Stage Six people, there is no distinction between Creator and creation, between self and other, between heaven and earth. There is no limit to the sacrifice Stage Six people are willing to make on behalf of others. Stage Six people may practice a particular tradition, but are likely to honor all tried-and-true spiritual paths as valuable roads to divinity. More than this, however, they spend themselves in the service of others, becoming activists for their unitive vision, tirelessly working to alleviate suffering and to raise people's consciousness of divine things.

COMPARISON OF MYSTICAL STAGES WITH FOWLER

Christian Mysticism	Fowler's Faith Stages
3. UNION	Stage 6: Universalizing Faith
2. ILLUMINATION	Stage 5: Conjunctive Faith
1. PURGATION	Stage 4: Individual-Reflective Faith
0. AWAKENING	Stage 4: Individual-Reflective Faith
	Stage 3: Synthetic-Conventional Faith
	Stage 2: Mythic-Literal Faith
	Stage 1: Intuitive-Reflective Faith
	Stage 0: Primal or Undifferentiated Faith

References

Opening *epigraph*: John Anthony McGuckin, *The Book of Mystical Chapters* (Boston: Shambhala, 2003), 96.

Introduction

Epigraph: Adapted from David O'Neal, ed., *Meister Eckhart, from Whom God Hid Nothing* (Boston: Shambhala, 1996), 93.

1. Adapted from Julian of Norwich, chap. X in *Revelations of Divine Love*, trans. Grace Warrack, http://www.ccel.org/ccel/julian/revelations.html (originally published 1901).
2. Quoted in Evelyn Underhill, *The Mystics of the Church* (NY: Shocken, 1964), 236.
3. Harvey Egan, SJ, *An Anthology of Christian Mysticism* (Collegeville, MN: Pueblo/Liturgical Press, 1991), 300.
4. Matthew Fox, ed., *Meditations with Meister Eckhart* (Santa Fe: Bear & Co., 1983), 45.
5. Egan, *Anthology of Christian Mysticism*, 298.
6. Quoted in Gabriele Uhlein, ed., *Meditations with Hildegard of Bingen* (Santa Fe: Bear & Co., 1983), 72.
7. Adapted from Norwich, chap. XLI in *Revelations*.
8. Bernard McGinn, ed., *The Essential Writings of Christian Mysticism* (NY: Modern Library, 2006), 12.
9. For more on alternative ways of viewing the process, see pages 117–20.

Chapter One

1. Hal Bridges, *American Mysticism* (NY: Harper & Row, 1970), 26–27.
2. Adapted from Norwich, chap. XLVI in *Revelations* (see intro., n. 1).
3. Ibid., chap. XXXVI.
4. Ibid., chap. XXXIII.

5. Ibid., chap. XVIII.

6. Ibid., chap. XI.

7. Brendan Doyle, *Meditations with Julian of Norwich* (Santa Fe: Bear & Co., 1983), 48.

8. Norwich, chap. XXVII in *Revelations*.

9. Clifton Wolters, ed., *Revelations of Divine Love* (NY: Penguin Books, 1966), 169.

10. Ibid., 170.

11. Ibid., 173.

12. Ibid., 68.

Chapter Two

1. Evelyn Underhill, *Mysticism: A Study in the Nature and Development of Spiritual Consciousness,* 12th ed. (London: E. P. Dutton, 1930), 212–13.

2. McGuckin, *Book of Mystical Chapters*, 32–33 (see opening epigraph).

3. Helen Bacovcin, trans., *The Way of a Pilgrim* (NY: Image, 1992), 18.

4. Ibid., 19.

5. Ibid., 24.

6. Luke 3:16.

7. O'Neal, *Meister Eckhart*, 35 (see intro, *epigraph*).

8. James Francis Yockey, ed., *Meditations with Nicholas of Cusa* (Santa Fe: Bear & Co., 1987), 63.

9. McGuckin, *Book of Mystical Chapters*, 39.

10. Luke 10:4, 8.

Chapter Three

1. My gratitude to Bishop Michael Milner for his assistance with this section.

Chapter Four

1. Alan Watts, *Behold the Spirit: A Study in the Necessity of Mystical Religion* (NY: Dutton, 1948), 82.

2. Timothy F. Lull, ed., *Martin Luther's Basic Theological Writings* (Minneapolis: Fortress Press, 1989), 322.

3. Psalm 62:1.

4. Norwich, chap. XXVII in *Revelations* (see intro., n. 1).

References

5. Friends' meetings do have an elected "clerk" and often several commit-
   tees, each of whom have some measure of power, but—among unpro-
   grammed meetings, at least—nothing analogous to other denominations'
   pastors or bishops.
6. Luke 2:29–32.
7. Acts 17:28.
8. Sue Woodruff, *Meditations with Mechtild of Magdeburg* (Santa Fe: Bear &
   Co., 1982), 42.
9. Egan, *Anthology of Christian Mysticism*, 298 (see intro., n. 3).
10. Fox, *Meditations with Meister Eckhart*, 21 (see intro., n. 4).
11. Ibid., 40, 44.
12. Ibid., 52.
13. Ibid., 46, 45.

Chapter Five
1. I'm grateful to my training at the Mercy Center, Burlingame, CA, for this
   idea.
2. A fine film depicting this event is *God on Trial*, directed by Andy de
   Emmony. The event may have been witnessed by a young Elie Weisel,
   who reset it in another time period in his play *The Trial of God*.
3. Job 2:9.
4. Thomas Merton, *The Thomas Merton Reader* (NY: Doubleday Image,
   1974), 402.
5. Unfortunately, I have not been able to locate a source for this quote. If
   you know it, please contact me at apocryphile@me.com.
6. Adapted from Underhill, *Mysticism*, 12, 55 (see chap. 2, n. 1).

Chapter Six
1. Augustine of Hippo, *Confessions*, X: 6.
2. Charles Upton, ed. and trans., *Doorkeeper of the Heart: Versions of Rabia*
   (Putney, VT: Threshold Books, 1988).
3. Underhill, *Mysticism*, 502 (see chap. 2, n. 1).
4. Matthew 27:46.
5. Apostles' Creed.

References

6. John of the Cross, "Living Flame of Love," from *The Collected Works of John of the Cross*, trans. Kieran Kavanaugh (Mawah, NJ: Paulist Press, 1987), ii.10.
7. Camille Campbell, *Meditations with Teresa of Avila* (Santa Fe: Bear & Co., 1985), 135.

Conclusion
Epigraph: Doyle, *Julian of Norwich*, 36 (see chap. 1, n. 7).
1. Campbell, *Teresa of Avila*, 140 (see chap. 6, n. 7).
2. For an introduction to Fox's work, I recommend *Original Blessing* (Santa Fe: Bear & Co., 1982) or *Creation Spirituality* (HarperSanFrancisco, 1991).

Questions and Answers
1. http://dictionary.reference.com/browse/mystic.
2. John R. Mabry, *Faith Styles: Ways People Believe* (Harrisburg: Morehouse Publishing, 2006).
3. Quoted in Underhill, *Mystics of the Church*, 231–32 (see intro., n. 2).
4. Quoted in McGinn, *Essential Writings*, 277 (see intro., n. 7).
5. Pierre Teilhard de Chardin, trans. René Hague, *Writings in Time of War* (San Francisco: Harper & Row, 1968), 134.
6. A certificate program in interfaith spiritual direction at the Chaplaincy Institute for Arts and Interfaith Ministry (www.chaplaincyinstitute.org).
7. An accredited master's degree program in interfaith spiritual guidance at the Institute of Transpersonal Psychology (www.itp.edu).
8. Matthew 18:21.
9. Luke 5:8.
10. Quoted in Underhill, *Mystics of the Church*, 218.
11. This has some resonance with the Dynamic Ground theory of transpersonal psychology put forth by Michael Washburn mentioned in the last chapter.
12. www.pelagia.org/htm/b24.en.life_after_death.07.htm.
13. Thank you, Jeremy Taylor.
14. M. Scott Peck, *The Road Less Travelled* (NY: Touchstone, 1998), 15.
15. Karl Rahner, *Encounters with Silence*, trans. James M. Demske, SJ (Westminster, MD: Newman, 1966), 8.

References

16. Thank you, Friedrich Nietzsche.

17. Luke 12:34.

18. Thomas Merton, *New Seeds of Contemplation* (NY: New Directions, 1961), 1–2.

19. See Astrid O'Brien, "Lucie Christine: Nineteenth-Century Wife, Mother, and Mystic," in Paula Jean Miller, FSE, and Richard Fossey, *Mapping the Catholic Cultural Landscape* (Oxford: Rowman & Littlefield, 2004), 145–53.

20. Fox, *Meditations with Meister Eckhart*, 90 (see intro., n. 4).

21. Charles Williams, *Religion and Love in Dante* (London: Robert Maclehose, 1930), 40.

22. McGuckin, *Book of Mystical Chapters*, 102 (see opening epigraph).

23. O'Neal, *Meister Eckhart*, 107–8 (see intro., epigraph).

24. David A. Sylvester, *Recovering the* Via Purgativa: *How the 12-Step Program Revives the Christian Tradition of Spiritual Formation* (Berkeley, CA: Jesuit School of Theology, 2009). Unpublished Master of Theological Studies' thesis. Available at http://appliedspirit.wordpress.com/ and http://davidasylvester.wordpress.com/. David describes his research this way: "The 12-Step program does focus on a kind of moral and spiritual self-examination and purification that is similar to practices in the *Via Purgativa*, the first stage of the mystical search for union with God. But the 12-Steps don't go far enough or deep enough. The ultimate spiritual focus of the 12-Steps is on recovery, not on union with God—and this is a crucial difference, because it's too easy to get stuck in the 12-Steps focusing on life in this world rather than on transcendent life. The 12-Steps approach may give the impression that God is the means by which we get a better life on earth rather than recognize that our life on this earth is the means by which we can forge a better relationship with God. This journey to God depends on the next two stages of the mystical path, the *Via Illuminativa* and *Via Unitiva*. These are the next two stages of enlightenment and union with their painful dark nights of the senses and the soul. For the Christian, progress along these would not be possible without the living presence of Jesus."

25. I'm grateful to my friend John C. Robinson for suggesting this point and even some of this language.

26. I am grateful to my friend and colleague Bishop Michael Milner for suggesting this possibility.

27. M. Scott Peck, *The Different Drum: Community Making and Peace* (NY: Touchstone, 1998).

28. Gerard Manley Hopkins, "God's Grandeur," in the *Norton Anthology of English Literature*, vol. 2 (NY: Norton and Co., 1986), 1581.

29. Baruch Spinoza, *The Chief Works of Benedict de Spinoza*, vol.2; revised ed., trans. R. H. M. Elwes (London: George Bell and Sons, 1901), "Letter 60 to Hugo Boxel" (1674), 387.

30. Emanuel Swedenborg, *A Compendium of the Theological Writings of Emanuel Swedenborg*, ed. Samuel M. Warren (NY: Swedenborg Foundation, Inc., 1875), 80.

31. William Blake, "The Divine Image," in the *Norton Anthology*, 35.

32. See Richard D. Patterson, "Metaphors of Marriage as Expressions of Divine-Human Relations," *Journal of the Evangelical Theological Society* 51, no. 4 (December 2008), 689–702.

33. Isaiah 54:5, 6–7.

34. Jeremiah 2:2–3.

35. Ezekiel 16:1–14.

36. Ephesians 5:25–27; Rev 21:2, 9.

37. Matthew 25.

38. George A. Maloney, SJ, trans., *Psuedo-Macarius: The Fifty Spiritual Homilies and the Great Letter* (Mahwah, NJ: Paulist Press, 1992), 145.

39. Luther, for instance, referred to both *deus revelatus* and *deus absconditus*. I am grateful to my friend Dr. Martha Stortz for this insight.

40. McGuckin, *Book of Mystical Chapters*, 48.

41. 1 John 1:8.

42. Woodruff, *Mechtild of Magdeburg*, 121 (see chap. 4, n. 8).

The Mystics, in Their Own Words

1. O'Neal, *Meister Eckhart*, 4 (see intro., epigraph).

2. George Fox, *An Autobiography* (London: Edward Marsh, 1850), 92–93.

3. Quoted in Underhill, *Mystics of the Church*, 225 (see intro., n. 2).

4. Anne Fremantle, ed., *The Protestant Mystics* (Boston, MA: Little, Brown and Co., 1964), 51–52.

References

5. Woodruff, *Mechtild of Magdeburg*, 113 (see chap. 4, n. 8).

6. Thomas Merton, *Asian Journal* (NY: New Directions Publishing, 1975), 308.

7. Yockey, *Meditations with Nicholas of Cusa*, 33 (see chap. 2, n. 8).

8. Rahner, *Encounters*, 9 (see Questions and Answers, n. 15).

9. Karl Rahner, *The Practice of Faith* (NY: Crossroad, 1983), 84.

10. Underhill, *Mystics*, 253 (see intro., n. 2).

11. George A. Maloney, SJ, trans., *Hymns of Divine Love by St. Symeon the New Theologian* (Denville, NJ: Dimension Books, 1976), 17.

12. Teresa of Avila, *The Interior Castle*, ed. Benedict Zimmerman (London: Thomas Baker, 1921), II:1:5.

13. Evelyn Underhill, *Mysticism: A Study in the Nature and Development of Spiritual Consciousness* (NY: E.P. Dutton, 1911), 197.

14. Augustine Baker, "Holy Wisdom," Treatise ii., Sect. i., cap. 3, quoted in Underhill, *Mysticism*, 218.

15. Hartmann, "Life and Doctrines of Jacob Boehme," p. 50, quoted in Underhill, *Mysticism*, 226–27.

16. "An Apology for Mrs. Antoinette Bourignan," pp. 269–70, quoted in Underhill, *Mysticism*, 212–13.

17. "Vitae Dottrina di Santa Caterina da Genova" cap. ii, quoted in Underhill, *Mysticism*, 182.

18. "Trattato di Purgatonio," caps. ii and iii, quoted in Underhill, *Mysticism*, 202–203.

19. Archimandrite Lazarus Moore, trans., *St. John Climacus: The Ladder of Divine Ascent* (NY: Harper Bros, 1959), 108.

20. Ibid., 130.

21. Ibid., 115.

22. O'Neal, *Meister Eckhart*, 113.

23. Fox, *Autobiography*, 71.

24. *Evagrius Ponticus*, 65.

25. Ibid., 66–67.

26. Ibid., 79.

27. Ibid., 79.

28. George Fox, *A Journal* (London: Richardson and Clark, 1765), 8.

References

29. G. E. H. Palmer, Philip Sherrard, and Kallistos Ware, eds. *Essential Writings, The Philokalia: Volume I* (London: Faber & Faber, 1983), 183.

30. Ibid., 194–95.

31. McGuckin, *Book of Mystical Chapters*, 21 (see opening epigraph).

32. John of the Cross, *Ascent of Mt. Carmel* (NY: Image Books, 1962), XV.5.

33. Camille Campbell, *Meditations with John of the Cross* (Santa Fe: Bear & Co., 1989), 15.

34. "Subida del Monte Carmelo" l.i.cap.iii., quoted in Underhill, *Mysticism*, 211.

35. McGuckin, *Book of Mystical Chapters*, 120.

36. Doyle, *Meditations with Julian of Norwich*, 49 (see chap. 1, n. 7).

37. Ibid., 26.

38. Palmer, Sherrard, and Ware, *Philokalia II*, 53.

39. Ibid., 63.

40. Ibid., 107.

41. Ibid., 107.

42. Ibid., 120.

43. Woodruff, *Mechtild of Magdeburg*, 112 (see chap. 4, n. 8).

44. Ibid., 71.

45. Merton, *New Seeds*, 34–35 (see Questions and Answers, n. 18).

46. Thomas Merton, *Conjectures of a Guilty Bystander* (NY: Doubleday, 1966), 224.

47. Ibid., 158.

48. Yockey, *Meditations with Nicholas of Cusa*, 37.

49. Underhill, *Mysticism*, 204.

50. McGuckin, *Book of Mystical Chapters*, 77.

51. Palmer, Sherrard, and Ware, *Philokalia IV*, 150; quoting Ephesians 4:13.

52. Adapted from Swedenborg, *Theological Writings*, 181 (see Questions and Answers, n. 30).

53. Teilhard de Chardin, *Writings*, 135 (see Questions and Answers, n. 5).

54. Ibid., 144.

55. Pierre Teilhard de Chardin, trans. Gerald Vann, OP, *Hymn of the Universe* (NY: Harper and Row, 1965), 14.

56. Ibid., 20.

57. Teresa of Avila, *Interior Castle* I:1:10.

58. Campbell, *Teresa of Avila*, 44 (see chap. 6, n. 7).

59. Ibid., 45.

60. Ibid., 54.

61. Teresa of Avila, *Interior Castle* I:2:10.

62. Palmer, Sherrard, and Ware, *Philokalia II*, 21; quoting 1 Timothy 6:10.

63. Underhill, *Mysticism*, 199.

64. Ibid., 204.

65. Ibid., 207.

66. Ibid., 208–10.

67. Simone Weil, *Waiting for God*, trans. Emma Craufurd (NY: G. P. Putnam & Sons, 1951), 29.

68. McGinn, *Essential Writings*, 127 (see intro. n. 7).

69. Campbell, *John of the Cross*, 74.

70. Ibid., 76.

71. Ibid., 12, 42.

72. Ibid., 77.

73. Ibid., 44.

74. Palmer, Sherrard, and Ware, *Philokalia II,* 315.

75. Adapted from Norwich, *Revelations*, LXVIII.7 (see intro., n. 1).

76. Ibid., LXXXIII.

77. Fremantle, *Protestant Mystics*, 124.

78. Maloney, *Psuedo-Macarius*, 195 (see Questions and Answers, n. 38).

79. Campbell, *Teresa of Avila*, 47 (see chap. 6, n. 7).

80. Quoted in Underhill, *Mystisicm*, 252.

81. Johann Arndt, *True Christianity*, trans. Peter Erb (Mahwah, NJ: Paulist Press, 1978), 45.

82. I Aug. Conf., bk. iii. cap. 6, quoted in Underhill, *Mysticism*, 250.

83. "Saul," xvii, quoted in Underhill, *Mysticism*, 255.

84. Palmer, Sherrard, and Ware, *Philokalia I*, 275.

85. Fox, *Meditations with Meister Eckhart*, 14 (see intro., n. 4).

86. Ibid., 14.

87. O'Neal, *Meister Eckhart*, 4–5.

88. Fox, *Meditations with Meister Eckhart*, 23.

89. *Evagrius Ponticus,* 66.

90. Ibid., 33–34.

References

91. Ibid., 63.

92. Ibid., 68.

93. Palmer, Sherrard, and Ware, *Philokalia I*, 47.

94. McGuckin, *Book of Mystical Chapters*, 74.

95. George Herbert, "The Elixer," *Oxford Book of English Mystical Verse*, selected by D. H. S. Nicholson and A. H. E. Lee (Oxford: Clarendon Press, 1917), 29.

96. Palmer, Sherrard, and Ware, *Philokalia I*, 185.

97. Uhlein, *Hildegard of Bingen*, 63 (see intro., n. 6).

98. Hopkins, "God's Grandeur," *Norton Anthology*, vol. 2, 1581 (see Questions and Answers, n. 28).

99. Ibid.

100. Hugh of St. Victor, "De Arrha Animae" (Migne, Patrologla Latina, vol. clxxvi), quoted in Underhill, *Mysticism*, 245–46.

101. McGuckin, *Book of Mystical Chapters*, 121.

102. Campbell, *John of the Cross*, 92.

103. Norwich, *Revelations*, VI.

104. Adapted from Norwich, *Revelations*, XI.

105. Doyle, *Julian of Norwich*, 47.

106. Ibid., 60.

107. Norwich, *Revelations*, LIV.

108. Adapted from Norwich, *Revelations*, LVII.

109. Fremantle, *Protestant Mystics*, 341–42.

110. Richard J. Foster and James Bryan Smith, eds., *Devotional Classics* (NY: Harper Collins Publishers, 1993), 120.

111. Timothy F. Lull, ed., *Martin Luther's Basic Theological Writings* (Minneapolis, MN: Fortress Press, 1989), 321–22.

112. Ibid., 321.

113. Adapted from Underhill, *Mystics*, 234–35.

114. Palmer, Sherrard, and Ware, *Philokalia II*, 55.

115. Woodruff, *Mechtild of Magdeburg*, 29.

116. Ibid., 30.

117. Ibid., 77.

118. Mechtild of Magdeburg, *The Flowing Light of the Godhead* (Mawah, NJ: Paulist Press, 1998), II.19, 83–84.

References

119. Thomas Merton, *The Hidden Ground of Love: Letters* (NY: Mariner Books, 1993), 63–64.
120. Quoted in David Steindl-Rast, "Recollections of Thomas Merton's Last Days in the West," *Monastic Studies* 7, no. 10 (1969), 2–3.
121. Merton, *Hidden Ground*, 627.
122. Yockey, *Meditations with Nicholas of Cusa*, 29.
123. Palmer, Sherrard, and Ware, *Philokalia IV*, 151.
124. McGuckin, *Book of Mystical Chapters*, 171–72.
125. Palmer, Sherrard, and Ware, *Philokalia IV*, 151.
126. Fremantle, *Protestant Mystics*, 109.
127. Rahner, *Encounters*, 9 (see Questions and Answers, n. 15).
128. Underhill, *Mystics*, 255.
129. Swedenborg, *Theological Writings*, 5.
130. Teilhard de Chardin, *Hymn*, 19.
131. _____, *Writings*, 118.
132. Ibid., 120.
133. Ibid., 121.
134. *Vida*, cap. xviii. § 20. "Letters of St. Teresa" (1581), quoted in Underhill, *Mysticism* (1911), 243.
135. Fremantle, *Protestant Mystics*, 139.
136. Palmer, Sherrard, and Ware, *Philokalia II*, 306.
137. Bridges, *American Mysticism*, 55 (see chap. 1, n. 1).
138. Thomas Traherne, "The Rapture," *Oxford Book*, 68.
139. Underhill, *Mysticism*, 260.
140. Ibid., 320.
141. McGinn, *Essential Writings*, 68.
142. Pred. lvii, quoted in Underhill, *Mysticism*, 389.
143. McGinn, *Essential Writings*, 416.
144. Ibid., 417.
145. Egan, *Anthology of Christian Mysticism*, 299 (see intro., n. 3).
146. *Evagrius Ponticus*, 66.
147. Palmer, Sherrard, and Ware, *Philokalia I*, 177.
148. Campbell, *John of the Cross*, 51.
149. Ibid., 62.
150. Palmer, Sherrard, and Ware, *Philokalia I*, 275.

151. Underhill, *Mystics*, 247.

152. Maloney, *Psuedo-Macarius*, 195.

153. Woodruff, *Mechtild of Magdeburg*, 60.

154. Ibid., 61.

155. Ibid., 107.

156. Ibid., 75.

157. Merton, *New Seeds,* 291–92.

158. McGinn, *Essential Writings*, 146–47.

159. Rahner, *Practice*, 83–84.

160. Teresa of Avila, *Interior Castle* 6:1:20.

161. Simone Weil, *The Notebooks of Simone Weil*, vol. 2, trans. Arthur Sills (UK: Routledge, 1976), 638.

162. Charles Williams, private correspondence, quoted in Gavin Ashenden, *Charles Williams: Alchemy & Integration* (Kent, OH: Kent State University Press, 2008), 215–16.

163. Palmer, Sherrard, and Ware, *Philokalia I*, 262.

164. Egan, *Anthology of Christian Mysticism*, 301.

165. Palmer, Sherrard, and Ware, *Philokalia I*, 190.

166. Uhlein, *Hildegard of Bingen*, 56.

167. Ibid., 92.

168. Campbell, *John of the Cross*, 77.

169. Norwich, *Revelations*, VI.

170. Adapted from Norwich, *Revelations*, V.

171. Ibid., XLIII.

172. Doyle, *Julian of Norwich*, 75.

173. Ibid., 85.

174. Adapted from Norwich, *Revelations*, LVIII.

175. Doyle, *Julian of Norwich*, 113.

176. Fremantle, *Protestant Mystics*, 110.

177. Underhill, *Mystics*, 245.

178. Ibid., 245.

179. Maloney, *Psuedo-Macarius*, 56.

180. Ibid., 87.

181. Ibid., 238.

182. Woodruff, *Mechtild of Magdeburg*, 46.

183. Ibid., 35.
184. McGuckin, *Book of Mystical Chapters*, 169–70.
185. Maloney, *St. Symeon,* 17.
186. Ibid., 17.
187. Ibid., 17.
188. Teilhard de Chardin, *Writings,* 143.
189. Ibid., 125.
190. Ibid., 139.
191. Campbell, *Teresa,* 117.
192. Teresa of Avila, *Interior Castle* VII:2:5.
193. Arndt, *True Christianity,* 21.
194. Ibid., 256.
195. Fox, *Meditations with Meister Eckhart,* 85.
196. Ibid., 91.
197. Ibid., 93.
198. Ibid., 116.
199. Ibid., 120.
200. *Evagrius Ponticus,* 78.
201. Uhlein, *Hildegard of Bingen,* 106.
202. Ibid., 128.
203. Ibid., 69.
204. Campbell, *John of the Cross,* 31.
205. Adapted from Norwich, *Revelations,* XLVII.
206. Maloney, *Psuedo-Macarius,* 142.
207. Ibid., 231.
208. Woodruff, *Mechtild of Magdeburg,* 83.
209. Ibid., 119.
210. Ibid., 122.
211. Ibid., 129.
212. Swedenborg, *Theological Writings,* 181.
213. Teilhard de Chardin, *Writings,* 128.
214. _____, *Hymn,* 15.
215. Campbell, *Teresa,* 41.
216. Teresa of Avila, *Interior Castle* V:3:8.
217. Campbell, *Teresa,* 73.

218. Palmer, Sherrard, and Ware, *Philokalia II*, 306.
219. Quoted in Underhill, *Mystics*, 230.
220. Although Anglicans (Episcopalians in the United States) are both Catholic and Protestant at the same time (the only denomination that can claim this distinction) I have listed them under "Protestant," as most people usually do.

Appendix A

1. Mark 13:24–26.
2. Many mystics of the medieval period, such as St. Teresa of Avila, existed for long periods on the nourishment of Communion alone. I do not recommend this, of course, but it is part of our mystical history.
3. John 14:20, 17:21.

Appendix B

1. James Fowler, *Stages of Faith: The Psychology of Human Development and the Quest for Meaning* (NY: HarperOne, 1995).
2. Fox, *Meditations with Meister Eckhart*, 67.

Index

Bold for illustrations and figures

Index

Index

Index

Index

Index

Index

Index

Index

Index

Index

Index

Index

Index

Quest Books

encourages open-minded inquiry into
world religions, philosophy, science, and the arts
in order to understand the wisdom of the ages,
respect the unity of all life, and help people explore
individual spiritual self-transformation.

Its publications are generously supported by
The Kern Foundation,
a trust committed to Theosophical education.

Quest Books is the imprint of
the Theosophical Publishing House,
a division of the Theosophical Society in America.
For information about programs, literature,
on-line study, membership benefits, and international centers,
see www.theosophical.org
or call 800-669-1571 or (outside the U.S.) 630-668-1571.

Related Quest Titles

The Cross and the Grail, by Robert Ellwood

The Divine Seed, by Pekka Ervast

Godseed, by Jean Houston

Hidden Wisdom in the Holy Bible, by Geoffrey Hodson

Jesus Christ, Sun of God, by David Fideler

A Rebirth for Christianity, by Alvin Boyd Kuhn

To order books or a complete Quest catalog,
call 800-669-9425 or (outside the U.S.) 630-665-0130.